D0547384

WALKS OF
CALIFORNIA

WALKS OF CALIFORNIA

GARY FERGUSON

Illustrated by Kent Humphreys

PRENTICE HALL PRESS • NEW YORK

Contents

THE FOREST   141

THE MOUNTAINS   211

About This Book

If it is true, as Henry David Thoreau claimed, that "the world is but canvas to our imaginations," then how fantastic must be the collection of daydreams that has been painted on the state of California. Imagine the fear with which travelers faced these deserts, the joy they felt at the feet of these soaring mountains. How many people have stood awe-struck in the shade of a forest where each tree weighed 5,000 tons, or drowsed by the seaside, lulled thoughtless by the whisper of waves against the sand. Perhaps it was in part the effects of several generations having been wrapped in this wild grandeur that led O. Henry to conclude that "Californians are a race of people; they are not merely inhabitants of a state."

Inside the covers of this book are a few bits and pieces of nature lore and history that will allow you to spill your own bright colors of imagination across some choice pieces of California canvas. To this end, there were several important considerations that went into the selection of the eighty walks that follow.

First of all, be aware that this is not a book for those looking to bag superlatives. These paths will not necessarily take you to the lowest, highest, or largest of anything. In fact, where you end up is often of no consequence at all. The turnaround points for many of the walks are arbitrary, and it makes little difference if you reach the place you set out for, go past it, or become sidetracked along the way. This is not a collection of destinations, only of gentle journeys.

Second, some of you will be surprised to find that while many of the walks are located in the forests and mountains surrounding the more popular national parks, there are relatively few

Crescent City
Alturas
Weed
Redding
Leggett
Truckee
Sacramento
San Francisco
Bishop
Fresno
Monterey
San Luis Obispo
Bakersfield
Needles
Barstow
Los Angeles
Riverside
Borrego Spgs
Santa Catalina
San Diego

KH

within the parks themselves. The reason for this comes down to a simple but very important matter of elbow room. While there is far more solitude to be had in the backcountry of a place like Yosemite than you might imagine, that is not true on the easier, more accessible walking paths. And, because Mother Nature usually doesn't talk much above a low murmur, you're more likely to get the full effect of what she's saying if you don't have a lot of background commotion to contend with. (Do keep in mind, however, that nature centers and staffs of trained naturalists do make national parks wonderful places in which to learn.)

Eighty easy walks in this book are distributed equally among four different environments: desert, coast, forest, and mountain. These environments are then broken down into four regions, most of them containing five walks. The four regions for each ecosystem will allow you to explore the same environment in a variety of locations, while clustering the walks in small groups will ensure that there arc always several other walks fairly close to the one you're taking. You'll find a map at the beginning of each five-walk section showing the general location of each trail. If the town names on these sectional maps aren't enough clues to tell you exactly where you are, check them against the state map located on page 2. Specific directions for finding the actual trail heads are given at the beginning of the walks themselves.

Though it would be nice not to have to bring up any caveats in what is essentially a book of fancy, there is a particularly sorry situation that you will almost certainly have to deal with on some of your forays into the California wild lands. For the past several years there has been a general refusal to fund even basic Forest and Park Service field-level maintenance programs. Many areas of this state are subjected to ferocious winter storms on a fairly regular basis, some of which leave trails all but impassable by knocking down dozens of trees and covering the trails with mud slides. The majority of the foot trails were built fairly cheaply during the 1930s, but at the current rate of deterioration it will not take more than a few harsh winters to push many to the point where repairing them is no longer cost-effective. It seems particularly unfortunate that we are letting our trails disappear at the same time that demand for recreational use of these lands is climbing steadily. In the years ahead there will unquestionably be fewer choices of backcountry routes to walk, which of course means that your encounters with the wilderness will not offer nearly the degree of solitude that they once did.

Another problem related to low field-level budgets is that forest road and trail signs that are stolen (a frequent occurrence) or damaged by storms are not always promptly replaced. The loss of a road sign can be particularly frustrating. Many California national forest maps are quite old, and most reflect only a few of the additional logging roads that have been put in during the last ten years. Coming upon an unmarked fork in the road that is not even shown on the map is becoming a routine, albeit ridiculously unnecessary, inconvenience.

Given such conditions, it is more important than ever to check with nearby ranger stations to confirm the conditions of roads and trails that you intend to use. This is also the time to pick up maps, ask about other walking paths in the area that might interest you, and fill out any of the free permit forms that may be required for you to build fires or enter wilderness areas. (Though not yet common, there are some wildernesses, like San Gorgonio, that require permits even for day hikes.)

Another effect of low field-level budgets is the fact that crews to collect trail litter are in many places already a thing of the past. Whatever trash you leave in the environment will be there for a long time to come. Therefore, it is imperative that you do your part to pack out what you pack in. Like it or not, we are rapidly being faced with taking responsibility to pick up other people's trash ourselves (or convince them to clean up their act), if we want to maintain a pristine walking environment.

Such things are extremely frustrating to any lover of the out-of-doors, especially considering that payments of higher fees for day use and overnight campground use have brought millions more dollars into the national recreation areas of California than was available to them several years ago. Unfortunately, more of this money than you might think only passes through an individual park or forest on its way to Washington, bound ultimately for government programs that have nothing at all to do with outdoor recreation. It is here, at this high level of government, where change

4

must be urged. Nearly every field-level park and forest recreation officer who helped with this book (and there were many) was hopelessly underfinanced for the job that he or she had been given to do—this, mind you, in some of the most heavily used recreation areas in the United States. Most said they would keep plodding along as long as their jobs lasted, but they shook their heads sadly when confiding that the integrity of the resource that they love is crumbling before their eyes.

These walks will take you to place after place where, at least for a short while, it might seem that you've somehow slipped through a crack in time, back to the untrammeled glory days of old California. Off the trail, though, realize that pressures are being exerted here that could soon eliminate the chance for nonbackpackers to savor the untarnished beauty and quietude that have been a hallmark for so many of California's recreation lands. For countless generations the wild tapestries of this state have satisfied anyone who has come to them looking for spiritual nourishment. It is past time that we return the favor.

THE DESERT

To many people the desert seems an unfortunate wasteland—a splash of beggarly scenery thrown in to offer contrast to purple mountains' majesty and amber waves of grain. Motoring across such vast expanses offers these people about as much thrill as a long elevator ride. Instead of staring at floor-number lights flashing on and off above the doors, they watch green mile markers drifting by ever so slowly on the far side of the windshield.

But as anyone who has managed to grasp the subtle grandeur of the desert will tell you, it is a place that must be approached on foot. It takes a good hour of measured stride before the enormity of that yawning space finally begins to sink in. By then, even the most robust of hikers catch on to the fact that the desert is not merely a piece of topography to be crossing on the way to somewhere else. That simple realization is usually enough to slow them down, perhaps even completely to stop them in their tracks. Their attention shifts from *ahead* to *around*. Much of the desert's fascination, they discover, lies not at the end of the trail but rather in the tiny nooks and crannies of life and landscape found along the way.

I will warn you now that should you decide to give the desert that first chance, you may find it to be extremely habit-forming. Experiencing it is not totally unlike listening to a classical symphony; though enjoyable enough at first, the more you immerse yourself in it, the more genius of form you will discover. Take a moment to consider some of the more incredible movements unfolding right now in the arid heart of the North American desert lands.

Any "terrific trivia" book that manages to squeeze in a fact about barren real estate will probably tell you that at 500,000 square miles, the North American desert ranks fifth largest in the world. The problem with such a numerical approach is that it promotes an impression that this big swath of space is all pretty much the same. Nothing could be farther from the truth. The Mojave, Colorado, and Great Basin deserts of California are as different as the Cascade Mountains are from the Rockies. Each is controlled by a very different set of environmental conditions, which means that each has a very different group of life forms that make their homes there.

So, throwing the "if you've seen one . . ." philosophy to the vultures, let's consider two basic characteristics of every desert: heat and lack of water. Applying these conditions to the plant life you see on your walks through the California deserts will go a long way toward helping you fit all the pieces of this ecosystem together.

One of the most common first impressions of the desert is that it seems *stark*—a place where vegetation is barely able to survive. In fact, the plants that grow here are very productive. The widely scattered distribution pattern is simply a response to the small amounts of available water. Remember, not only do most deserts receive less than 10 inches of rain per year but much of what does fall simply runs through the sandy, nonretentive soil or runs off hardpacked soil in flash floods. Unlike a forest, there are no colonies of earthworms here to aerate the ground. (Decades ago small burrowing animals used to produce a similar effect, but many were killed off because they were competing with cattle for native grasses. Ironically, fewer animal burrows has meant less water retention for desert soils, which has wiped out some of the very grasses the ranchers were trying to save.)

But scattered distribution is only the beginning. The thing that makes desert plants so fascinating is the ingenious methods they've developed for obtaining, and then keeping, every drop of water that happens to dribble by.

Many cacti have shallow roots that soak up rain over a large area. Some cacti are even able to produce special "rain roots" immediately after a shower. Other plants, such as the creosote bush, make sure they get their fair share of moisture by emitting a

10

poison into the soil to keep other plants from coming too close. Some even try to bypass the problem completely by putting down root systems that go all the way to the water table, sometimes located more than 100 feet below the surface of the ground.

As you might expect, the survival rate for new plant life in the desert is not very high. It would seem that the best way to beat poor odds in favor of sprouting would be to produce plenty of seeds, as the tumbleweed does, which turns them out by the millions. But many of the plants in the desert, especially those that each spring splash the sandy floor with a riot of color, have yet another strategy. Their seeds have a special coating on them that prevents germination if they have not been adequately soaked. Only when the rains have been sufficient to insure a good supply of water will the seed be able to break free of its coat and get on with the business of growing. Recent research has suggested that some of these special chemical inhibitors can even gauge the difference between a rather worthless summer downpour that runs off quickly and the more lasting soak provided by a gentle shower.

Trees that grow along desert washes (dry streambeds) may tackle the reproduction problem from yet another angle. Their seeds have very hard coats that must be cracked open by an outside force before germination can occur. About the only thing with power sufficient to achieve this is a flash flood, which will sweep the seeds down the wash, violently smashing them into rocks of every size. When it's all over, the seed is open, and the ground is wet enough to support life.

In some parts of the California deserts, well over a year may pass between rain showers. The problem then becomes not only how to get water but how to keep it. Several desert plants avoid dehydration by opening their "pores" to exchange gases only at night. And few have what may be considered "traditional" leaves. If indeed they have any leaves at all, the leaves may be rolled up to reduce evaporation, or else they have the ability to turn themselves parallel to the intense rays of the sun. Under drought conditions, some plants even drop their leaves to conserve water. The creosote bush goes even further, letting loose entire branches.

A walk among desert plants, then, is a journey through some of the most finely tuned organisms in the world. Nowhere does so

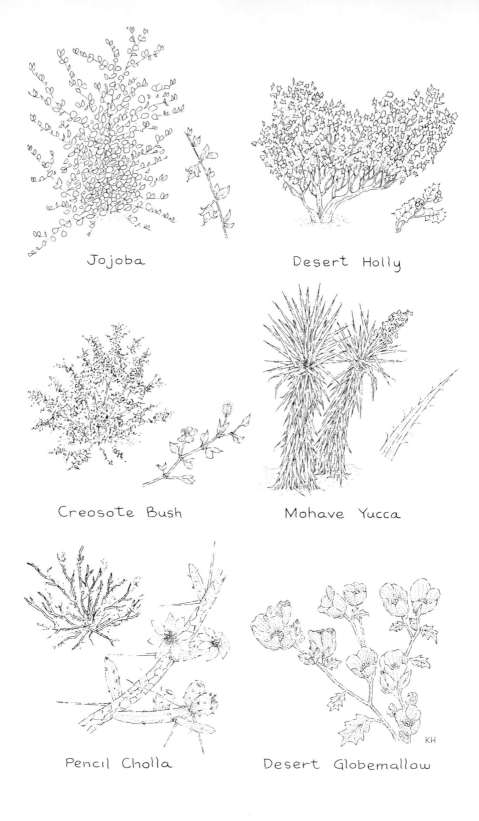

Jojoba   Desert Holly

Creosote Bush   Mohave Yucca

Pencil Cholla   Desert Globemallow

much life flourish with so little to support it; it is nature's most Spartan economy.

Since a few flowers (usually cactus) open only at night, plan to begin your walk as early in the morning as you possibly can. (This time of day is also good for catching glimpses of desert wildlife.) If your adventures are slated for the early spring, look for color on south-facing slopes of hills and mountains. Later on, or if it has been a year of poor rainfall, aim for the north side, where precious moisture is not evaporated so quickly by the sun. Finally, remember that elevation plays a key role in the plant life of any environment. If your walks are well above the desert floor, you'll find a different set of plants, blooming at a later time.

The animals of the desert are regulated by the same extreme conditions that rule the plants. But unlike their rooted counterparts, when the going gets hot they can simply move to a more favorable location. Without question, the best place to go in such conditions is down. When the ground temperature is 150 degrees (not uncommon), 2 feet below the soil it will be around 85 degrees. Since few mammals can stand a body temperature of much above 100, many will hole up during the day and emerge only in the cool of darkness.

Of course you have a problem if you don't happen to be a burrowing animal or if the temperatures are still a bit high for you when it's time to go about the business of the day. If you were a jackrabbit, you'd lay those big long ears across your back to deflect the sun from your body. If you were a coyote, you'd hang out in the shade and do a lot of panting. A burro would be able to store several degrees of heat in his body, and "let off steam" at night.

But dealing with heat is one thing; dealing with a lack of water is quite another. Not surprisingly, pockets of standing water are the social hot spots for a host of desert dwellers. Some may need to return to water holes only occasionally, but there is no doubt that their lives are inescapably linked to them. Others, like the spadefoot toad, hole up in the ground for ten months nursing their body water and then emerge at the first good rain of the season.

Of all the creatures involved in this constant struggle to keep supplied with the essence of life, there are a fortunate few

13

who seem to have come amazingly close to escaping the struggle. One of the best known of these is the kangaroo rat. During a life of eating nothing but dry plant food, never once does this tiny rodent need to take a drink of water. What little liquid it needs comes from the minuscule amounts available in its food, as well as from water produced by certain processes in metabolism. These little creatures come out only at night, literally walling themselves in their burrows after sunrise to avoid dehydration.

Since so many of the desert's animals are nocturnal, any wildlife lover would do well to schedule a walk on a moonlit night. If possible, plan to reach a secluded place above a water hole just after sunset. Should there be any kind of breeze, make sure that you're downwind. The quiet and patient observer will be amazed at the wildlife that saunters up for a slow drink and then disappears again into the shadows of the night.

A quick word about photography, since the desert is not an easy place to capture on film. Harsh sunlight reflecting off the sandy soil and rock walls can really play havoc with long-range pictures. There just isn't as much light on your subject as the camera thinks there is. Using a manual camera and no light meter, set the camera so that the picture appears to be slightly overexposed. Alternatively, you can walk up to within 3 to 5 feet of the subject and set the exposure from there. Return to your shooting spot and snap the picture at that setting.

Remember that this light is not as harsh during the early morning and evening hours. Also, the desert winds that set long-stemmed wild flowers dancing will be calmer at these times. If you have just one day for shooting, start out with the long-stemmed wild flowers in the morning and move to the sturdier cactus flowers in the afternoon. Scenic views can then be captured in the soft, red light of evening.

Finally, it should go without saying that hiking in the desert requires some precautions. Though none of the walks here require much physical effort, remember that your body will nonetheless be continually cooling itself off as perspiration evaporates. (The dry atmosphere may make it seem that you aren't perspiring at all.) Unlike some desert mammals, who can lose nearly 50 percent of their body weight in water and still survive, humans cease to think rationally after losing just a tenth of that. Hiking in hot, arid climates requires that you carry along at least 1 gallon of water per person per day. That's the one time you won't complain about the weight in your day pack.

Another thing to remember about desert hiking is the danger of sunburn. The clear air and reflective surface of the ground can fry you in no time. Take along a good sunscreen and use it!

Also, the combination of dry heat and afternoon winds is not exactly kind to skin moisture. Unless you have a particular desire to look like a sourdough prospector, take along a good body lotion (aloe vera works fine), and apply it twice a day when you're out on the trail. If your skin is particularly sensitive, plan also to wear a light-colored, thin cotton shirt and pants. These garments also will allow you to lose less body moisture through perspiration. And finally, don't forget a comfortable, wide-brimmed hat.

East Mojave
National Scenic Area

KELSO DUNES

Distance: 1 mile
Location: From Interstate 40, approximately 64 miles west of
Needles, head north for 12.3 miles on the Kelbaker Road.
There is a sign on the left pointing to Kelso Dunes, the parking
area for which lies 3 miles to the west. The road to the parking
area is fairly rough, so go slow. Just beyond the trail-head area
is a sign by the road that reads: "Danger, Aircraft Landing
Strip. Keep Out." An alternative route to Kelso Dunes is to
head south from Baker for 39 miles on the Kelbaker Road.

The beautiful Kelso Dunes form the third largest collection of sand
dunes in America; the tallest peaks rise more than 500 feet above
the desert floor. Your first steps into the foothills of these sand
mountains can leave you feeling as if you had somehow been transported into a scene from an old Lawrence of Arabia film. Person-
ally, I wouldn't have been the least surprised if a band of nomads
had suddenly topped the peaks, heads wrapped in cloth, tents and
cookstoves strapped to a string of sagging camels.

In order for desert sand dunes to form, eroded particles of
surrounding mountain ranges must first become airborne on a consistent wind flow. When something then happens to interrupt this
air pattern—a change in topography or clashes with winds from
other directions—the prevailing wind drops its load of particles. It's
usually fairly easy to tell the direction of the winds that formed the
dunes. The windward side will be a gentle slope, whereas the lee
side will be a sharp drop. As new sand is deposited it will roll down
the steep front flanks, causing the dunes to "migrate" in the direction of the prevailing wind.

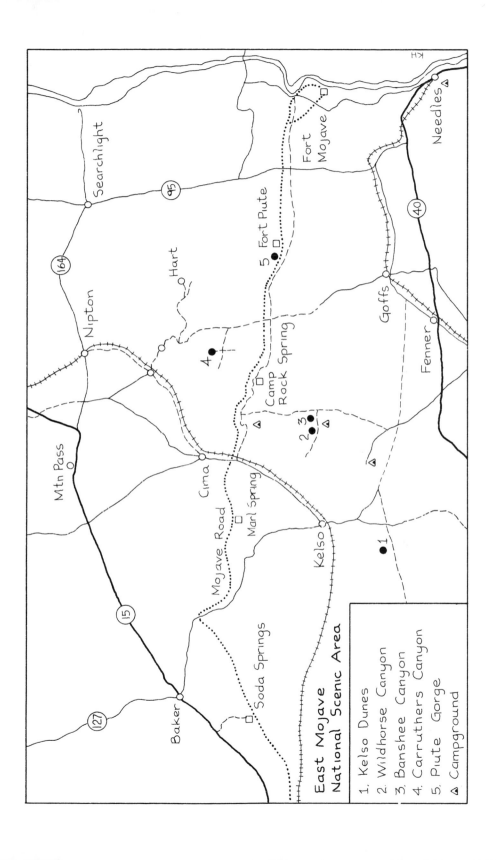

East Mojave
National Scenic Area

1. Kelso Dunes
2. Wildhorse Canyon
3. Banshee Canyon
4. Carruthers Canyon
5. Piute Gorge
△ Campground

The sand that formed Kelso Dunes begins 35 miles to the west, at the mouth of Afton Canyon, and is blown across a broad plain known as the Devil's Playground. It so happens that the shape of the land here allows strong winds from the east, south, and north to collide with the sand-laden westerlies, causing them to drop their cargo and form this magnificent collection of dunes.

Even in this apparently harsh ecosystem, a variety of life forms have taken hold. In the sandy flats immediately below the dunes, the opportunistic honey mesquite has sunk its long, spindly root fingers all the way down to the water table 50 feet or more below the surface of the ground. Although mesquite was held in contempt among many white settlers for its tendency to take over abused rangeland, it was for many desert Indian tribes the most important of all plants. In fact, it appears likely that large mesquite groves provided so much food that they allowed people such as the Cahuillas to trade the rigors of nomadic life for permanent settlements—a transition that is usually credited only to agricultural economies. The harvesting of blossoms, green pods, and finally mature pods, or beans, lasted from April through August.

You'll notice a few creosote bushes hanging on to the higher, more unstable foothills, but soon even they are left behind. From here rice and big galleta grass are common, their supple stalks continually bent and twisted round by the wind until they have etched a pattern of concentric circles in the soft sand. With ample rains, patches of sand verbena and evening primrose appear seemingly out of nowhere, dotting the shifting hills with splashes of lavender and white.

One of the most interesting aspects of dune walking (particularly in the early morning) is the amazing number of tracks preserved in the sand. There are those of ravens and kestrels, kangaroo rats and pocket mice, sidewinders, leopard and zebra-tailed lizards, and a host of others. These tracks provide a wonderful opportunity to figure out what was going on the night before. For instance, you might see a line of rodent tracks that ends abruptly. Look for wing tip disturbances around the end of the tracks, suggesting that Mr. Mouse was unexpectedly seized as dinner by a hungry hawk or eagle. Elsewhere, notice how tracks of a lizard moving at a leisurely pace will have a line in the center of them etched by a dragging tail. Since lizards hold their tails off the ground when running, the disappearance of this line would indicate a sudden shift into high gear.

What is unique about Kelso Dunes is their singing ability. Yes, their singing ability. Taking steps on the steep upper slopes of the dunes results in an amazing medley of deep, vibrating tremolos—a sound rather like an Italian tenor clearing his throat. When these dunes are very dry, pressure on the sand grains will cause air to resonate across loosely compacted pockets, creating sounds in much the same way that breath across a reed instrument produces music.

WILDHORSE CANYON

Distance: 3 miles
Location: Take the Essex Road exit off of Interstate 40, approximately 42 miles west of Needles. Go north 9 miles, then right on Black Canyon Road 8.2 miles to Wildhorse Canyon Road (just south of Hole-in-the-Wall Campground). Turn left. Go 1.05 miles to a small parking area outlined with rocks on the north side of the road.

Wildhorse Canyon offers a perfect opportunity for a leisurely stroll through the open desert, a stroll especially appropriate for those trying to become familiar with some of the more typical plants of the Mojave Desert. The first 0.75 mile of trail winds through a rather handsome neighborhood of buckhorn cholla, foxtail, and Mojave yucca. You'll find that just knowing the common names of desert plants—especially those in the cactus family—can be a big help in identifying them in the field. The long, fuzzy spines of old man cactus, for instance, do look a great deal like the grizzled white beard of a senior miner just down from the hills. Beaver tail cactus, which has no visible spines showing on its joints, does indeed look like the business end of a beaver, albeit a green one. It doesn't take much imagination to see the pear shape of prickly pears, and it takes none whatsoever to see the prickly part.

Nineteenth-century white man's loathing of the desert—"a

19

sweltering, longing, hateful reality," as Mark Twain called it—kept him from ever becoming very familiar with the sustenance aspect of this environment. To the desert Indian, the jumping cholla produced delicious buds, which, when cooked in a pit of hot stones, could nourish him throughout the winter. To the pioneer, the same plant produced nothing but despicable spiny balls that continually found their way into a horse's fetlocks. A prudent wagon-train leader would continually caution his hungry immigrant charges not to steal from Indian food caches, when the very same foods lay at their feet, hidden in all that "grotesque" desert vegetation.

At 0.75 mile, the trail begins a gradual climb. On your right notice the tilted outcropping of black-brown rocks that follows the trail toward the pass to the north. This dark coloration, which you'll see often in the deserts of the Southwest, is known as "desert varnish." The color is caused by a coating of clay, iron, and manganese oxides and typically requires more than a thousand years to form. (That is a small drop in the bucket, when you consider that these outcroppings cap a ridge of rock that is more than 600 million years old.)

It's just under 0.75 mile from where you first join the varnished rock to the low saddle that marks the turnaround point for this walk. As you near this pass, the trail may become faint in places. Keep to the shallow valley formed by rugged pinnacle rocks on the left and the line of varnished rocks to the right. At 0.4 mile from the saddle you'll see a beautiful garden of barrel cacti growing among the jagged outcroppings. As you may have heard, these cacti have saved the lives of more than a few parched travelers, though a 3-foot-high plant typically yields only about a pint of bitter juice. The procedure for obtaining this liquid was to slice off the top of the cactus and dig the pulp out of the trunk. The liquid from this pulp was then squeezed back into the open cavity. So leak-proof is this plant that Indian tribes could dig out the interior pulp and, using hot stones, boil water in the hollowed vessel.

When you finally gain the pass 1.5 miles from the trail head, you'll be looking north into a grand swell of lonely desert landscape. From here it's easy to imagine that you're the only person on earth—wind, sun, rock, and sky your closest companions.

Take note of all the juniper trees before you, whereas behind you there are almost none. This pattern of growth, like so many in nature, is determined by exposure to the sun. The slope that holds these trees faces north and consequently is shaded from the intense summer sunlight. Less sun means that more moisture is retained in the soil—an important ingredient if you want to grow junipers in a hot desert.

As you head back toward the trail head you'll see a wonderful panorama of mountain ranges and mesas. Just to the southwest is Wildhorse Mesa; behind that, the mineral-rich Providence Mountains. Directly ahead of you is the long stretch of the Clipper Valley, bracketed in the distant south by the rusty lilt of the Clipper Mountains. This is an especially wild, little-known section of California—a small part of what Bureau of Land Management people affectionately refer to as "the Lost Triangle."

BANSHEE CANYON

Distance: 1.3 miles
Location: Take the Essex Road exit off Interstate 40, approximately 42 miles west of Needles. Go north 9 miles, then right on Black Canyon Road 8.4 miles to Hole-in-the-Wall Campground. Park on the north side of the campground.

Hole-in-the-Wall Campground lies against an intriguing collection of 20-million-year-old rocks (mere teenagers, really), which have been sculpted by wind and water into a twisted medley of quiet chasms and egg-shaped boulders. From the north side of the camping area, walk by the entrance route back out to Black Canyon Road, and turn right. Before you lies the long, yawning reach of the Clipper Valley—a silent sweep of landscape that can lull the viewer into the finest daydreams. As you stand here wrapped in the Mojave Desert, consider that it has taken less than 140 years for such expanses to evolve from scenes that put knots in the stomachs of the pioneers, to rich sources of tranquility for denizens of a hurried world.

In 0.2 mile, make a right turn onto Wildhorse Canyon Road.

On the western horizon lies a small tip of the Providence Mountains. This range was given its name by immigrants during the 1850s, who believed that the many springs they found here had been "sent from Providence." A decade later the first miners began to roll into these mountains, following rumors of rich silver lodes. In the early years of mining, this was definitely not a place you could make a two-bit strike and walk away with money in your pocket. The remoteness of the Providence Range meant that you paid several hundred dollars a ton just to have your ore hauled to a processing site. Supplies, on the other hand, came all the way from San Francisco—first by water to the port of Wilmington, then eastward 175 miles on horse-drawn freight wagons, and finally to the mine sites themselves only after several days on a burro's back. Operations became more profitable when the Santa Fe Railroad was completed through the area in 1884. Unfortunately, just nine years later the silver market crashed, and with it the dreams of many a Providence miner.

Down Wildhorse Canyon Road 0.6 mile a small roadway heads off to the right from the west side of a cattle guard. For the next 0.3 mile you'll traverse a pleasant carpet of typical Mojave desert plants. There's the plentiful creosote bush, which Southwest Indians have used for treating nearly as many diseases as the white man has treated with penicillin. Only fifty years ago, researchers at the University of Minnesota extracted a chemical from the creosote known as NDGA, which even today is considered one of the most effective agents for keeping butter fats and oils from turning rancid.

Elsewhere along this stretch of trail you'll see the spindly cholla cactus, with its unmistakable Tinkertoy construction. Chollas can spread simply by dropping one of their prickly joints onto the ground, where it will take root and begin a new plant. This propagation plan is often thwarted, however, when some industrious pack rat comes along and takes the thorny joint back to his nest to fortify it against predators. The pack rat is not the only creature that takes advantage of this type of armament. The tiny cactus wren often builds his nest in the cholla's thorny branches. Also in this area are prickly pear cactus, catsclaw, and during the spring, the splashy reds and blues of Indian paintbrush and lupine.

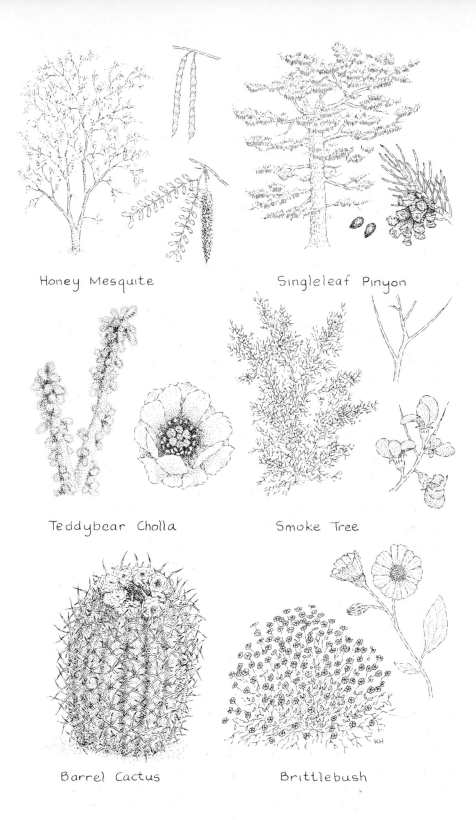

Honey Mesquite

Singleleaf Pinyon

Teddybear Cholla

Smoke Tree

Barrel Cactus

Brittlebush

At a point 0.3 mile from the cattle guard, take the right fork of the road, which by this time has become rather faint. You'll follow a small wash (dry streambed) that runs northeast toward the tall, red cliffs standing before you. Here is the mouth of Banshee Canyon, an eroded wonderland of narrow twists and tiny caverns. This rock is known as rhyolite, which is actually a type of lava that was crystallized beneath the earth's surface from a hot liquid state millions of years ago. As you advance up the canyon, notice how cool it is in the depths of this passageway and how different the plant life is from that of the warm flats you left behind.

About 200 yards from the mouth of the canyon you'll come to a steep corridor where iron rings have been sunk into the rock to aid your passage. This is a very short section and should not prove difficult for those who take their time. Past the iron rings 0.1 mile is the parking area at the head of the canyon where you began your walk. Before you leave, walk about 40 yards south from the head of the canyon to a trail that heads west into a mass of giant rocks. Follow it in a few feet to an observation platform that affords cozy views of a stunning site.

This gorgeous, vase-shaped amphitheater, perhaps 20 yards across, is a true inner sanctum sculpted out of rose-colored rock. On the far side you can see where streams of water have carved small bowls into the horizontal ledges. Brittlebush clings for life in the tiny cracks that run down the sheer rock walls. Enough soil has formed at the very bottom of the theater to support a lush green carpet of grass.

To walk into this theater is a splendid experience—typical of the way an apparently impassive desert can suddenly enchant you with an unexpected thread of beauty. It's interesting that this canyon was named Banshee, which comes from an Irish word for a special "family elf" that had the power to warn of approaching death. Within these rocky chasms, there indeed seems to be just enough magic, just enough mystery, for an old-world spirit like the banshee to find a home.

CARRUTHERS CANYON

Distance: 2.6 miles

Location: Exit on Mountain Springs Road off Interstate 40, 28 miles west of Needles. Go north 27.4 miles (the road turns into Ivanpah-Goffs Road at Goffs) to New York Mountains Road, which is 5.4 miles past a telephone booth. (New York Mountains Road heads west directly across from several OX Cattle Ranch buildings.) Go west for 5.6 miles, then north for 1.85 miles (you'll pass a large water tank). Park in a forested area with many turnouts, just past a wash filled with heavy brush.

It doesn't take long to realize that the New York Mountains ecosystem is entirely different from any other we've been exploring in the East Mojave National Scenic Area. The air is cool and bright. There are large, beautiful trees, and the skies are filled with bluebirds, hawks, and flickers.

These dramatic changes from the comparatively sparse plant and animal communities you left behind in the Lanfair Valley are all the result of an increase in altitude. Higher elevations usually snag more moisture from passing storm systems, and their cooler conditions result in a slower rate of evaporation. Plants that find it too dry down in the valley can flourish up here. (As far as plant communities are concerned, each additional thousand feet of elevation is like traveling several hundred miles northward. Thus, many plants found in the high mountains of the Sierras are the same ones that grow profusely in Canada or even the Arctic.)

In the first 0.1 mile notice the occurrence of rabbit brush along the roadsides. This is a very common resident of higher elevations in the Mojave and belongs to a genus that is found only in western North America. Navajo Indians still extract a bright yellow dye from the flower heads, and several Southern California tribes claim that a tea made from boiling the twigs relieves coughs and chest pains.

About 50 yards from the parking area is a roadway heading off to the right. Stay on the left. A gradual climb begins about 0.25 mile in, and a glance back during rest periods will afford you superb views south toward Table Top Mountain. For the next 0.5 mile you'll be surrounded by house-size boulders to the east and tow-

25

ering granite protrusions to the west, which rip through the vegetation like shards through a canopy. In 0.3 mile you will come to a Y fork in the road. The right branch dead-ends in 0.2 mile at an old mining shack and an abandoned car that have spent more than their fair share of time baking in the summer sun. Stand in the doorway and try to imagine what life would have been like for most men here, scratching metal out of the ground in exchange for a modest paycheck, which collected dust until the time came for another of those blessed trips to Hardyville.

The surest way back to our route (we want to take the left fork at the Y intersection) is to return the way you came. The more adventurous among you, though, may opt for shooting a line westward from this old cabin across the rocks to intersect the left fork without backtracking.

You'll cross a wash 0.6 mile from the trail head, which is often studded with pools of quiet water. From here the road begins to climb a bit more severely, crossing the stream bed again in 0.1 mile and a short way past that reaching a gigantic boulder that has fallen across the road. Rest assured that you'll have plenty of peace and quiet beyond this point. The beautiful gray-green foliage of desert holly can be seen along this stretch. Desert holly is used a great deal for indoor decorating, and is one of the most salt-tolerant of all the desert plants. On alkali-heavy alluvial fans, it will often be the only plant able to grow at all.

You'll reach a low saddle in 1.2 miles, which will offer fine views to the north into an extremely rugged basin of granite rock outcroppings. You'll cross a wash, again strung with blue pools of water, immediately after which you'll see a road taking off to the right. It will take you to a series of old gold mine shafts. Mining activity began in the New York Mountains in the 1860s, well before just about any other part of the region had felt the sting of the pickax. Mining, followed by cattle ranching, was the main economic base for the area well into the twentieth century.

Besides undergoing the hardships of living and working in a remote area under primitive conditions, early miners in Carruthers Canyon were not exactly welcomed by the Indians, who had called that place home for hundreds of years. The murder of a mining recorder in the canyon in 1866 resulted in all kinds of additional bloodshed, with the frustrated whites finally setting out sacks of sugar laced with strychnine to "get hold of those natives [Piutes] who never would stand and fight."

PIUTE GORGE

Distance: Part One, 2.8 miles; Part Two, 2.2 miles
Location: From Interstate 40, exit at Mountain Springs Road (28 miles west of Needles). Head north (at Goffs this becomes the Ivanpah-Goffs road) for 22 miles to Cable Road, which is on your right, 50 yards past a phone booth (it's the only phone for many miles). Head east for 10 miles on Cable Road (it follows a buried cable) to a junction with a north-bound road located just west of a range fence line. Park here. (Note: There is a fork on the Cable Road 3.8 miles east of the Ivanpah-Goffs Road. Stay right. 1.65 miles farther is another fork, at which you will again stay to the right.)

Piute Gorge offers an exceptional two-part walk—a wild, lonesome slice of desert spiked with enticing bits of western American history. By all means try to do both parts of the walk, which together cover a bit more than 5 miles. (Part One can actually be driven, though of course many of the more enjoyable sensations will be lost.)

Part One. The first part of the walk begins in the lower reaches of the Lanfair Valley. This rather attractive mesquite and bunch grass desert climbs slowly to the northwest until it reaches the stout eastern flanks of the New York Mountains. You'll find that there's a unique, timeless feeling to this corner of the National Scenic Area—a special tranquility borne in on the shoulders of the west wind.

Walking north along a dirt road, in 0.5 mile you'll intersect the Old Mojave Road. While it may not look like much, this humble pathway holds more tales of adventure and romance than you could ever hope to unravel. Originally it was a trade route connecting the Mojave Indians, who lived along the Colorado River, with tribes on the coast. Later the Mojaves served as guides for outsiders bound for the Pacific Ocean. Father Francisco Garcés was among the first of these in 1776, followed fifty years later by the mountain man Jedediah Strong Smith. The trapper Kit Carson and the explorer John C. Frémont were among many other nineteenth-century celebrities traveling various parts of this pathway. The first efforts to turn the Mojave Trail into a road came between 1857 and 1860 with the assistance of the U.S. Army's infamous camel brigade, a rather gangly, shaggy group of desert specialists who served under a land-locked former Navy man named Edward Beale.

Farther up the road 0.35 mile you'll come to a splendid old livestock pen (Piute Corral), which belongs to the OX Cattle Company. Despite its obvious age the structure is still used today and should not be molested in any way. Although cows still tend to run things here, it was really a hundred years ago that the area was neck deep in the glory days of East Mojave cattle ranching. The grand operator at that time was the Rock Springs Land & Cattle Company, or the "88 outfit," which referred to a double-eight brand designed to mark its beginnings in 1888.

With careful management, a good supply of money, and a few hired guns thrown in for good measure, the 88 outfit was able eventually to increase its operations to more than 10,000 head of cattle spread over a million acres of land. Things cooled off considerably early in the twentieth century, however, and around 1930, the 88 Outfit faded from the scene, and the OX boys took over.

In the next 0.5 mile you'll be walking through a classic creosote community, where shrubs are spaced so perfectly that you would swear they had been hand planted. This is a splendid example of how water calls the tune of life in the desert. The creosote bushes have established the minimum distance between themselves in order not to overuse the scant water resources. They are often so good at this spacing that they leave little or no moisture for other plants, which is why the life here seems so homogeneous. If you take a close look at the creosote bush's branches, you'll notice a waxy coating on the leaves. This is a special adaptation, which is a great help in reducing evaporation. In a serious drought, creosote bushes will drop all of their mature leaves, keeping only the small, partially developed ones to carry on the plant's basic functions.

On the right side of the road 1.4 miles from our starting

point you'll see a parking area perched on the very edge of a spectacular 800-foot canyon. This is Piute Gorge. It is a fantastic tapestry of polished chasms and hidden springs, a slice of heaven for any lover of the wilderness.

Part Two. Piute Gorge is a geological fantasy land, a pathway into 1.5 billion years of earth history. Those who walk it will have the chance to rub elbows with some of the oldest rocks in western America, to peer into a Precambrian melting pot a full one-third as old as the world itself.

The trail for Part Two of this walk begins at the right edge of the parking area and overlook. You'll head down to the north for 0.2 mile into a sandy wash at the bottom of the canyon. This is a fairly sharp descent, with the last 100 yards being the most severe. Take a right into the wash—one of the most delightful natural walking paths you'll ever find. Keep an ear out here for bird song, from the quick, tinkling ditties of the black-throated sparrow to the clear, down-the-scale whistles of the canyon wren. If you turn your eyes skyward occasionally, you'll likely spot a golden eagle or two cutting circles high above the gorge.

Just 0.1 mile after joining the wash, the canyon walls begin to close in. From here to the turnaround point you'll be in a silent rock cathedral, adorned with hanging boulders and strange, smooth tongues of green and lavender rock flows.

Notice the healthy stands of barrel cactus 0.4 mile into the wash on the north side of the canyon. In the sand immediately beneath such colonies often lie huge specimens that have been knocked off their perches by falling rocks. If you find a fairly fresh one, carefully nudge the end and note how heavy it is from the moisture being stored in its tissues. The buds of this cactus are definitely edible, but they tend to be bitter unless first boiled with several changes of water.

From here you will pass beautiful pour-off basins. Evidence of the power and grace of water running against rock is everywhere. The wash in this central section of the canyon is littered with rocks of every imaginable shape and color. Animal tracks—from kit foxes to mountain lions—form intriguing patterns in the sand.

The sight of the head of Piute Creek, which is reached after approximately 1 mile of walking in the wash, hits you like ice water

29

on a hot day. One minute you're in the depths of a stark, rocky labyrinth where life is handed out a drop at a time. Then a small stream rises from the depths of the earth, and all of a sudden life runs thick and green across the land, stone drunk on the possibilities of water.

This is the head of Piute Creek. It runs about a mile before sinking into the sand as suddenly as it appeared. That's enough, however, to give it the distinction of being the only year-round watercourse in this part of the state. Beautiful cottonwoods fly their leaves in the late afternoon breezes, and birds of every description flit among the willows and tall grasses. Toads can be seen hiding in the reeds, waiting for hors d'oeuvres to fly by.

Spend some time here, and gain a real appreciation for one of life's most precious ingredients.

Anza-Borrego Desert
State Park

BORREGO PALM CANYON

Distance: 3 miles

Location: Behind the park visitors' center and adjacent to Borrego Palm Canyon Campground. (Take Palm Canyon Drive west out of Borrego Springs, following signs for the campground.) The trail parking area is located at the far end of the campground, and the trail itself takes off north from a point near the entrance to this parking area.

The Borrego Palm Canyon walk goes a little against an important tenet of this book: to provide you with slices of nature that offer a great deal more peace and quiet than can be found on most developed nature trails. To gain such tranquility in Borrego Palm Canyon one must go very early in the morning, especially during winter holiday weekends. In spite of this requirement, I decided to include the trail for the simple reason that I doubt anyone could design a more beautiful walk if he or she had the hand of God Himself as an aid.

The hike begins at the open end of a letter V formed by two abrupt spines of rock skyrocketing 3,000 feet above the desert floor. Each step brings with it a sense of excitement for the mysteries that seem to be waiting up ahead, in the nooks and narrow passageways of the upper valley. Things begin to get particularly interesting less than 0.1 mile up the path, when you meet a seasonal stream bubble-dancing its way down the valley, acting more like bumper crop runoff from a Sierra snowpack than a rare, measured line of moisture coursing its way through a Spartan desert.

From 0.1 mile on you'll see beautiful examples of a large

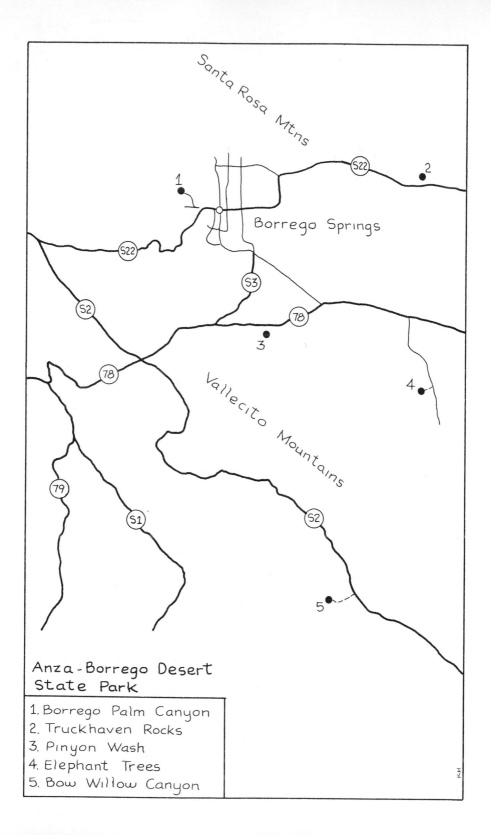

Santa Rosa Mtns

1

2

S22

Borrego Springs

S22

S3

S2

78

3

78

Vallecito Mountains

4

79

S1

S2

5

Anza-Borrego Desert
State Park

1. Borrego Palm Canyon
2. Truckhaven Rocks
3. Pinyon Wash
4. Elephant Trees
5. Bow Willow Canyon

KH

number of plants common to the Anza-Borrego landscape, as well as a respectable collection of plants that grow only where they can rub elbows with a good supply of running water. Keep an eye out for desert lavender, brittlebush, ocotillo, mesquite, willow, ironwood, cholla, beavertail cactus, and the beautiful red flowers of the chuparosa. (Such red blossoms, by the way, are where you'll most often spot feeding hummingbirds.)

Like many oases located in rugged mountain areas, this canyon system is a favorite haunt of desert bighorn sheep. Each year many observant visitors are lucky enough to spot these nimble creatures scampering up and down the stark rock walls that line this pathway. The desert bighorn is a true sheep, consuming a diet of yucca and desert shrub leaves early in the morning, around noon, and again during the evening hours. Nights are spent in well-worn bedding sites, most of which are located in the most rugged and inaccessible country imaginable.

A short way up the valley you'll begin winding around the first of many gigantic boulders. Notice here how different plants have very strong preferences for either shaded or well-lighted portions of the rocks' perimeters. The way that the sun falls on the ground will greatly affect the amount of moisture present in the soil. If as a plant you plan to live in a hot, sunny niche, you'd better be able to hold onto a good share of whatever water comes your way. The champions at this game are the miserly cacti, which instead of growing water-wasting leaves, manufacture their food through the chlorophyll present in their green stems. Another way to survive the hot seat is to be able to sink your roots way down deep, like the creosote bush, to collect what moisture you can from the available supply of ground water.

An interpretive sign about 1 mile up the trail tells about the groups of fan palms that you'll be coming across as you make your way up the path. From the sign you can just see the fuzzy tops of the first palm grove about 0.5 mile ahead in the narrow slit of the upper canyon. Though from this point the grove may not look like much, if you've never been to a fan palm oasis you'll be astounded at the exotic beauty that surrounds these remnants of a much earlier, much wetter climate. For a good part of the year tall reeds, sedges, and rushes line silky pools of water. The air is cool and

33

moist, stitched through with a bright medley of bird song and waterfalls.

The majority of the hundreds of palm trees found in this canyon system are in the upper reaches of Borrego Palm Canyon, as are some exquisite waterfalls. These delights are substantially more difficult to reach, however, and should be attempted only by those willing to scramble for their scenery.

TRUCKHAVEN ROCKS

Distance: 3 miles
Location: North side of County Road S22, 9.25 miles east of Pegleg Smith Monument, 100 yards west of the turnoff to Arroyo Salado Primitive Campground. If conditions are good (no recent rains), you may want to park 0.5 mile up Coachwhip Canyon, which will reduce the round-trip distance for the walk by 1 mile.

The actual name of this wash is Coachwhip Canyon, "coachwhip" being another name for the spindly ocotillo plant. Despite its stark, badland appearance, this western side of Truckhaven Rocks can provide you with a fascinating study of wind and water architecture.

The first 0.5 mile of the walk away from County Road S22 is through a wash garden of smoke trees, those misty-looking plants that encase their seeds in hard coats, which will open only under the violent action of flash floods. Notice the soft, sandy texture of the wash, which indicates that sandstone is being steadily worn away up the canyon. It is interesting to consider that because of this wearing action, Anza-Borrego's flatlands to the south are already much higher in elevation than they used to be. Water and winds carry away entire mountain ranges down washes like these, a particle at time. If internal movements in the earth do not push the mountains upward at the same rate that they are being worn away, the area will again turn into a flat, largely featureless landscape. (In fact, an artery of the San Jacinto Fault, a crack in the earth that allows for vertical as well as horizontal movement, is located at the base of the Santa Rosa Mountains immediately to the north.)

The wash forks 0.7 mile from County Road S22. Stick to the left, which in 50 yards will take you through a narrow passageway in the slab rocks on the west side of the wash. Despite the severe lack of vegetation on these dry, unstable hills, this protected catchment basin often sports a healthy crop of lush green grass.

Another 0.5 mile will bring you to the Swiss Cheese Rocks. This is a strange collection of yellowish sandstone that has been eroded into bizarre shapes riddled with holes of varying sizes. Strong desert winds and rainwater will sometimes hollow adjacent chambers to the point where they become joined together, forming a single passageway framed by a delicate outside arch.

The unstable character and low nutritive quality of these sedimentary foothills have restricted opportunities for plant growth to only the most efficient contenders. Smoke trees and brittlebush dot the wash bottom, where groundwater is more accessible, but on the stark, grainy slopes, only ocotillo and cholla cactus appear with any regularity. To see them in late spring unleashing their red and yellow blooms against this bleak canvas hints at the grand powers held in smallest slices of life.

PINYON WASH

Distance: 4 miles
Location: On the south side of State Highway 78, approximately 3.5 miles east of the intersection with County Road S3. Coming from the east, the wash will be 0.5 mile west of the Narrows Earth Trail.

Of all the ways to see the desert, wash walking is perhaps the most enjoyable. Unusual plants, as well as the variety of animals and birds they support, are plentiful along these sandy water courses. There are always chances of finding oases of cool, clear water and, in the mountains, mysterious stone galleries and towering cathedrals of polished stone. The constant drift and meanders of most washes keep your exact destination a secret, yet there is an obvious pathway to take you safely out again.

Of course you should never walk in any wash when rain is threatening, even if the storm is isolated in a mountain range many miles away. Most of the rainwater simply runs off the nonabsorbent desert soil, forming great liquid walls that go careening down the ravines at breakneck speed.

As devastating as these flash floods can be, some plants have evolved to take advantage of this rather violent side of desert life. One such plant that you'll see along the first 0.25 mile of this walk through Pinyon Wash is the smoke tree, named for the gray-green branches that appear like smoke or haze when viewed from a distance. The seeds of the smoke tree are encased in an extremely hard coat, which must be broken before germination can begin. About the only force strong enough to accomplish this, as noted earlier, is a rampaging ride in the arms of a flash flood, smashing against one rock after another. The beauty of this system is that afterward, when smoke tree seeds get down to the business of sprouting, the flood waters will have provided enough moisture in the soil for roots to grow strong and hearty.

If the smoke tree deserves acclaim for creative sprouting, then a small animal you'll surely see in Pinyon Wash, the antelope ground squirrel, should win the award for creative cooling. When the hot summer sun threatens desert animals with overheating, many will simply burrow down to cooler temperatures or sit in the shade and pant. The antelope ground squirrel, however, has discovered that by drooling on his chest fur and facing into the wind, he can create his own evaporative cooler! Look for this chipmunk-size fruit and seed eater all along this walk, usually scampering across the wash with his tail held over his back.

Up the wash on the right about 1.25 miles is a beautiful forest of ocotillos. During the months of March through June, clusters of delicate scarlet blossoms hover on the tips of the plant's spindly branches. This is a particularly fine slice of desert to explore outside of Pinyon Wash.

Just past the ocotillos is a junction with Nolina Wash, which heads straight south while Pinyon breaks off to the east. Keeping to the pathway on the left, you'll soon come to a superb collection

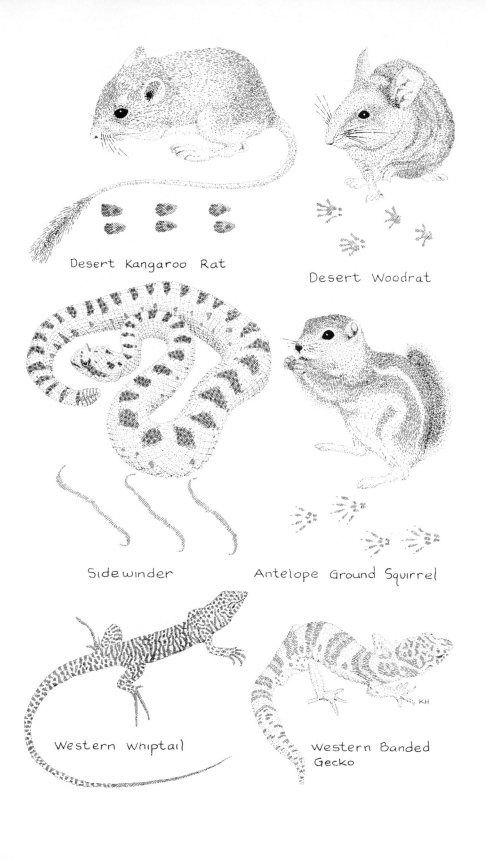

Desert Kangaroo Rat

Desert Woodrat

Sidewinder

Antelope Ground Squirrel

Western Whiptail

Western Banded Gecko

of agaves on the south side of the wash. Agaves are most easily recognized by their single 10- to-15-foot-tall flower stalks, so strong that they have often been used for ridge poles in house construction. In June through August the upper stalks of some agaves will bear large oval flowers that look like yellow islands hanging in the sky. Each agave requires many seasons before it eventually flowers, though the notion that this happens only once every hundred years (hence their nickname of "century plant") is incorrect.

Southwest Indians have long considered the agave to be one of Grandmother Earth's most precious plants. In fact, for many desert-bound cultures the agave held the same great importance as a food source as did pinyon nuts and acorns for other California tribes. For this reason the agave harvest was a time of great excitement and celebration. Leaves were steam-roasted or baked for later use and blossoms dried in the sun retained their flavor and nutritional value for many years. The most relished part of the plant was the stalk, which when roasted tastes like very rich molasses.

In addition to a food source, the extremely strong fibers in agave leaves were separated from one another by pounding them with rocks, after which they were dried and combed. The fibers were then used in the construction of everything from skirts, sandals, and bowstrings, to mats, snares, and baby cradles. The plant's thorns, which are located at the tip of each leaf, made perfect sewing needles with which to weave the fibers.

The turnaround point for this walk has no distinct markings, but you will have gone about 2 miles at the point where Pinyon Wash swings from a southeast heading to go straight south. From here you will be surrounded by clusters of beautiful desert lavender and tall foothills covered with great tilted slabs of rock. Behind you to the northwest is a magnificent panorama of Anza-Borrego desert running down to the Mescal Bajada.

Were you to continue up the wash another 3.5 miles you would come to the bowl-shaped valley of Harper Flat, one of the most heavily used and longest-occupied Indian camps in the park. As the white man's push westward began to uproot the lives of Southern California Indians, Harper Flat became a kind of secret meeting place in which people from many tribes came to pray and dance, to ask from the sacred powers some kind of understanding of what was happening to their people. The wash where you now stand was a major route of travel to and from the flat during this period. In this sense, Pinyon Wash was not so much a trail of tears as it was a pathway of hope for those seeking a spiritual center in a world thrown horribly out of balance.

ELEPHANT TREES

Distance: 3.2 miles
Location: From State Highway 78 just east of the park boundary, head 6 miles south on Split Mountain Road. Turn west on a dirt road leading to the Elephant Trees Nature Trail. (Note: The 1.5-mile-long entrance road to the nature trail is quite rocky and rough. Take your time.)

The Elephant Trees walk, which combines a 1.5-mile, self-guided loop trail with 2 miles of wash walking, has enough variety to please even the most demanding desert aficionado. The interpretive loop will allow you to learn or reacquaint yourself with seventeen of the more common Anza-Borrego Desert plants. Included among these is the rare elephant tree, so called because of its greatly swelled trunk. The elephant tree is a member of a relatively small family of plants from the tropics, and this happens to be the northernmost collection on the continent. Though prospectors reported seeing these plants around the turn of the century, it took dedicated botanists more than thirty-five years to verify their existence.

Cahuilla Indians believed the elephant tree to have great power. The tree's red sap, which was sometimes referred to as blood, was supposedly an effective treatment for skin diseases when rubbed on the body. Because of its potency, elephant tree sap was usually administered only by tribal medicine men.

After you've finished walking the self-guided loop, go back up the trail and follow the wash that runs westward between interpretive stops no. 5 and no. 6. (A row of rocks has been placed across the wash at this point.) It's possible to become slightly confused 0.1 mile after leaving the nature trail, since here the stream bed starts to intermingle with several islands of vegetation. Just keep veering at a shallow angle toward the low hummock hills ahead of you on your left. Note the rock and mud construction of these sedimentary walls, so perfectly layered that it's hard to believe they weren't laid down by a stone mason.

The now obvious wash continues westward, through beautiful collections of ocotillo, desert lavender, mesquite, and smoke tree. These large shrubs form a prime habitat for birds, especially since they are protected from the sun by the line of north-facing hills. If at all possible, plan to do this trip in the early morning hours. This is also the best time to photograph the silky light and shadow shows that flow across the handsome Vallecito Mountains to the west.

You may notice tiny holes in the bottom of the wash that have been surrounded by circular walls of pebbles, sand grains, or bits of vegetation. These are the homes of rough harvester ants, who can be seen collecting seeds and grains from the edges of the wash to fill their underground pantries. If you are here in hot weather, you may find entrance holes that have been plugged. While this is sometimes done to protect against invaders, desert ants have adopted this technique to keep out the heat, as well as to maintain humidity levels within the range that the colony needs to survive.

As you near the end of the hills on your left, the wash becomes a quiet, totally secluded pathway filled with a profusion of birds, plants, and animal tracks. As the hills come to an end, the wash continues west southwest for about another 0.5 mile, finally breaking up into several smaller washes in the middle of one of the most peaceful, appealing slices of desert to be found anywhere in the park. The thick vegetation here offers fine camouflage for wildlife watchers to sit and wait for action.

If you want to add to the distance of this walk but not necessarily the difficulty, when you reach the edge of the hills on your way back, follow them around to the south for about 50 yards. Here you'll come to a delightful little park nestled against the western edge of a group of sedimentary hills—the perfect place for naps, picnics, or pretending you're a chilly whiptail lizard by sprawling across the hottest slab of rock you can find.

BOW WILLOW CANYON

Distance: 5 miles
Location: From State Highway 78, 5 miles east of Banner, head south on County Road S2 approximately 30 miles to a dirt road heading west toward Bow Willow Campground. A parking area and seasonal ranger station are at the west end of the campground.

Archaeologists have widely differing opinions as to precisely when humans began living in Anza-Borrego, but even the most conservative estimates place paleo-Indian tribes in the region about 7000 B.C. This is more than two thousand years before the earliest recorded date on the Egyptian calendar and almost nine thousand years before the first European—Lieutenant Pedro Fages of the San Diego military post—happened to stumble into the area in pursuit of a small group of army deserters.

The path that you'll be following into Bow Willow Canyon was an important trail to a group of Indians known as the Kumeyaays. Living in this area from about A.D. 1000 to the beginning of the twentieth century, the Kumeyaays were the very last of a long chain of native peoples that had achieved an enduring harmony with this frugal land. They would spend the months from autumn through spring here on the desert floor, gathering foods from native plants and hunting rabbit and bighorn sheep. Then in late spring the Indians would follow this trail up into the Laguna Mountains to the west, where they would subsist on nuts and berries, as well as on game such as bear and mule deer.

The first 0.25 mile of this walk is through a stark landscape—hummocks of rust-colored boulders sharp against a cobalt sky. At 0.5 mile the wash begins to narrow slightly. Scattered across the sandy floor are the olive greens of brittlebush. This plant, which is quite common on dry slopes and in washes below 3,000 feet of elevation, produces a fragrant resin that was used as an incense in many of the churches of Baja California. In addition, Cahuilla Indians heated the resin and applied it to the chest for relief of localized pain. During the months of March through June, brittlebush explodes with a full crown of brilliant yellow flowers.

Notice that as the canyon narrows and the walls become

41

steeper, plants in the bottom of the wash become more plentiful. This is a good place to grow, since whatever rains come during the year will certainly be channeled right down this canyon. In addition, moisture remains here longer because the steep walls allow only a limited amount of harsh sunlight to reach the floor of the wash each day. If you look in the shade of willow branches and other fairly dense shrubs, you'll even see rich carpets of green grass. Take careful note of how plants grow according to their orientation to the sun, and it won't be long before you'll be able to predict what kind of life certain niches will contain.

At 1 mile into this walk, the shrub vegetation has become so robust that it completely obliterates views of the wash edges. You can wander at will among the plants without any kind of feeling that you're being channeled in a certain direction. Along with this hardy plant community comes an abundance of bird life. (Ardent bird watchers should hit this trail early in the morning.) Keep eyes and ears open for the Say's phoebe, verdin, northern flicker, black-throated sparrow, and, farther up the wash, the tiny Costa's hummingbird.

About 2 miles up the wash the canyon walls will close in to their narrowest point. Notice the appearance of barrel cactus and ocotillo on the right (west) side of the canyon. The number and size of leaves on the ocotillo's branches is a good indication of how recently it has rained. As the soil dries out the plant will drop its leaves to reduce moisture loss and then grow a new set after the next rainstorm. This cycle is particularly easy to track during the hot months of summer. Some Indian tribes soaked the ocotillo's blossoms in water to make a tangy drink, and later in the year, they parched the seeds and ground them into flour for cakes. The plant's long stems are still used as slats for fences and corrals throughout the southwestern United States and Mexico.

Joshua Tree
National Monument

FORTYNINE PALMS OASIS

Distance: 3 miles

Location: Turn south on Canyon Road, located about 5 miles west of the city of Twentynine Palms. Caution: This road will not necessarily be marked. It lies just to the west of the High Desert Animal Hospital, which is on the southeast corner of this intersection, and is several miles east of the turnoff to Indian Cove. Follow Canyon Road for 1.7 miles to the parking area and trail head.

Although the walk to Fortynine Palms Oasis requires a 400-foot climb on the way in and another 300 feet going out, it will provide you with an unmatched opportunity to slip your tired spirit into the magic cradle of a desert oasis. It was likely in just such a place that nature writer George Wharton James found that "mind and soul are soothed and quieted, and one is able to see how to use the added strength and rugged power he has absorbed from the rude and uncouth, but loving and generous bosom of the desert mother."

The climbing part of the walk is limited to about the first 0.7 mile, following an old Indian trail through a stark, rock-strewn landscape to a ridge high above the town of Twentynine Palms. Jojoba and calico cactus can be found here, and you can see wonderful splashes of lichens staining the rocks with unheard-of colors. Lichen is a unique partnership (symbiosis) of algae and fungus, with each member bringing a separate, life-sustaining function to the partnership. Chemicals released by lichen actually erode the rock underneath, and on horizontal surfaces, their decaying tissue combines with crumbling rock and windblown debris to form the

43

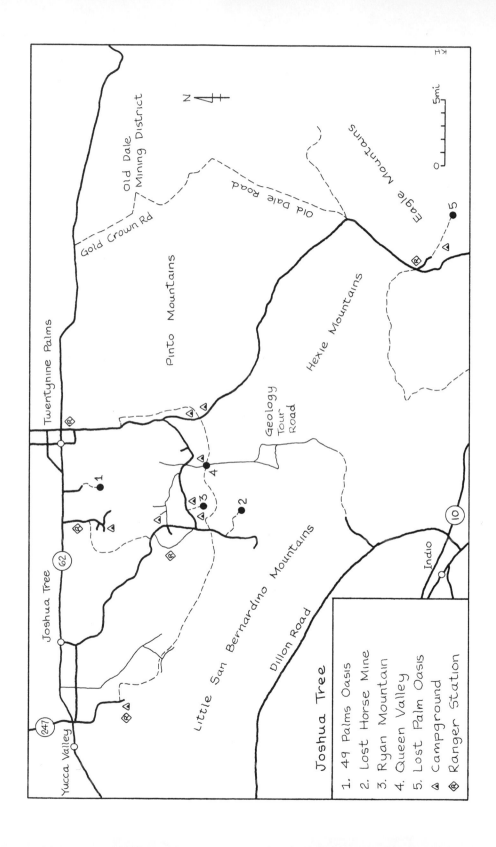

Joshua Tree

1. 49 Palms Oasis
2. Lost Horse Mine
3. Ryan Mountain
4. Queen Valley
5. Lost Palm Oasis
▲ Campground
⊗ Ranger Station

N

0   5mi

Twentynine Palms

Old Dale Mining District

Gold Crown Rd

Old Dale Road

Pinto Mountains

Eagle Mountains

Hexie Mountains

Geology Tour Road

Little San Bernardino Mountains

Dillon Road

Joshua Tree

Yucca Valley

247

62

10

Indio

first hints of soil. The organism is adversely affected by pollutants of any kind, so many people consider a profuse mosaic of lichen to be an excellent indicator of clean air.

Just after topping the ridge at 0.7 mile, note the fantastic collection of barrel cacti, one of the finest to be found anywhere in the area. Barrel cacti have suffered greatly in some American deserts from thieves who steal them to sell to urban landscapers. Also working against them is the fact that some species have succulent fruit that lends itself to being sweetened into a mildly raging novelty called "cactus candy." (The fruit is also occasionally pickled.)

It really is surprising how much moisture the inner tissues of the barrel cactus can hold. In fact, it isn't uncommon to find a plant that has gone two or even three years without any access to water, still putting on a blooming good flower show.

About 1 or 1.5 miles to the southeast you can see the junction of two extremely steep and rugged canyons. It's at the bottom of this apparently lifeless labyrinth that water has bubbled to the surface and made it possible for an oasis to form. This group of fan palms, along with those at the Oasis of Mara at Twentynine Palms, forms the northernmost collection of native *Washingtonia filifera* in the western hemisphere.

The trail soon begins to descend through a boulder-strewn landscape dotted with mesquite, brittlebush, and desert trumpet (a small woody plant with swelled joints below its branches). As you approach the first set of palms, you'll note that the trunks of many of them have been blackened by fire. In fact, this grove has been burned three times since the 1940s. It appears that an occasional burning can actually help the fan palm by clearing away undergrowth (often mesquite) that is competing with the trees for water. For some desert Indian tribes, burning the trees every so often was considered part of the routine maintenance of a healthy grove.

Work your way back to the upper groves. Here the palms seem to rise from a fairyland—giant boulders huddled into chambers that echo the tick-tock dripping of cool water; stands of rich green reed grass and the fuzzy brown heads of cattails swinging like metronomes in the canyon breeze; and best of all, deep, clear pools framed by weavings of maidenhair fern.

On your way back out, stop for a minute on the high ridge

overlooking the city of Twentynine Palms. It is easy to forget that its survival, like that of the oasis, hangs on the constant drip of water. Some scientists are already concerned that we are pushing this resource too far, too fast. The many wells in this area seem to be contributing to the lowering of the region's groundwater at a rate of about a foot a year. Surface pools have already disappeared from Lost Palms and the Twentynine Palms Oasis. When the water slips to more than 20 feet below ground level, the oasis, as well as many of the life forms that are sustained on its riches, will die. And they will take their magic with them.

LOST HORSE MINE

Distance: 3.2 miles
Location: Go south on the main entrance road at Twentynine Palms. Take the first road heading west for approximately 10 miles to a T intersection. Go south on Keys View Road a little more than 2 miles to a dirt road running east to the Lost Horse Mine. The parking area is a little more than 1 mile from the pavement. The wash you'll be walking up is just to the right of the "Trail" identification sign, located a few yards from the parking lot.

A trip to Joshua Tree National Monument wouldn't be complete without dabbling a bit in the strange tales of fortunes lost and found in the lonely pursuit of gold. There are many different versions of how the Lost Horse Mine came into being, most of which, appropriately, do involve a lost horse. One of most commonly accepted tales says that at a camp about 4 miles east of the present mine site, a horse belonging to a feisty German named Johnny Lang decided to wander off into the sunset. While Johnny was trying to track his mount down, he was met by a local rancher named McHaney, who matter-of-factly informed him that his horse was "no longer lost" and that he should vamoose to an area known as Witch Spring, where another German named Frank Diebold happened to be camped.

Diebold told Johnny about a rich gold vein he had discovered nearby but admitted that he couldn't work it because of harassment by McHaney's roughshod cowboys. Johnny later checked out the vein and found it enticing enough to buy out Diebold for an even one thousand dollars. Johnny formed a partnership to develop the mine in the faces of McHaney's hooligans. Then, in 1895, all the partners except him sold their shares to two brothers named Thomas and Jep Ryan, and Johnny became manager of the night shift. Unfortunately, one night he got caught in the mill building pilfering gold, and Jep Ryan offered him a choice: go to jail or sell out for twelve thousand dollars. Johnny never did think much of jails.

Under the leadership of the Ryans, the Lost Horse Mine became the most successful gold operation in the area. In the mine's sporadic forty-year history, of which 1896–1899 were the peak years of production, it produced 9,000 troy ounces of gold worth about 350,000 dollars. Twenty-five men worked at the mine site, while almost a dozen more had full-time employment scavenging for wood to fire the big, noisy steam engine that ran the 8,500-pound stamp mill. (Notice that the rolling hills surrounding the mine are covered with blackbrush and scrub vegetation. There was a time, though, when they supported healthy stands of pinyon and juniper, all of which went up in smoke.) To avoid being ripped off by road bandits during the early years, gold ingots produced at the Lost Horse Mine were hidden in freight wagons and hauled 25 miles to Indio.

Instead of walking to and from the mine on the old wagon road, it's much more enjoyable to make a circle trip out of this journey by heading up the wash just to the right of the first trail marker sign (adjacent to the parking area). This is a delightfully secluded little watercourse filled with a surprising variety of plants as well as an abundance of bird life. About 0.2 mile from the trail head the wash is wrapped in a heavy cloak of pinyon and oak; keep a close eye out here for Gambel's quail.

At 0.3 mile in you'll see a large plant resembling yucca growing along the more open, rocky banks of the wash. This is the nolina, and it can be most easily distinguished from the Mojave yucca by the fact that its leaves do not have loose white fibers curling up from their edges. Some desert Indians used to bake the stalk of this plant by placing it in a pit lined with hot rocks and ashes and then covering it with sand. The result was a food more tender than you might think but with a definite bitterness to it.

About 0.6 mile into the walk the wash will enter an open area and split into two forks. Follow the left-hand fork upward about 50 yards until you reach the Lost Horse Mine Road and take a right (this road has been above you all along). The roadway twists and climbs, affording you your first view of the Lost Horse Mine stamp mill about a mile away.

Although the Park Service has filled in most of the mine pits in this area, be careful as you're walking around that you don't stumble into one. The stamp mill forms the centerpiece of the historical relics at Lost Horse Mine, surrounded by an assortment of amalgamation tanks and mine shafts. Ore was crushed to powder under the enormous weight of these stamps, and the gold was then separated from the worthless material by amalgamating it with mercury, or, during later years, with a cyanide solution. Even with the aid of the stamp mill the early mining days were just plain hard work. Besides the actual extraction of rock from the ground, someone had to break up pieces of promising-looking ore with a sledgehammer constantly and feed them into the battery boxes of the stamp mill. The actual amalgamation process also required constant attention to assure that as much gold (or silver) as possible would be retrieved by the mercury bath.

For a few years around the turn of the century, the partners of the Lost Horse Mine were making the tidy sum of three thousand dollars a day—certainly enough to take the edge off even the most trying manual labor. Shortly after the turn of the century, however, the vein played out and was never found again.

RYAN MOUNTAIN

Distance: 3 miles
Location: Head south on the main park entrance road at Twentynine Palms. Take the first right turn (heading west) toward Queen Valley. The parking area for Ryan Mountain is a little more than 0.3 mile west of Sheep Mountain Group Campground.

Though fairly short, the Ryan Mountain walk is one of the steepest trails in the entire book and therefore may not be appropriate for people with health problems. The reward for a slow, steady uphill effort, however, is one of the finest desert views in the state.

The first 0.1 mile of trail will take you between two sets of enormous rock outcroppings. These sculpted blocks and towers of quartz monzonite (a rock very much like granite) are among the most intriguing aspects of the Joshua Tree Monument landscape, and their story is one worth telling. Many years ago—about 80 million to be more specific—the material that makes up these piles of rocks was a molten liquid oozing its way upward from deep inside the earth. Though it was pushed up a great distance, when the journey ended the fiery hot fluid was still thousands of feet beneath the earth's surface, where it eventually cooled and hardened, forming igneous rocks.

The rocks were slowly uplifted, and, during a period when the climate was much wetter, endless rivulets of groundwater coursed down the joints of the buried rock, rounding off their sharp edges in the process. As the desert climate took over, flash floods began to rip through the area, carrying away layer after layer of valley soil finally to reveal this intriguing collection of inner-earth sculpture.

If you have visited the much lower, eastern part of the park, you may remember that the plants of that area were somewhat different than those you see here. Much of the change is due to a gain in elevation, which results in a temperature decrease of about 3 degrees for every thousand feet climbed. Higher elevations often receive more precipitation, and what they receive they retain longer owing to the cooler temperatures. Also, notice that this side of the mountain is facing north, which means it gets the least amount of

49

moisture-stealing sun during the year. All these things put together mean that plants that find it too dry really to thrive at lower elevations—such as juniper and certain types of grasses—manage to do quite well here.

The path intersects the trail from Sheep Mountain Campground at about 0.2 mile. Huff-n-puff stretch no. 1 begins here and lasts about 0.2 mile, at the end of which you're rewarded with 30 or 40 yards of flat walking. While your lungs are doing their best to revive you, sit down and enjoy the expansive views of the Queen Mountains to the north and the carpets of Joshua trees rolling far into the distance. Huff-n-puff stretch no. 2 begins shortly after this, heads south for a time, and then turns again to rise westward along the flank of the mountain. Although your climbing isn't exactly over, this shift to the west marks the end of the worst.

If you go early in the morning before the winds begin, you will never find a quieter stretch of trail than this. Except for an occasional car throwing back the morning sun at you from the bottom of the Queen Valley, it would be easy to think that you were the only person alive on earth.

From here on up take your time. Notice the thin, dark coating of iron and manganese—commonly referred to as "desert varnish"—that has been deposited on many of the rocks during centuries of weathering. Look for brightly colored lichens. See how some of the boulders are beautiful compositions of many different types of rocks, mixed together like marble-cake-batter swirls.

At 1 mile the trail heads south through a narrow notch dotted with hardy pinyon pines. The nuts of the pinyon are very rich and delicious, with a caloric content similar to that of almonds or peanut butter. Though the quantity of each year's nut crop is very unpredictable, Indian tribes of the Southwest have always placed great importance on their harvest. Besides being a valuable addition to their own food supply (in some tribes the nuts were important as nourishment for infants), a pinyon crop was also a precious trade item.

Soon out of this notch, at about 1.35 miles you will gain the first sweeping views of the landscape to the south—the grand tilt of the Queen Valley, the enticing wildness of the Little San Bernardino Mountains.

Desert Bighorn

It is only a short 0.15-mile stroll to the top of Ryan Mountain. From here the entire world seems to open up into a crumpled, windswept tapestry of browns and rusts and greens. To the west is Lost Horse Valley, to the east and south, Queen and Pleasant valleys, as well as the holes of the Lost Horse Mine. Look to the western horizon and you'll see fall lines from two north-south mountain ranges dipping toward each other to form a distinct notch. This is San Gorgonio Pass, which for well over a century has been the principal route connecting these vast, unbridled deserts with the rich coastal valleys of southwestern California.

QUEEN VALLEY

Distance: 5 miles

Location: Head south on the main entrance road at Twentynine Palms, and take the first spur heading west toward Queen Valley. In about 5 miles you'll come to the Geology Tour Road, which heads south. Take this until you reach the California Riding and Hiking Trail. There is a trail sign here, as well as a sign-in board and parking lot on the east side of the road. The walk follows the trail to the west. (A sign at the beginning of the geology road says "4-wheel drive recommended," but there is no need for it up to this point.)

I remember often wishing as a young boy on vacation with my family that we could stop the car along some open highway and just walk off into the middle of nowhere. The desire could strike in almost any unpopulated area, but it seemed especially common when we were in a nondescript landscape whose only real significance was that there was so much of it and so little of anything else. There was something incredibly enticing about all that open space—as Willa Cather said, "Something soft and wild and free; something that whispered to the ear on the pillow, lightened the heart, softly, softly picked the lock, slid the bolts, and released the prisoned spirit of man into the wind."

This walk through the open reaches of the Queen Valley is such a fantasy come true. While there are not necessarily any "wow!" spots here, there is a wild vastness of truly healing proportions. Thousands of Joshua trees cloak countless miles of landscape, their expanse ultimately broken by the Queen Mountains to the north, the Pintos to the east, and the great swell of the Little San Bernardinos to the south and west. Yuccas, chollas, mound cacti, juniper, bunch grass, desert trumpet, and great collections of blackbrush fill in the remaining ground space as close to one another as the water supply will allow.

This walk may provide you with your first opportunity for a close look at a Joshua tree. The famous explorer Captain John C. Frémont called it "the most repulsive tree in the vegetable kingdom." Another desert explorer wrote that the Joshua tree was "more like some conception of Poe's . . . than any work of wholesome Mother Nature. One can scarcely find," he went on to say, "a term of ugliness that is not apt for this plant."

Try as I might, I can come up with no such contempt for this stalwart member of the agave family. Besides blessed shade, the Joshua tree offers its sharp pointed leaves to wood rats, who use them to fortify their nests. Its flowers and fruits provide food for small mammals. More than two dozen species of birds use the giant plant as a nesting site, including cactus wrens, ladder-back woodpeckers, Scott's orioles, and screech owls. Lizards and night snakes make homes in its dead branches. A bird known as the loggerhead shrike takes lizards it has caught and skewers them on the Joshua's sharp leaves for later dining.

Interestingly, the very existence of the Joshua tree depends on the tiny female yucca moth, the only creature that can transfer pollen from one flower to another for the production of seeds. Keep in mind that it's really by "accident" that most bees, flies, and moths carry pollen from one flower to another—a simple result of their continual search for food (nectar). But here is a moth that eats neither nectar or pollen yet purposely goes out and collects pollen and then deliberately places it on the waiting organs of the Joshua flower! There is, as you might have guessed, a significant payoff to the moth. She lays her eggs directly in the flower's ovary, with the result that her young can then feed off the Joshua tree's developing seeds. This relationship has worked so remarkably well that over thousands of years the Joshua tree has lost all other means of reproduction.

A short way into this walk you'll come upon a post with a number 12 on it. These are mile markers that have been installed along the California Riding and Hiking Trail, and the numbers increase as you walk west. Among the bunch grass and juniper trees past mile marker 12, you may notice a slender little plant with very swollen joints beneath its branches. This is a fairly common resident of arid lands known as the desert trumpet. The rather sour-tasting stems of the plants were regularly eaten by Indians, who also occasionally dried the hollow, swollen stems for use as tobacco pipes.

I chose to end my walk on top of a small hill about 0.25 mile past mile marker 14. From here you can have a grand view of the tablelands that run south to the flanks of the Little San Bernardino Mountains. It's interesting to consider that the valley before you is simply the result of a different type of rock. Those under what are now the flatlands happen to be "softer" than those that make up the surrounding mountains. Millions of years of water erosion have turned a rather homogeneous uplifted landscape into the combination of plains and peaks that lie before you. (The piles of jumbo rocks to the east, however, have a story all their own. For a special discussion of these, see the Ryan Mountain walk.)

LOST PALMS OASIS

Distance: 7.4 miles

Location: Take the park entrance road north from Interstate 10 for about 7 miles. Follow signs to Cottonwood Springs, which is located on a spur road heading southeast from the Cottonwood Visitors' Center. A backcountry sign-in board and alternate trail head lie along this spur road 0.25 mile before you reach the actual springs. Go ahead and sign in here, but do not take this trail, as it adds 0.5 mile to an already long walk. (You can also begin at Cottonwood Campground, but this route is longer by 0.4 mile.)

Although longer than most of our treks, the Lost Palms Oasis walk is worth every single step. The vast majority of visitors to Joshua

Tree Monument see only the western, Mojave Desert side of the park. The Lost Palm Oasis Trail winds through a part of the monument dominated by the more eastern Colorado Desert—lower in elevation and laced with some of the most ruggedly beautiful desert scenery you will ever lay eyes on.

The walk begins at lovely Cottonwood Springs, an important stopover for prospectors and freight haulers during the late nineteenth and early twentieth centuries. While today the spring may flow at 20 or 30 gallons an hour, seventy-five years ago it spewed forth its precious liquid at five times that rate. The fine fan palms you see here are not native but are thought to have been planted around 1920. In addition to an occasional piece of water pipe and the faint tracks of old wagon roads, it's not hard to find evidence of much earlier visitors to Cottonwood Springs. Where the Lost Palm Oasis Trail first leaves the palm grove on the east, for example, you'll discover grinding mortars worn deep into the rocks by the labors of uncounted generations of desert Indians.

The first thirty-five minutes of this walk is a rather up-and-down affair through several small wash systems peppered with juniper, creosote bushes, cholla, and yucca. The trail settles into a more horizontal run after reaching the junction of Mastodon Peak Trail at 1.1 miles. Notice how the desert here has a bright, scrubbed look to it. Plants grow in pleasant spacing patterns that are somewhat less congested than in the higher, wetter Mojave Desert to the west. The different shrubs with their various shades of green have an especially rich, healthy appearance against the cinnamon-and-sugar-colored gravel. The most carefully planned desert botanical garden never looked better.

As you make your way across this engaging stretch, keep an eye out for the leathery, lobe-shaped leaves of the jojoba plant. Indian tribes in the area collected the plant's small seeds and either ate them raw or ground them into a powder, which produced a coffeelike drink. Unlike most native desert plants, which are rarely harvested anymore on a significant scale, the jojoba is once again coming into its own as an important resource to man. The small fruits of the plant contain nearly 50 percent oil. What's more, this oil has the somewhat rare quality of not being weakened by bacteria and is one of few substances that could completely replace the high-grade oils produced from dwindling populations of sperm whales. The United States is currently producing more than 200 tons of jojoba oil a year, which is finding its way into everything from cooking to car wax to lubricants for machinery.

Surrounded by high rock ridges that are slowly fracturing into giant slabs, the path makes its way eastward through a series of fine washes. In one of these, located at about 1.75 miles, the trail traverses what would best be described as a small forest of desert willows. Willows were one of the primary woods used by many desert Indian peoples to construct their houses and granaries and to make strong, flexible bows. From here the path enters an increasingly rugged country of eroded ridges framing narrow, lonely ravines. Daydreams of lost Indian tribes begin to surface, and of horse camps filled with grinning banditos counting bags of gold plucked from the Indio stage.

After climbing out of a rather steep wash at about 2.6 miles, you'll wind around a large hummock and gain a far-reaching view of the Salton Trough 25 miles to the south. Here lie 2,000 square miles of dry land below sea level, the largest such pocket to be found in the entire western hemisphere. On the floor of this basin is the Salton Sea, created in 1905 when the Colorado River was accidentally diverted into the Salton Trough through irrigation canals. When the mighty river was finally restored to its original channel in 1907, what had been dry land had become a 400-square-mile lake nearly 80 feet deep.

Dropping through a series of rocky ravines and washes, the trail reaches the Lost Palm Oasis Overlook in another 0.8 mile. The fan palm oasis is in the bottom of a sheer canyon, approximately 300 vertical feet and 0.2 mile below the overlook. Though this is the most strenuous part of the walk, it should not prove to be taxing to walkers who take their time. This is one of the two largest groups of native palms in the monument and certainly one of the most beautiful groups in the entire state. It is an unforgettable experience to lie here in the cool shade, listening to the music provided by the fingers of the wind stroking the palm fronds high overhead.

Death Valley
National Monument

LITTLE HEBE CRATER

Distance: 1 mile
Location: Northern edge of the monument, 5.2 miles north-west of the Grapevine Ranger Station. (Be careful that you make the left turn just past the station, and do not accidentally take State Highway 267 to Scotty's Castle.)

Although traffic can be rather heavy at times at the parking area adjacent to Ubehebe Crater, your walk up to Little Hebe Crater will leave most of the crowds behind. A series of connecting ridges with sweeping views of Death Valley are accessible from Little Hebe, and extending the walk to follow one or more of these crests is a sure path to peace and quiet.

From the interpretive sign at the edge of 500-foot-deep Ubehebe Crater you'll see a trail to your right climbing up a slope of loose cinders. It is about 0.5 mile from this point (adjacent to the parking area) to the western edge of Little Hebe.

The magnificent relics of volcanic activity before you are sometimes referred to as explosion craters. They were formed when hot magma rising inside the earth encountered groundwater, producing powerful blasts of steam that ripped through the earth with incredible fury. What is particularly surprising about Little Hebe Crater, which was blown into the broken edge of a cone formed much earlier, is its youth. Some geologists now think it to be no more than a thousand years old, which is only a tiny drop in the bucket when you consider the millions of years that have passed since the vast majority of Southern California desert rocks were formed.

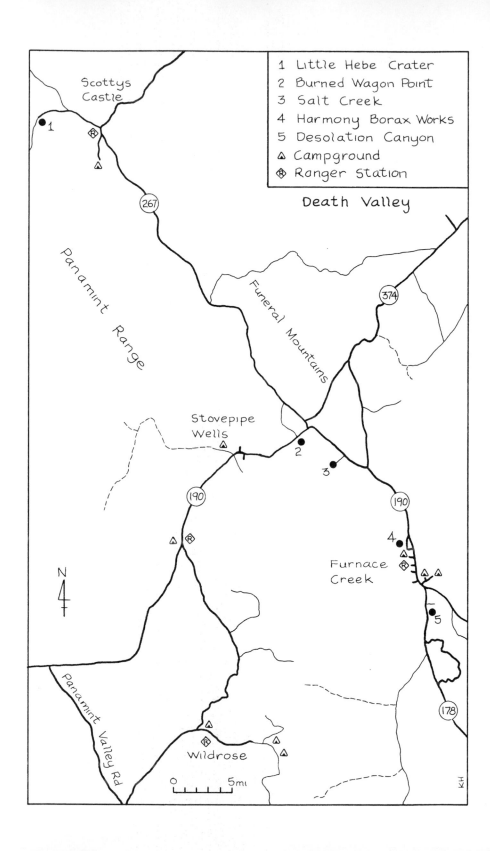

1 Little Hebe Crater
2 Burned Wagon Point
3 Salt Creek
4 Harmony Borax Works
5 Desolation Canyon
△ Campground
® Ranger Station

Death Valley

Scottys
Castle

1

267

Panamint Range

Funeral Mountains

374

Stovepipe
Wells

2

3

190

190

4

Furnace
Creek

5

N

Panamint Valley Rd

178

Wildrose

0   5mi

KH

Once you slog your way up a section of loose gravel at the very beginning of this walk, the trail eases up a bit, giving you a chance to explore leisurely some of the plants that manage to eke out a living here. (By the way, you'll want to stop at a point about 50 yards up from the parking area, where you will have a spectacular view back down into the beautifully striated rock lines of Ubehebe Crater. This is one of the best early morning photographic vantage points you'll find, with the rugged walls of the Last Chance Range providing a dramatic backdrop to an already impressive scene.) From here up you'll see scattered clumps of the tenacious mesquite plant growing on the small flange of land separating Little Hebe from Ubehebe. Besides being an extremely important food source for desert Indian tribes, the seed pods of the mesquite are also a favorite of browsing animals, who inadvertently help propagate the plants by passing the seeds through their waste.

Beneath much of this mesquite you'll also see a light brown to gray-green plant with very swollen joints. This is the desert trumpet, whose rather sour tasting stems were eaten on a fairly regular basis by desert Indians and also were used as tobacco pipes. Finally, rising brightly above this parched soil is one of the true champions of survival in a dry land—the desert holly, whose beautiful, light greenish white leaves are often dried and used for indoor decoration.

Take the short amount of time required to walk around the perimeter of Little Hebe Crater, which will offer you not only good opportunities to study the strange erosion patterns of the depression but will give you grand views of the beautifully desolate, windswept country lying to the west and south. Even the names of the geological features could make a thirsty man a little nervous: Dry Mountain and the Last Chance Range to the west and Dry Bone Canyon to the south. This is a landscape as harsh as any in America; and while at first it may make you strangely uncomfortable, the more time you spend among these warmly colored flutes of eroded rock, the more you will perceive the subtle beauty of this untamed desert terrain.

BURNED WAGON POINT

Distance: 4.5 miles
Location: The trail heads south on an old roadbed located along the south side of State Highway 190, just across from the turnoff to the Sand Dunes Picnic Area. (This is east of Stovepipe Wells.) It can be a bit hard to locate the beginning of the path. If you were to stand in the middle of the Sand Dunes Picnic Area road (north side of highway) looking south, it would be directly across the highway and about 10 yards to your left.

Take time to ponder the surroundings as you leave Highway 190 behind and strike southward on foot through the thirsty heart of Death Valley. Imagine the fears that this austere, ironclad landscape must have kindled in those lost pioneers of 1849. Along this same corridor many of them struggled, sunburned and famished, a desperate group of late autumn travelers that, ironically, had elected this more southerly route from Utah to the gold fields in order to avoid the horrors of ice and snow that had overcome the Donner-Reed party as they crossed the Sierras just three years earlier.

About 0.6 mile in, the old roadway passes a series of sand hummocks now colonized by healthy stands of honey mesquite. This deep-rooted plant seems particularly fond of staking its claim to life in precarious environments, even occasionally in landscapes marked by nothing but drifting dunes, struggling to grow at a rate just ahead of that at which the sand around it is accumulating. As for water, the mesquite gets its fair share through a system of very long roots, tapping supplies 50 feet or more below the surface of the ground.

This plant contributed a great deal to the sustenance of Indians of the area, as was described under the Kelso Dunes walk. The mesquite's spring blossoms, new pods, and finally the beans that dried on the vine during the summer were all harvested. They had a variety of uses, from making nutritious drinks to making flour. The beans themselves, which can be stored for well over a year, are 50 percent carbohydrate and nearly 10 percent protein, with a lesser, though still healthy amount of fat.

About 1.5 miles into the walk you'll come to a collection of gravelly-looking hills. The obvious roadway continues to the south-

60

east, but a small, westbound wash cuts between a large, long ridge on your right and a small escarpment just to the north of it. Follow this wash a short way to the other side of the hills, where it will join a faint roadway heading roughly south. You'll see these hills from a long way off; just remember that you will eventually want to end up on the west side of them, where there will then be nothing between you and the Panamint Mountains.

It's another 0.75 mile from the wash to Burned Wagon Point, which is marked by a metal sign. It was here in 1849 that a hapless group of men belonging to a group known as the Jayhawkers, decided to kill their oxen and dry the meat over fires built from their wagons in the hope that it would sustain them during their westward tramp to civilization. Three months passed between the time the Jayhawkers left the Old Spanish Trail for this "shortcut" that took them to the edge of death, and their fortunate deliverance to a cattle ranch in the San Fernando Valley.

Just west of Burned Wagon Point is a small, brackish pool known as McLean Spring, thought to have been used by the Jayhawkers as a water supply. A primitive trading post made out of marsh reeds stood here during the 1930s, though no sign of it remains today.

Walk about 100 yards south to have a closer look at the spongy, salt-laden ecosystem that surrounds the Salt Creek drainage (the Salt Creek Nature Trail is 1.5 miles to the southeast). Two plants—salt grass and pickleweed—are the dominant forms of life. Pickleweed, a shrub with fleshy green stems made up of tiny joints, is one of the most salt-tolerant plants in the United States, able to grow in environments with nearly twice the salinity level of sea water.

Common table salt can be found on the surfaces of the salt grass you see in this area. Some California Indian tribes used to obtain their supplies of this condiment from the ashes of burned salt grass. The stiffness of the plant also made it an effective scrubbing device.

SALT CREEK

Distance: 2 miles
Location: Salt Creek Interpretive Trail, located on the west
side of State Highway 190 about 13 miles north of Furnace
Creek. The trail begins from a parking area located at the end
of a dirt road heading southwest from the highway.

Nothing in Death Valley is more astonishing than to see the clear,
gurgling waters of Salt Creek rolling across the parched salt pan.
Despite the inviting appearance of this stream, however, don't rush
to fill your canteen from it. About twelve thousand years ago, the
enormous snowmelt lake that had filled this valley for thousands of
years began to dry up. As it grew smaller and smaller, the salinity
of the remaining water increased, bringing an end to thousands of
plants and animals that had depended on a freshwater environment. Those that adapted, particularly the pupfish you'll see in
these waters, are as significant an example of evolutionary change
as you'll find anywhere in the world.

The Salt Creek pupfish, which are found in no other ecosystem on earth, have adjusted to an environment incredibly different from the one in which they once existed. What was formerly
fresh water has become as salty as the ocean. This means that
pupfish, which at one time while living in fresh water could meet
their daily water needs simply through body absorption, have had
to develop the ability to drink salt water, remove the excess salt,
and then excrete it through their kidneys or gills. In addition, the
temperature of the water, at one time fairly consistent, today varies
from 32 to nearly 100 degrees. During the winter months the stream
remains above ground for a distance of about 2 miles, but in the
summer it dries up to a scattering of pools surrounding McLean
Spring, located 1.5 miles to the northwest. While there may be a
million pupfish in Salt Creek during the spring, by late summer,
only about 3,000 will remain.

Pupfish are omnivores, eating both plant and animal particles as they become available. The female will typically lay only
one egg at a time, which if successful (once laid, it receives no
further care from the parents), will become a mature fish in only
two or three months. Young pupfish add nearly 10 percent new

Costa's
Hummingbird

Red-tailed Hawk

Ladder-backed
Woodpecker

Loggerhead Shrike

Black-throated Sparrow   Gambel's Quail

body weight per day. If you happen to be here in the spring, keep an eye out for the bright blue males, waiting to mate with any receptive female that crosses the boundaries of their territory.

When you reach a bridge at the northernmost point of the boardwalk loop, you'll see a small trail continuing north along the east side of Salt Creek. Following this pathway will afford you fine opportunities to view pupfish, as well as several species of birds that you may miss if you stay on the more crowded nature trail. The colors here are especially beautiful—stark green carpets of salt grass lining the stream, framed by the soft browns, beiges, and reds of the distant uplands to the north and east.

Keep an eye out along the shores of Salt Creek for the great blue heron, a magnificent fishing bird that stands 3 to 4 feet high. Herons are not as wary as some birds and can often be seen from close range if you are very quiet and slow-moving. Along this back trail you'll also see snipes probing in the mud for small organisms, and killdeer, which if approached will run across the salt grass feigning a broken wing in hopes of leading you away from their nests.

This is also a favorite area for the coyote, whose tracks can often be seen in the mud ledges along Salt Creek. Since the coyote is not particular about what he eats, the Salt Creek drainage area allows him to add a few bird dishes to his regular menu of desert rodents, roots, and even mesquite beans. Birds and rodents are brought whole to young coyotes still in the den. The process of tearing the food helps to strengthen their jaws for the day when they will accompany the adults on hunting expeditions. There are a few coyotes who have formed a rather strange alliance with another Death Valley mammal, the badger. This much smaller, though more vicious carnivore makes his way through rodent burrows, chasing the residents out of their homes and into the clutches of the waiting coyote. The two animals then split the feast between them.

Before you turn south for the walk back, take a close look at the country before you. Along this small pathway the famous gold field-bound Jayhawkers struggled in 1849, after having already survived two months of ordeal in the desert. To the north 1.5 miles is McLean Spring, where the Jayhawkers killed their oxen and built fires from the wood of their wagons to smoke the meat. It was to be their sole source of food for a grueling overland walk to civilization—250 miles to the west. At times their mouths were so parched and swollen that they could not produce enough saliva to eat the meat. Most of them, however, did in fact make it out alive. It was part of a trek that Americans would come to view as an ultimate struggle for life, against a land that offered no compromise.

HARMONY BORAX WORKS

Distance: 2.75 miles
Location: Harmony Borax interpretive display, west side of State Highway 190, just under 2 miles north of Furnace Creek.

Just as the saga of William Manly and the lost forty-niners tends to ignite some rather stirring Death Valley daydreams, so can the tales of hell-bent hardship found in the early days of mining borax, the "white gold" of the desert. At the time Aaron Winters first discovered borax on the valley salt pan in 1881, the substance was being sold for a respectable thirty-five cents per pound. Winters sent borax samples that he had taken along Furnace Creek to William Coleman, a San Francisco investor who was providing the financial backing for several borax mines in Nevada. Since Winters and his wife, Rosie, were living at the time in a dirt-floor dugout at the edge of the Armagosa Desert, they were thrilled when Coleman bought their rights to the Furnace Creek borax fields for twenty thousand dollars.

Coleman wasted little time in building the Harmony Borax Works, an operation that rested heavily on the strong backs of Chinese laborers who gathered the borite "cottonball" by hand into large baskets. At an on-site refinery, the substance was crystallized onto iron rods that had been suspended in large vats. At that point it was ready to be transported to the railhead in Mojave, 165 miles away. It was the miserable transportation conditions that prompted superintendent J.W.S. Perry to build special 16-foot-long ore wagons to be hauled by ten pairs of mules in tandem. The total weight

65

of each load, which included 1,200 gallons of water, was more than 72,000 pounds. Off men and beast would go, trudging 16 miles a day for ten days through some of the loneliest, most forlorn country in America.

Thus was born the romantic, Wild West image of "twenty-mule teams." That particular term was copyrighted as a trademark of Coleman's company by a young borax salesman named Stephen Mather, who later became one of the most celebrated directors of the National Park Service.

Today borates are still used throughout the industrial world for the manufacture of glass, ceramics, antifreeze, fertilizers, cosmetics, and especially fiberglass.

The path out to the salt-marsh mud flats, where borax was first mined in the 1880s, traverses some of the most tortured-looking soil surfaces you'll ever set eyes on. Beneath you are 3,000 feet of sediment carried by water into this basin from the surrounding mountains. These layers, in turn, sit on 6,000 additional feet of soil and volcanic debris. And yet this valley—closed on both ends—is a long, long way from being filled.

About 0.3 mile into the walk there are three distinct washes. It is perhaps easiest to stick to the center wash, although all of them will rejoin again shortly. Continue to follow this rutted pathway until, at about 1.3 miles, the trail end is marked by a wooden post. From here it's only 100 yards or so to the edge of the actual salt marsh, where faint remains of borax mining activity can still be seen. By 1889, only eight years after Aaron Winters first came across these borate-bearing muds, the resource had played out, and operations at Harmony Borax Works came to a close.

While scenes of Chinese laborers pulling sledges filled with borax may be hard to imagine, even harder to comprehend is the geologic history of this salt pan. Fifty thousand years ago, for instance, this wide, windswept sink was filled with cool, fresh water. At that time a much colder climate had choked the Sierras with snow and ice, the meltwater of which filled the valleys to the west, eventually pushing its way across the Panamints at Wingate Pass. This flow, along with the Mojave and Armagosa rivers, created a vast lake 600 feet deep and more than 100 miles long.

Today, however, the only liquid that remains is that which

underlies the muddy marsh in front of you—water saturated with salts, borite, and carbonate of soda. Here, in fact, lie nearly 1,000 feet of soil soggy with water, yet nowhere is there a drop fit to drink.

DESOLATION CANYON

Distance: 4 miles
Location: Approximately 3 miles south of Furnace Creek Ranch on the Badwater Highway. Park along the main road across from the large sign marking Desolation Canyon. Begin the walk on the dirt road which heads east from this point.

One of the most enchanting things about the beginning of the Desolation Canyon walk is the rainbow of colors staining the rugged foothills of the Black Mountains to the east. The various hues belong to deeply eroded hummocks that were formed from the mud and gravel of ancient lake bottoms, later streaked by flows of molten rock. The hills nearest to you are thought to be about 10 million years old.

Notice that the first part of this roadway climbs up a broad slope composed of loosely compacted soil and gravel. This material has all been carried by water from the mountains and foothills to the east. Rain falling on the nonabsorbent soil of the desert creates tremendous flash floods, which race down canyons and gullies carrying hundreds of tons of soil and rocks. Immediately upon reaching an open area, the water and its cargo spread out, losing momentum in the process. The largest rocks are dropped almost immediately, near the mouth of the canyon. Smaller stones and soils continue their downward ride, eventually spreading out into fan-shaped swells like the one you are now walking on.

Largely because of the alkali nature of this alluvial fan, there is very little plant life to be found here. The one exception you'll see is a small, greenish white shrub with sharply pointed leaves. This plant is called desert holly and is one of the most hardy pieces of greenery to be found anywhere in the Southwest. The unique greenish white color, which can range from white to pur-

67

plish, is actually formed by a very thin coating of dry airsacs that protrude from the outer cells of the leaves. Desert holly is often dried and used as an interior decoration.

The road splits at 0.5 mile, and you should take the left fork. This route will climb up gently and curve to the south, ending in another 0.5 mile amid a series of heavily eroded hills. The Desolation Canyon wash lies 50 yards to the east of these hills and can be reached via a fairly well-worn pathway. A cairn (a small pile of rocks) has been built in the center of the wash, so you'll know where the end of the roadway is on your way out. Once you reach the wash, take a right and follow it up into the foothills.

You will have gone no more than 0.3 mile in this wash before the walls of the canyon, perhaps 150 feet high, begin to close in. A little farther up are places so narrow that you can put one hand on each side of the canyon and so twisted that your line of sight is no more than 15 feet. Plant life has for the most part fizzled out. Notice that beneath their outer coatings, some of these walls look as if they were built by mud wasps—they form strange collections of beautiful stone debris suspended in a soil that crumbles to the touch. Water slices through these hills like a hot knife in butter, creating a ruddy gray, vertical world capped by a thin blue streak of sky.

You should stay generally to the right in order to follow the main wash, though some of the side canyons heading off to the left also have some interesting tales to tell. Farther up 0.6 mile the main wash climbs over a couple of 4- to 5-foot-high pour-offs that are easy to negotiate but in which caution should be used to avoid slipping on the loose, crumbling rock. The end of the walk is marked by a small box canyon located about 1 mile up from where you first left the dirt roadway.

The walk out along the road will offer you fine views of the Furnace Creek area, as well as the soaring, brawny flanks of the Panamint Mountains to the west. It was this range of peaks that, in 1849, held William Lewis Manly and an ill-fated party of westbound pioneers on the brink of death.

Exhausted and famished after a two-month ordeal of trying to reach snow-capped Telescope Peak (the tall pinnacle 20 miles to the southwest), the travelers could find no suitable wagon route over the Panamints.

Desperately, Manly and John Rogers left a haggard band of nineteen men, women, and children at the base of the Panamints in a heroic race to find food and water. What they thought would be a ten-day journey became a tribulation that lasted nearly four weeks, taking them across more than 500 miles of rugged mountain terrain. When Manly and Rogers finally returned, only eight people remained. All of the other party members had struck out on their own; one of them, a Captain Culverwell, was found dead from thirst. Miraculously, the others did struggle back to civilization, battered, but alive.

Most of today's visitors to Death Valley are utterly fascinated by the vast, shimmering desert that surrounds them. Yet in the right mood and moment, this uncompromising landscape can uncover a tiny pang of fear, still pounding in some dark, forgotten corner of the human heart.

THE COAST

For thousands of years man has stood on the coastlines of the world, humbled by the power and mystery loosed in the coupling of earth and sea. In ancient times these edges of the continents represented the end of the known world—a threshold over which came either the gentle rains that brought life to a withering countryside or the fiery, savage storms that slapped the face of the earth with unparalleled fury. Here also could be had green plants and strange swimming creatures to fill man's belly and, of course, the predictable currents and winds that would one day carry him to unknown places.

Today we still flock to the coast, inspired by its beauty, soothed by the rhythms of the ocean waves as they roll to shore. Although California is the most populous state in the country and the coast is its most popular region, the shoreline here is so expansive that there is hardly a time when you cannot find somewhere some degree of solitude as you walk the line between land and sea. (The general north-to-south distance of the state along the coast is about 840 miles. The actual tidal shoreline, however—bays, sounds, creeks, and rivers measured to the head of the tidewater—is a remarkable 3,427 miles!)

While coasts have often been thought of as arenas where earth and sea engage in fierce battle, they may just as easily be considered corridors of creation. Waves press against the shore with relentless patience, eroding mainland peninsulas into fabulous sculptures of cliffs and pinnacles, and, with the aid of currents, turning rocky headlands into long, silky beaches. Each day tiny pieces of the interior mountains slip back into their salty birth water via the fast-dancing currents of coastal rivers. The enormous plate of land known as the Salinian Block, which not only contains California's two largest cities but a vast collection of mountain ranges, slips slowly northward along the San Andreas Fault.

One of the strangest but most striking examples of how this coastline is a zone of astounding change can be seen by looking far into the past. For there was a time when the present coast was not part of the continent at all but a layer of muddy sediment lying a thousand miles away, on the dark, cold surface of the ocean floor.

Geologists believe that there is a place in the middle of the Pacific that serves as a release point for molten rocks that have reached such incredibly hot temperatures inside the earth that they rise and break through the surface of the earth's mantle. From this enormous vent, which is known as the midocean ridge, the mantlerock fans out to the east and west like the overflow from a pot of melted chocolate bars, the leading edges solidifying as they move slowly away from their source of eruption.

These moving pieces of earth mantle, which are now thought to be drifting at a rate of about 2 inches each year, actually have the potential to move entire continents or sections of continents with them. The earth's mantle does not flow in one piece but in many pieces, which sometimes grate against one another along bands known as faults.

Some 200 million years ago, an eastward-flowing mantle collided with the western edge of the continent, and needing somewhere to go, began to slide under the western rim much the same way that the moving steps of an escalator disappear beneath a metal plate at the top of the staircase. As the mantle continued to slip beneath the continent, the thick blankets of muddy sediment that lay on top of it were deposited along the edge layer upon layer, building the land toward the west into the sea and creating what we now know as the state of California. The mantle, still moving beneath the land mass like the belt of a conveyor, sank back toward the hot core of the earth. Here it melted once again, providing the molten material that would eventually boil up and help form the interior mountain ranges of the state.

Of course, like us, the life forms that live on the coast tend to be more concerned with immediate ebbs and flows than they are with slow movement of the earth's mantle. Over countless millen-

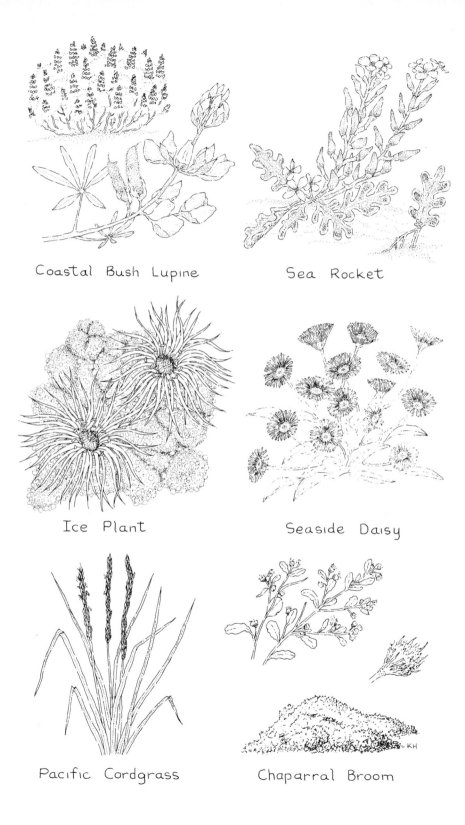

Coastal Bush Lupine

Sea Rocket

Ice Plant

Seaside Daisy

Pacific Cordgrass

Chaparral Broom

nia, nature has devised ingenious ways for organisms to deal with this unstable mix of land and water. Creatures such as periwinkles and barnacles, for example, which would normally be dessicated by the salt air and sun, have developed a door called an operculum that can be tightly sealed off from the outside world.

For those living along the tide line below what is commonly referred to as the Splash Zone, a more immediate problem than dessication is how to deal with the destructive force of ocean waves. Some organisms fasten themselves to rocks with muscles, some use suction, and still others, like the mussel, hold fast with strong filaments. One of the most competent of the anchoring specialists is undoubtedly the horse barnacle, whose ability to seal itself against any and every available surface has for years seemed a curse to those who didn't appreciate hitchhikers on the bottoms of their fishing boats. So desperate a problem were these sticky creatures that at one point a group of frustrated boat owners went to a major chemical company in hopes that a surface coating could be developed that would be impervious to the barnacle's sealant. The chemical company agreed to the project and set to work. What they found was incredible. The glue manufactured by horse barnacles was determined to have a strength of roughly 7,000 pounds per square inch and could withstand temperatures of more than 400 degrees! After trying and failing with virtually every trick in the book to develop a coating that the horse barnacle could not fasten itself to, the chemical company finally raised the white flag. Shifting gears, instead they developed a glue based on a formula similar to the one used by the barnacle, which they now sell to the medical community to mend broken bones and rebuild damaged teeth.

While both the problems and solutions of life at the edge of the sea may seem strange, it's important to remember that organisms here have developed along the same basic patterns that we have come to associate with life forms on land. (In fact, they probably perfected the survival game in the first place.) Seaside plants and animals exist according to well-defined food webs. Where on land a base layer of plants and seeds serves as the anchor point for all life forms above them, in the ocean this level is filled by vast collections of tiny algae and plankton known as diatoms. On land the plants that form this base are eaten by small animals, such as meadow mice or pocket gophers, which may then be consumed by snakes. The top organism of the food chain might be, say, a golden eagle. In the ocean the diatoms are consumed by tiny, floating animal organisms known as zooplankton, and these in turn are eaten by small fish. This ocean food chain is topped by carnivores such as the Steller's sea lion.

In addition to this hierarchy in which life flows from those who can make their own food to those who then feed off the food producers, you should also recognize the familiar pattern of organisms existing in fairly well-defined niches. While some plants and animals, of course, are capable of existing in a variety of environments, each evolves to take advantage of specific locations and techniques of obtaining food and shelter. For example, just as a whiptail lizard will not be found on the high crest of the Sierras, a starfish cannot exist by free floating in the middle of the sea. As lodgepole pines will not survive in the dry lowlands of the Central Valley, neither will rock lice be found at the bottom of a tidal pool.

To those of us who grew up far from the shore, perhaps it is the singing of these familiar earth songs in a new and dazzling language that pulls us back again and again to the edge of the sea. Here it seems we are once more like children, wide-eyed at the mystery of nature, tuned once again to the rhythm beneath the reason. As T. S. Eliot suggests, when we leave the coast, a part of it travels inside us.

> What seas what shores what gray rocks and
> what islands
> What water lapping the bow
> And scent of pine and the woodthrush singing
> through the fog
> What images return
> O my daughter.

North Coast

POINT ST. GEORGE

Distance: 1 mile
Location: Just northeast of Crescent City, exit west off U.S. Highway 101 onto Washington Boulevard. Past the airport this route becomes Radio Road. Continue to the parking area at end of road.

From the parking lot at Point St. George, a small dirt road descends through a lovely swell of coastal hills covered with thick mats of perennial grasses and wild flowers. You'll reach the beach itself in 100 yards or so, beside a freshwater stream. From here head southeast, making your way toward the most obvious rock peninsula.

This rough headland area (perhaps too rough for walking with very small children) is more than 100 million years old—formed, like most of California, by the head-on collision of the continent overriding the eastward-moving ocean floor. Water has eroded these shales and sandstones into complicated jumbles of deep cups and pockets, many of which remain filled with water when the tide recedes. These places are called tide pools, and they comprise the ecosystem with the single largest concentration of visible life forms on earth.

Scientists have broken tidal areas into five different zones. The highest of these is the Splash Zone, which consists of plants and animals that are really more bound to earth than to water. The biggest task for most of the residents here, such as the periwinkle, is to avoid drying out, which they do nicely by sealing themselves off from contact with the air. Below the Splash Zone are the Upper

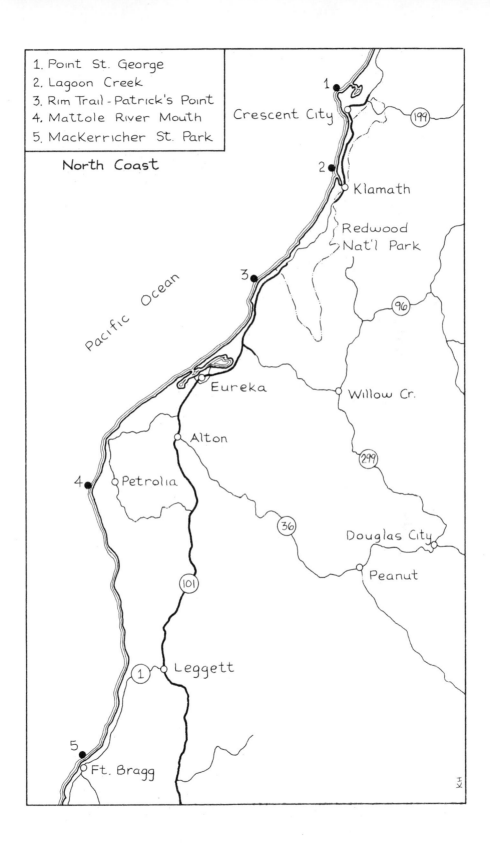

1. Point St. George
2. Lagoon Creek
3. Rim Trail - Patrick's Point
4. Mattole River Mouth
5. MacKerricher St. Park

North Coast

1

Crescent City

199

2

Klamath

Redwood
Nat'l Park

Pacific Ocean

3

96

Eureka

Willow Cr.

Alton

299

4 Petrolia

36

Douglas City

Peanut

101

1 Leggett

5
Ft. Bragg

KH

Intertidal Zone, which low tides expose twice a day, and the Lower Intertidal Zone, which, owing to the slight variance in daily tide levels, is exposed only once every twenty-four hours. The fourth zone is exposed only twice a month in ocean levels called "extreme tides." The last and lowest region is the Subtidal Zone, which is continually under water. As is true with inland ecosystems, the plants and animals that live in these tidal regions have evolved to fill these specific niches in the environment.

Of course to gain the most benefit out of a tide-pool hunt, or any type of beachcombing, for that matter, you should plan your walk for low tides. At these times the full range of intertidal magic will open up to you. If this walk is your first attempt at such exploration, you could hardly have chosen a better place. As it happens, the coastal community surrounding Crescent City is among the richest on the North American continent. Take your time, and you'll be able to see subtle changes in life as you make your way from the inland beach out across the rocky spur. (By the way, be aware that tidal pools tend to have fewer organisms in them immediately following storms.)

One of the first out-of-water creatures you're likely to encounter is the acorn barnacle, which avoids the harsh pounding of the surf by anchoring itself to rocks. During high tide it will open its tightly sealed hatches and feed on rich plankton that has been carried in by the rising waters of the sea. Here also are the beautiful spiral shells of the periwinkles, as well as the oval shells of the limpets. Some of these creatures will be on the sides of rocks, while others can be seen by carefully turning rocks over with your hands, being sure to replace them afterwards.

As you progress to the various tidal pools themselves, the forms of life become a rich collection of shapes and colors. Besides other types of snails and barnacles, here you will see urchins, anemones, crabs, and, who knows, perhaps even an octopus. If you happen to spot a plant swaying in the pools that looks like lamplit green silk, it's likely to be sea lettuce, which grows abundantly from Alaska to South America. Sea lettuce is used in oriental cooking and is extremely high in vitamins and minerals. Kelp and sea palms are two other permanent residents in these pools and are also deliciously edible. (Unfortunately, there are just too many people visiting such tidal areas to make harvesting of such plants a good idea.)

Perhaps the most easily recognized resident of the tidal pools is the starfish, or sea star. The most common starfish in (and sometimes above) these pools is the thick-limbed ochre sea star. These handsome creatures can range in color from yellow and salmon red to purple, though in these pools the reds seem to be most common. Like all starfish, the ochre sea star is carnivorous. It will typically clamp itself around a mussel or barnacle and then proceed to pry the creature's shell apart. Not being equipped with a mouth, the starfish consumes its prey by simply unfolding its stomach around it.

In the deepest tide pools, you may also find the much bigger sunflower star, a twenty-four-armed wonder that often measures more than 2 feet across. This is not only the largest but also the fastest *Asteroidea* on the entire coast. Starfish move by means of small tube feet, and the sunflower star has to coordinate more than fifteen thousand of them to go where it wants to go.

You may wish to leave the headland after your tide-pool explorations and head a bit farther south, hugging the cliffs along the way. In the spring you'll see a delightful series of little streams cascading off these grassy hummocks, giving life to fern and plant gardens that grow against the dark gray headland walls. On the beach beneath these hanging gardens are vast collections of drift-wood, as well as an occasional section of bull kelp (bullwhip kelp). These may appear and feel like pieces of rubber or plastic tubing, but rest assured that they were once a living seaweed. Bull kelp often grows to 100 feet in a single season, and it is topped with an air-filled float chamber, on which herons perch while fishing. Though it may not appear very tantalizing when you see it on the beach, it is indeed quite edible when harvested fresh.

LAGOON CREEK

Distance: 4 miles
Location: At Lagoon Creek Fishing Access, 5 miles north of
Klamath on the west side of U.S. Highway 101.

Lagoon Creek is a wonderful walk, which takes off southward
along the Coastal Trail from the Yurok Loop self-guided nature
path. You'll cover the first half of this nature trail going out and the
second half coming back, so be sure to pick up one of the interpretive brochures adjacent to the parking area.

The name Yurok was one given to the Indians of this area by
the white man, and like many such names, it would make little
sense to the Indians themselves. *Yurok* was simply a word that a
group of Indians farther up the Klamath River used to mean
"downstream." So the white man, eager to name and categorize,
wasted little time in christening the coastal people the Yuroks. The
Indians from whom they learned the word ended up being called
the Karoks, which was simply their word for "upstream." This
region of California was especially frustrating to the calculating
Anglo pioneer, because there really were no political organizations
among the Indians. The rich bounty of the land and sea left little
need to develop nations or tribes, the populace existing instead
simply as individual families. In this area, chiefs and tribal groups
were mere figments of the white man's imagination.

It was along this section of coast that the famous mountain
man Jedediah Strong Smith plodded northward on a trapping expedition in 1828, the first white man ever to see this part of California. Four miles to the south from where you now walk, near
Requa, Smith's bedraggled party stumbled out of the forest onto
the beach, having been so hungry the day before that they had to
kill a young horse for rations. From there it took four long days for
the party to struggle 18 miles to the site of what is now Crescent
City.

The Coastal Trail branches toward the right off the Yurok
Nature Loop onto a beautiful grassy pathway. The area is rich in
ferns, groundcovers, and beautiful fruit-bearing shrubs like the
pink-flowered salmonberry. Fine views can be had of stately head-

lands to the south. The first thirty minutes of the walk also offer
good opportunities to see migrating gray whales, especially during
their southward journeys in late fall and early winter, when they
tend to travel closer to shore.

Just under 1 mile into the walk you'll come to a fine grove
of red alders. These graceful trees often occur in nearly pure stands
from southern Alaska to central California. Besides using the bark
as a source of dye, Indians boiled it down to a liquid that was used
in everything from easing childbirth to keeping hemorrhoids in
check. In addition, the young shoots were considered to be an
acceptable material for making arrows. Today red alder is the leading hardwood of the region, used in pulpwood and for making
furniture and tool handles.

At 1 mile is the beautiful Hidden Beach. Even though
choked with tons of driftwood, it is a wonderful, lonely place to sit
and let your cares float out to sea. Camping is allowed here, by the
way, although it can at times be a challenge to find a suitable spot
among all the washed-up wood. For those with limited time or
energy, this is a good spot to turn around. The distance for such a
round-trip walk would be just under 2 miles.

As you've probably noticed by now, there are wooden posts
to mark your progress every half mile along the Coastal Trail. We
are going to the top of a sharp divide about another mile from here,
which is halfway from where you parked to the mouth of the
Klamath River at Requa. (The trip to Requa is a fine walk for those
with a shuttle car.)

The trail climbs steadily for the next 0.5 mile, surrounded
by thimbleberry, alder, and dense patches of false lily of the valley.
Groves of Sitka spruce often block out the views of the ocean, but
they afford a unique opportunity to fine tune your listening skills.
You can actually detect specific rhythms in the pounding surf far
below, and by the time you reach the divide you may be able to
predict just when the larger breakers will hit the beach—all without
ever laying eyes on them. These trees are the largest members of
the spruce family in the world, their range spreading from here up
to southeastern Alaska. In that state Sitka spruce is the most common commercially harvested tree.

Finally reaching the summit of the divide, you'll have gained a new appreciation for the trials that Jed Smith's heavily laden party must have gone through to make their way along this section of coast. A few days before reaching the point where you now stand, Smith wrote in his diary that "we have two men, every day that goes [sic] a head with axes, to cut a road, and then it is with difficulty we can get along." Two months later, most of Smith's eighteen men were slaughtered in southern Oregon during the Umqua Massacre. The four survivors, including Smith himself, barely escaped with their lives.

RIM TRAIL

Distance: 4 miles

Location: Patrick's Point State Park, west side of U.S. Highway 101, 5 miles north of Trinidad. Take the first right turn after the entrance station and follow signs to Palmer's Point.

Though parts of the Rim Trail can be fairly busy during the summer, it is nonetheless one of the most beautiful walks in the entire northern part of the state. So profuse is the vegetation during the first 0.5 mile that you may think you're strolling through a botanical garden. Salt air mingles with the spice of greenery—salal, salmonberry, sword ferns, and pines, as well as rich ground carpets of moss, trilliums, and false lily of the valley. Despite the lushness, occasional openings in the canopy appear, affording you spectacular views of giant headlands jutting into the surf far below. Spur trails will take you out to Abalone Point, Rocky Point, Mussel Rocks, Patrick's Point, Wedding Rock, and Agate Beach—the latter three being especially good places to watch gray whales migrating in the spring and late fall.

Bird life at Patrick's Point can be quite diverse, especially when migrating shore birds are present. The rest of the time several varieties of woodland birds will make themselves evident to travelers along the Rim Trail. One of the easiest to spot (here and throughout the West) is the Steller's jay, a rather large bird with a grayish black upper body and dark blue rear quarters. The real giveaway for this bird, though, is the large gray-black crest rising

Sea Fig

Wallflower

Beach Morning Glory

California Thrift

Silky Beach Pea

Yellow Sand Verbena

from the back of his head. The Steller's jays at Patrick's Point will be found in conifers, especially those near campgrounds, where they learn quickly to associate camping *Homo sapiens* with tasty crumbs. If you don't happen to see a Steller's jay, then you'll surely have no trouble hearing one. Their raucous "chack-chack-chack" is one of nature's loudest voices.

Another winged resident that is particularly easy to spot is the Wilson's warbler. This little golden-bellied bundle of energy can be seen searching for insects on the outer branches of shrubs and alder saplings. It will allow you to walk up quite close if you avoid making sudden moves; this is an interesting game to play and one that will teach you quite a bit about its special techniques for snatching tasty bugs.

The first spur trail you will come to goes out to Abalone Point; there the more northern Yurok Indians once had a summer village, which was used as a base to harvest seafood and game. It's interesting to note that most of the rocky promontories and sea stacks that you see along this coast had hunting-and-gathering rights assigned to them by various Indian families or groups of families. The same was also true with certain forest groves. This was not land ownership per se but rather an arrangement by which specific groups or individuals would husband the resource and in return harvest a reasonable portion of its bounty. Simply to go out and collect shellfish or acorns anywhere you pleased was hardly well thought of.

Although there are plenty of directional signs along the Rim Trail, some of them can be rather confusing. Just keep in mind that while heading north, you'll want to stay to the left as much as possible without inadvertently following a headland spur trail. (It's usually easy to tell when you've strayed on a spur path, since they tend to have abrupt climbs and descents; the Rim Trail is generally level.)

A little more than halfway to the turnaround point at Agate Beach is a beautiful grove of red alder trees, named for the red inner bark and heartwood of the tree. As beautiful as the alder is, it is only a temporary resident here, a pioneer in disturbed soil that will eventually be replaced with conifers. Alders are like peas, beans, and clover in that they are legumes, or plants that have special nodules on the roots that can actually take nitrogen out of the air and turn it into fertilizing compounds that help the tree to grow.

Two miles from the Palmer Point parking area you'll reach Agate Beach Campground. From here a short, steep trail descends to the beach itself, an interesting, crescent-shaped strand that contains great amounts of driftwood, as well as some fascinating semiprecious stones that have been polished through years of abrasion by sand and water. Also adjacent to the campground are some fine groves of majestic Sitka spruce. In some areas this largest of the spruce trees may grow to more than 150 feet high, and its straight, broad trunk can attain a base diameter of 5 to 7 feet.

If you haven't done so on the outbound walk, take the time on your return trip to walk out on one of the many headland spur trails. There is a peculiar timelessness to this stretch of California coast. How long did it take for the ocean to turn what was once a series of long rock promontories into the solitary stacks you now see rising out of the sea? Will these rough headlands eventually be smoothed by the relentless pounding of the waves? Even as you stand here there are pressures inside of the earth moving the dark ocean floor toward you at the rate of 2 inches per year. Without such internal rumblings the world would have long ago eroded into a flat, featureless plain. In truth, the ebb and flow of the surf below is merely a reflection of a much larger pulse beating in the planet— creating and destroying, the sculptor of new earths to come.

MATTOLE RIVER MOUTH

Distance: 3 miles

Location: Head west off U.S. Highway 101 at Ferndale exit, just north of Fortuna. Follow signs to Petrolia. This is a long, twisting drive, not recommended for trailers. Go west on the Old Lighthouse Road, located on the south side of Petrolia, to the parking area at beach.

The Mattole River Mouth walk lies on the western edge of a rugged section of land commonly referred to as California's "Lost

Coast." You'll need plenty of time and patience to navigate the route to the Mattole River mouth successfully. The roads here ride like rollercoasters over the deep cuts of the King Range Mountains—a true wilderness blanketed with a stunning blend of chaparral, oak, fir, sugar pine, huckleberry, laurel, and ferns. Here the clear, bright streams do fast dances to the sea. Ringtail, mink, bear, and bobcat move through the undisturbed interior forests, while Steller's sea lions and gray and killer whales range the wild, lonely coast. Those who are of the spirit to explore this primitive area will most certainly never forget it.

A Bureau of Land Management parking area is located along the beach at the end of Old Lighthouse Road, which runs southwest out of Petrolia. Begin your exploration by first walking 0.3 mile north to the mouth of the Mattole River. Here you'll very likely see harbor seals at work and play, swimming up the river a short way and then floating back out into the churning waters where river currents clash with the surf.

Harbor seals have a range that literally spreads around the world, from the Baltic Sea to the coast of China, from the Arctic Sea to Baja California. These handsome animals lead much more independent lives than sea lions do and also tend to be more wary of humans than their pinniped relatives. If you should happen to come upon a baby harbor seal alone on the beach, don't assume that it has been abandoned. The mother is probably watching frantically from the water, waiting for you to depart so that she can rescue her offspring. These seals are quite curious, however, and will often swim alongside a person walking the beach, holding their big, dark eyes just above the surface of the water.

Female harbor seals in this area bear their young between March and the first two weeks of May. The babies, which weigh about 25 pounds at birth, are often fully weaned and able to live on their own only a month after birth. This rapid development is an important survival mechanism. Unlike sea lions, harbor seals cannot move across the land by bringing their rear flippers forward—a fact that makes it impossible for them to reach the protection offered by high rocks. Birth occurs on a low-lying reef or sandbar, where predation is much more likely to occur.

As you turn toward the south to begin the major portion of

your walk, keep an eye to the ground and notice the differences in the types of rock that cover this beach. Near the river mouth are stones 3 to 4 inches across. A bit south of these are tiny pebbles a couple of times the size of sand grains, and finally, still farther south, is sand itself. Many factors contribute to the varying makeup of beach materials. Shores that are well protected by headlands tend to have flat beaches composed of fine-grained sand. Beaches exposed to the northwest (where violent winter storms come from) tend to be steeper and have coarser sand. Beach composition can also be affected by the type of headland rock that was eroded to form the beach, as well as by the presence of inlets and bays.

The walk south along this stretch of coast is pure magic. In the spring, waterfalls cascade down grass-covered cliffs, sand verbena and sea rockets splash the sand with color, and the entire beach is stroked by the firm hand of the north wind. At all times of the year there is a certain wild loneliness here—the kind that is rapidly becoming rare not only in California but throughout the West.

Though it is difficult to tell from this perspective, you are approaching the crest of a small headland known as Punta Gorda. Off this knob of land are collections of rock outcroppings that serve as rookeries for the Steller's sea lion. This is an entirely different creature from the harbor seal. Breeding, which, like most of their activities, takes place well offshore, is based on a complex social system, with males conducting fierce battles in late May to acquire harems. The young pups, born one to a litter in June or July, are much slower to develop than the young of the harbor seal. Some, in fact, may nurse for a full year.

Unlike harbor seals, all sea lions have rear flippers that can be brought up under the body to be used for moving on land. The waddle of the sea lion is not particularly graceful compared to the sleek movements they can perform in the water, but then a full-grown male may weigh in at a hefty 2,000 pounds, fully ten times the weight of a mature male harbor seal.

There are a few small tidal pools about 0.75 mile down the beach, and you may want to plan time to explore them, especially if there have been no storms over the past week. As to where this wonderful beach leads, you could actually walk a full 24 miles south to Shelter Cove, seeing very little but sea, land, and sky the entire way. No matter how far you go, enjoy the fact that you are on the most remote, peaceful stretch of coast left in the entire state of California.

MACKERRICHER STATE PARK

Distance: 2.5 miles
Location: North of the town of Fort Bragg on U.S. Highway 1, head west on Mill Creek Drive. (This road is located a short way north of the main entrance to the park.) Follow it to a point just past Cleone Lake, where the road splits. Turn right, following the road under a metal bridge trestle and into the parking lot. The trail starts near the south side of the parking area.

Although the first 0.5 mile of the Mackerricher State Park trail can be busy on summer weekends, it is nevertheless a delightful walk. The pathway clings to a ledge about 15 or 20 feet above the beach, winding around small coves and inlets framed by a tier of perennial grasses and mats of brightly colored succulents. In places where it's possible to descend from the trail to the beach itself, there are some superb opportunities for tide-pool exploration.

If you have the patience to look hard, these rich tidal pools can provide you with great opportunities for learning how organisms evolve to fill certain environmental niches. While the sea is extremely rich with tiny edibles, it nevertheless deposits only so much food in a single small area such as a tidal pool. When competition is great, an organism's best chance for survival is not based on beating up every other creature, as people often mistakenly believe. (It's important to remember that the much overworked statement "survival of the fittest" merely refers to the fact that the more fit members within a single species tend to survive longer.)

Rather than waste energy in constant battle, it's much smarter for an organism simply to find areas with slightly different environmental conditions, called niches, and concentrate on being as good as it can be at living within those parameters. Two slightly different species of warblers, for example, may develop surpris-

90

ingly compatible feeding habits—one concentrating on the lower half of trees while the other feeds up higher. Pelagic cormorants will nest on coastal ledges so narrow that they have to take off backwards, while their relatives stick to wider ones. As for these tidal pools, you can see certain types of barnacles appearing high on the tidal plane, while others have set up shop farther down. When you see similar organisms operating in the same area, they may well be eating different kinds of foods. While it would be a mistake to think that residents of tidal pools don't defend their territories, it's a far better strategy for them to capitalize on their own specialties than continually to be fighting every barnacle and its brother.

If you are here in the spring or summer, you'll be treated to the sight of beautiful mats of purple-flowered sea figs, the slender white or red petals of ice plant flowers, and the tight clusters of purple and pink seaside daisies. The plants with the narrow, erect, succulent leaves and purple flowers so plentiful here are not ice plants but sea figs. Ice plants have oval or spatula-shaped leaves and stems covered with tiny but obvious moisture beads. Near these mat plants are the lavender colors of sea rockets, California thrift, and morning glories, with a smattering of pink and white silky beach pea petals enlivening the display.

Visitors begin to thin out after 0.5 mile, giving you plenty of time for uninterrupted daydreaming. You happen to be walking along the southern limits of land once used by the Coast Yuki Indians. The origin of these people continues to pose a particularly frustrating puzzle to anthropologists, because their language is the only one in the entire state that has never been connected to that of any other tribe. The Yukis were part of what was essentially a linguistic island. For this reason many anthropologists consider them to be the oldest tribe of the region—California's "original Indians," as some say. How long the Yuki people actually lived in this area is still not certain, although three thousand years is probably a conservative estimate. For them this land—bountifully supplied with fish, game, and acorns—was as close to a place of milk and honey as could be found anywhere.

The most-prized fish was the salmon, which coastal Indians along the entire northern half of the state caught with baskets or spears as the fish migrated up coastal rivers to spawn. Once the salmon had been dried they were put into storage baskets, each layer covered with a layer of pungent laurel leaves. These spicy leaves are said to have kept out insects that would otherwise have laid eggs in the flesh. Shellfish provided another source of seafood and were sometimes dried and traded to tribes further inland. Edible shellfish included abalone, clams, limpets, cockles, mussels, oysters, scallops, chitons, and barnacles, to name but a few.

At 1 mile you will come to the turnaround point for the walk, a sandy beach that stretches to the south for about 0.25 mile. This is the first break you'll have from the more rocky tidal-pool areas, and it is a perfect place to do a little beachcombing or relaxing in the sand.

North Central Coast

BODEGA HEAD

Distance: 2 miles

Location: From the town of Bodega Bay, head west on Bay Flat Road, which then becomes Westside Road. Follow this to the end of Bodega Head, taking a right turn at the only fork. Walk on the trail that heads north from the parking lot, marked with signs for Salmon Creek and Horseshoe Cove.

The large metal fence near the parking area for the Bodega Head walk serves as a solemn reminder that had Bodega Head development gone according to original plans, you would now be standing near the cooling towers of a nuclear power plant. Fortunately the scheme was scrapped, leaving this wild, wonderful peninsula to the soaring birds and spirits of men.

Up the trail 0.4 mile you'll come to a fork. You will eventually be taking the right path, but first take a quick stroll up the left branch to the Horseshoe Cove Overlook. From here you will be afforded fantastic views of both the Sonoma and Marin county coastlines. Immediately to the north is the appropriately named Horseshoe Cove, followed by a sweep of sandy shoreline that includes Salmon Creek, Gleason, and Wright State beaches. The large building just this side of Horseshoe Cove is the University of California's superb Bodega Marine Laboratory, which is open to the public on a fairly limited basis. Keep in mind that the vast majority of land that you are walking through is used by the university for various types of ecological studies. It's important that you stay on the trails in order to help maintain the integrity of these experiments.

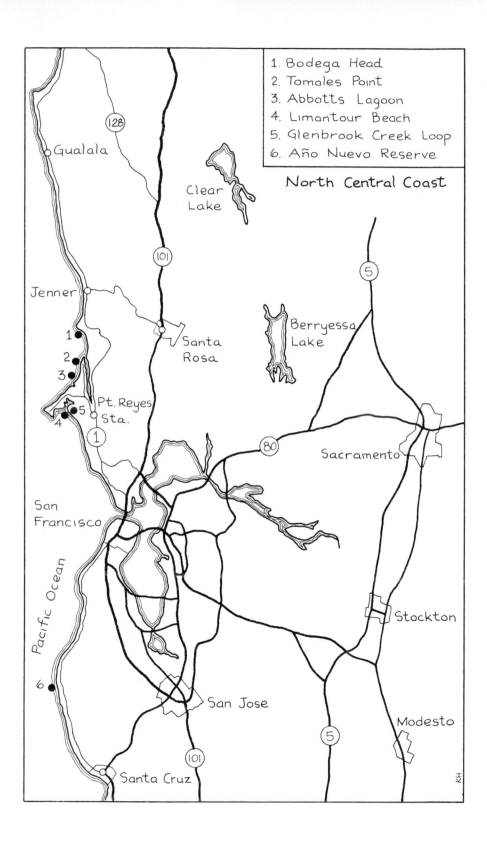

1. Bodega Head
2. Tomales Point
3. Abbotts Lagoon
4. Limantour Beach
5. Glenbrook Creek Loop
6. Año Nuevo Reserve

North Central Coast

Gualala

Clear Lake

128

101

Jenner

1
2
3

5
4

Pt. Reyes
Sta.

1

Berryessa Lake

5

80

Sacramento

San Francisco

Pacific Ocean

Stockton

6

San Jose

Modesto

5

101

Santa Cruz

Santa Rosa

KH

In the other direction lies the crescent coast of Bodega Bay, pierced in the south by a long finger of land that forms the northern tip of Point Reyes National Seashore. If you look directly offshore you can usually see bobbing white fishing boats working their way along the rich continental shelf that frames this coast.

Take one last deep drink of scenery, and then work your way back down the trail to the right fork mentioned earlier, where this time you will follow the sign pointing toward Bodega Dunes Campground. The large pocket of inland water visible to the east is Bodega Bay Harbor.

This part of the walk is extremely pleasant, winding through occasional patches of coyote bush and thick stands of tree lupine, a bushy plant with wheels of narrow leaves and strikingly beautiful blue or yellow pealike flowers. You may notice that at Bodega Head the tree lupine is growing in bigger, healthier stands than it is able to manage farther to the north. Lupine, incidentally, comes from the Latin word *lupus,* which means "wolf," a name that was likely bestowed on the plant because it was thought that it acted "wolfish" by quickly using up all the nutrients in the soil. In fact, lupine does no such thing but rather is very adept at growing on soils that are already poor. The plant establishes its sizable root system rather quickly, and it has been planted throughout the state to help stabilize shifting dunes.

The trail descends gently to the east, eventually crossing a paved road that leads to the Bodega Marine Laboratory. Keep a sharp eye out in these hills for soaring birds, which can frequently be seen hanging on the tops of onshore breezes that run up the west side of Bodega Head. The kestrel (sparrow hawk) will be looking for grasshoppers and meadow mice, as will the marsh hawk (northern harrier), who may also add a small bird or two to his daily fare. If you're lucky, during the evening you may even spot the beautiful, dark brown and ivory plumage of a short-eared owl, who, like his fellow carnivores, will be looking for small rodents. It's interesting to note that the marsh hawk has a sunken face similar to that of the owl; it is thought that this shape helps to direct the tiny sound of field mice squeaks into the birds' ears.

Shortly after it crosses the roadway to the Marine Lab, the trail becomes a little difficult to follow. About 0.1 mile to the east you'll see a large dish-shaped area of sand lying against the west side of a grass-covered hill. Given the lack of distinct pathways, this sandy area is a good turnaround point, and the walk over there will allow you to take a close look at how grasses and shrubs can be extremely effective in stabilizing what were once bare, shifting dunes. This little sandy hollow is a fine place to observe bird life in the early morning, and a cautious peek over the adjacent hill at this time of day may reveal a herd of deer.

TOMALES POINT

Distance: 6 miles
Location: Point Reyes National Seashore. From the visitors' center, head west on Bear Valley Road until you reach Pierce Point Road. Continue west to the trail head at the end of the highway.

It has been nearly four centuries since the Spanish explorer Don Sebastián Vizcaíno sailed north along these rocky headlands on the January festival known as the Feast of the Three Kings. He was not the first European to arrive here—Sir Francis Drake had sailed these waters twenty-four years earlier. But the name Vizcaíno gave this windswept peninsula—Punta de los Reyes, "the Point of the Kings"—is the one it still bears today—Point Reyes. (The specific point that Vizcaíno likely saw lies southwest of here, framed by Chimney Rock and Sea Lion Overlook.)

As you walk out toward the beautiful Tomales Point, it's easy to believe that Vizcaíno named this peninsula not so much for the day he first saw it but for the regal appearance of the land itself. These lush, rounded moors stretch to the north for more than 5 miles. Together they form a long, velvet perch from which the walker can survey a slice of the world as lonely and beautiful as any in America.

Beginning outside a cluster of fine, old dairy buildings at Upper Pierce Ranch, the trail climbs to the north for a little more than a mile. From there it flattens out for a way, finally making a steady descent to our turnaround point at the site of the Lower

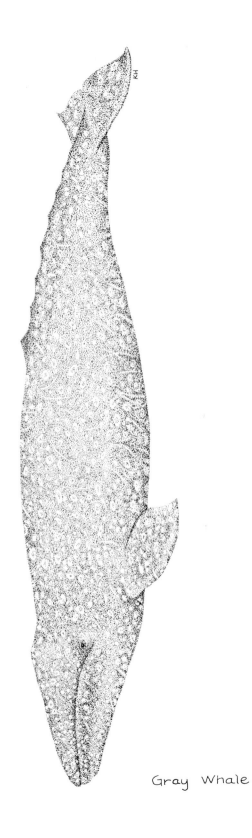

Gray Whale

Pierce Ranch. The climbing involved in this trip is hardly enough to detract from the feeling that this is somehow a summer stroll through a foreign land—the wind, the sea, the lupines, and the poppies diverting you from any concern about whether the dirt path is heading up or down.

Once you go a distance from the trail head ranch buildings, keep your eyes on the grassy ridge lines to the right for the appearance of tule elk. If there is any royalty in residence on "Point of the Kings" peninsula, these noble creatures surely must be it. Once the tule elk roamed in great numbers throughout the grasslands of California. But as the prairie lands fell to the plow, so did the elk populations. Some people claim that the total number of tule elk actually fell beneath a half dozen individuals and that conservationists' efforts to save them were only a frightfully short step ahead of extinction. The animals that originally resided on Point Reyes were hunted out of existence by the 1860s and were not residents there again until 1977, when the Park Service relocated several from the Owens Valley to the rich grasslands of Tomales Point.

The lush grass that covers this area makes it one of the state's most beautiful prairies, lying in sharp contrast to the impenetrable chaparral thickets that can be found in some other parts of the park. These rich wild pastures did not go unnoticed by nineteenth-century settlers. Cows that were brought into the area produced exceptionally high-quality butter and cream, much of which by the 1870s was being shipped to urban markets on cargo schooners.

Reduction in the numbers of cows in the area since it achieved national-park status has allowed this coastal prairie to grow out of its clipped appearance and back into a thick mat of shaggy, perennial grasses peppered with blue-eyed grass, cow parsnip, mariposa lilies, and Douglas iris.

Take a close look at the richly colored Douglas iris with its purple or dark pink petals and deep blue veins, commonly seen growing in small clumps on grassy patches 1.5 to 2.0 miles into the walk. (*Iris*, by the way, is Greek for "rainbow.") Besides being one of the park's most beautiful flowers, the iris was a very important plant for Indians of the area. The extreme edges of the leaves contain very resilient fibers, similar in strength and texture to silk. Indians used abalone shell scrapers to separate the strong, outer filaments from the rest of the leaf, after which they wove the filaments into rope that could be used for nets or snares for catching deer. So laborious was the process of making these ropes that a 12-foot section might take a month and a half to complete.

Not always noticed by many visitors to these parts are the thousands of harvest, meadow, and deer mice that feast on the seeds, stems, and green leaves of the coastal prairie plants. Midway in the food chain, these creatures in turn become feasts themselves; you should have no problem sighting hungry kestrels and marsh hawks soaring on the ocean breezes with their extraordinary eyes and ears tuned into the slightest squeaks and movements in the fields below.

At 3 miles you will come to a small pond, and just past this, a beautiful grove of eucalyptus, a rather common California tree that was first imported to the state about 150 years ago. Although there are no buildings left standing, this grove of trees marks the sight of the Lower Pierce Ranch. Solomon Pierce created a very successful dairy operation here in 1858, which remained in the Pierce family for the next seven decades. Solomon was probably too busy milking cows and making butter boxes to spend much time sitting and taking in the loveliness of this place. But it's the perfect location for such favorite lazy pastimes as snoozing and sky watching.

Those with any leftover energy may want to continue north on a dirt pathway for another mile to a high vista that provides wonderful views to the west of nearby Bird Rock. Here can often be seen great congregations of sea birds, including white pelicans and Brandt's cormorants. Cormorants do not have enough oil in their feathers to keep them from becoming waterlogged after prolonged soaks in the ocean. Those you see standing on Bird Rock flapping their wings vigorously are most likely in the process of drying out.

ABBOTTS LAGOON

Distance: 3 miles

Location: Point Reyes National Seashore. From the park visitors' center, head west on Bear Valley Road, which eventually joins Pierce Point Road. Continue west to the trail head at the end of Pierce Point Road.

The Abbotts Lagoon walk is great for bird lovers, leading through open grassland to a brackish lagoon and, a short distance from that, to a long, wonderfully quiet stretch of ocean beach. The distance to the beach itself is a bit more than a mile; the 3-mile distance listed for the walk is assuming that you'll put in at least another mile in a slow saunter along the ocean.

A hundred yards or so into the walk you will come upon a small, brackish pond on the left side of the trail. Though the edges of the water here are lined with thick mats of pennywort, water parsley, and other oxygen-producing greens, the water itself is not particularly rich in the oxygen needed to support aquatic life. Besides not being able to aerate itself by simple movement the way a tumbling stream would do, this pond is so shallow that the sun keeps it at a fairly high temperature. And, the higher the temperature of water, the less oxygen it is able to hold. As a result of this condition, the water insects you see living here have developed rather ingenious ways of supplementing the supply of oxygen.

Some insects simply absorb oxygen by extending parts of their bodies above the surface of the water, while a few have special breathing tubes that they can send up to the surface like the periscope on a submarine. Still others, beetles in particular, fashion bubbles of air from the surface of the pond, which they then either wear around their bodies or carry beneath their wings the way a scuba diver carries oxygen tanks on his back.

In the pasture land on the other side of this ridge you will almost certainly see a variety of airborne predators, one of the most common and beautiful of which is the marsh hawk. This bird appears rather slender in flight, with black wing tips and distinct horizontal bands on its tail. It does not tend to glide in circles the way some other birds of prey do but can often be seen tracing a wavy flight above the pasture.

Two things about this area are of particular interest to the marsh hawk. One is the grassy shoreline of the lagoon up ahead, which harbors a variety of nests with tasty young birds. The other item, even better, is the abundance of meadow and harvest mice that make their homes in the grassy pasture before you. While you may or may not spot an actual meadow mouse along this path, these fields are crisscrossed with the paths they have cut between their nests and choice feeding areas within their territory. (Meadow mice will rarely leave their own territory, even if faced with starvation.)

These busy little rodents will eat just about anything, including seeds, leaves, stems, bark, bulbs, and insects, and will typically consume their own weight in food every twenty-four hours. Females are capable of bearing litters at any time of year, and in twelve months time may produce seventy-five offspring in nine or ten litters. This proliferation of youngsters occasionally leads to severe overpopulation. With Point Reyes' sizable collection of hungry marsh hawks, owls, eagles, kestrels, coyotes, bobcats, and foxes, however, most meadow mice probably end up as dinner before the end of their first year of life.

The other, equally tasty ground goodie, to be found in the thicker mats of grass, is the harvest mouse. Harvest mice tend to be most active at night, but you may see one of their nests along the path, which consist of fairly large collections of carefully woven dried grass. The diet of the harvest mouse is a little less varied than that of the meadow mouse, with the majority of its meals restricted to various kinds of seeds and the green shoots of young grass. Propagation, from mating to adulthood, is amazingly quick. The female will give birth just three weeks after copulation, and, even though the newborn are completely blind and helpless, they are ready to strike out on their own just a month after birth.

In a little under a mile you'll reach the butterfly-shaped Abbotts Lagoon, named after two brothers who were ranchers here during the 1860s. Carlyle Abbott became a cowboy of somewhat legendary proportions when he supposedly rescued the frightened members of a wrecked clipper ship by lassoing them and dragging them out of the surf to safety. In this lagoon you will see a fine collection of coots, dowitchers, killdeers, terns, willets, and grebes. The long-necked western grebes discourage opportunistic birds of prey from eating their eggs and young by building floating nests out in the open water of the lagoon. The nests of coots will be just on the very edge of the open water.

Cross the lagoon at its narrow midpoint, then work your way to the ocean along the top side of the southern pool. Here grow a fine variety of dune plants, some of which, like the bush lupine, are very important in stabilizing drifting sand. You can see that there is a distinct difference between the plants growing on the firmer, wetter edge of the lagoon and those such as the sand verbena, sagewort, seaside daisy, and California thrift, which tend to be farther back in the foredunes (the dunes nearest the sea).

Look at the large, beautifully polished grains of sand that lie adjacent to the northwest corner of the south lagoon. The finer grains have been carried off by the wind, and you'll find them just a few feet away on the tiers of the foredunes. When you reach the ocean itself, note the steepness and the coarseness of the sand along the part of the beach that meets the surf. Beaches like this that are exposed to the full force of the northwest storms tend to be steeper and have larger grains of sand than those that are more protected. If you were hoping to stretch out on a flat beach with very soft, fine-grained sand, you'd be more likely to find it at Drake's Beach or Limantour Spit, both of which are protected from storms by the arm of Point Reyes.

LIMANTOUR BEACH

Distance: 3 miles
Location: Head south on the park entrance road (Bear Valley Road), located off of State Highway 1 just northwest of Olema. Turn left on Limantour Road and follow it to the end. (The Limantour Beach and Glenbrook Creek walks begin from the same point.)

Limantour Spit, named for a French trader whose ship was lost here, may be the ultimate walking beach. Clean, blond sands stretch westward for nearly 3 miles, kissed by surf on the south, and a short walk away on the north, by estuary waters incredibly rich in bird and plant life. Although the first 0.5 mile of the beach can be busy during spring and summer weekends, those who continue on to the western half of the spit will have no trouble finding peace and quiet.

As you walk down the beach, notice the difference in both the type and amount of vegetation on the windward side of the spit compared to that on the leeward side. Even though the dunes are relatively low, they do offer protection from the erosional power of sea storms. Without this sand buffer, life for many plants on the leeward side of the spit would be impossible.

Notice yet another important buffer from the ravages of the sea. Ahead of you to the west is the broad hook of land known as Point Reyes, crowned on the near tip by Chimney Rock. This headland is what catches most of the violent storm activity coming out of the northwest, protecting this spit and Drake's Beach (directly in front of you) from violent storm waves. In fact, tiny particles of rock torn from Point Reyes by waves and weather often end up as sand on Limantour Spit. In general, the best beaches— flat with fine grains of sand—will be found behind such protective headlands.

Limantour Spit may afford you a glimpse of migrating gray whales, especially if you happen to be here for their southward trek during late fall and early winter when the great mammals travel closer to shore. At that time they are en route to calving grounds near Baja California from feeding areas located far to the north in the Bering Sea. As large as these creatures are, it comes as somewhat of a surprise that they eat almost nothing once they are outside of their far north summering grounds. There they have dined well on millions and millions of tiny, bottom-dwelling crustaceans, which will fuel their long round trip to Baja California.

The first whales you will see heading south along Limantour Spit will be pregnant females, who conceived about eleven months ago. The newborn babies will be 15 or 16 feet in length, and though they will nurse for about seven months, they'll be ready to accompany their mother back north when they are only four to eight weeks old.

When this stretch of coast was still wild, and the great grays had not been slaughtered to near the point of extinction, they were a common sight. Although no Indian tribe on the California coast hunted ocean-going whales, the whales did occasionally end up beached, which meant great feasting for local tribes such as the Ohlone. Such an important bounty was a beached whale that medicine men even had special chants with which to call the whales onto shore. The Ohlones were not the only ones interested in the event, however, as several early explorers noted crowds of grizzly bears partaking in such feasts as well.

If you continue all the way to the end of the spit (about 3 miles), you'll come to a narrow water passage that separates Limantour from Drake's Beach. It is a lesson in the forces of change when you consider that only a century ago, this now tiny channel was sufficiently large to admit passage of large sailing ships. Loaded with grain and redwood, they would dock at the far northern reaches of the large body of water at the end of the channel called Drake's Estero. Then they would sail off again, their hulls filled with dairy products and livestock.

Keep an eye out all along the farther reaches of the spit for bird life, which is usually plentiful. Egrets, willets, godwits, and great blue herons are common.

This is sure to be a beach walk that remains in your mind for a long time to come. When pressures and worries build up, roll the tape of Limantour Spit—the long, long line of crashing waves, the fishing birds and blowing whales. The ocean strums a special melody along this strip of sand, soothing anyone who comes to listen.

GLENBROOK CREEK LOOP

Distance: 6.5 miles
Location: Head south on the park entrance road (Bear Valley Road), located off of State Highway 1 just northwest of Olema. Turn left on Limantour Road and follow it to the end. (The Glenbrook Creek and Limantour Beach walks begin from the same point.)

Although longer than most of our walks, the Glenbrook Creek Loop offers a very special sampling of Point Reyes fare. The beauty and diversity of bird life here is rivaled by very few places in the country. Besides the estuary near the trail head, there are hushed pockets of woodland and perches high in the hills where you can drink in great sweeps of unspoiled ocean views.

From the trail head west of the parking area, follow the signs toward Muddy Hollow. For the first 0.4 mile of the walk you will skirt a beautiful *estero* (like an estuary) teeming with bird and aquatic life. Try to reach this part of the walk early in the morning when the area is soaked in soft apricot sunlight, and activity is at its peak. There are several stretches through here where tall vegetation hides the trail from the lagoons below, providing you with good vantage points from which to watch and photograph the bird life.

This first stretch of pathway is a particularly good place to see how different bird species have their own special feeding habits. Some will be actively coursing back and forth in the water, trying to flush out food as they go. Others, such as the great blue heron, will stand perfectly still and wait for breakfast to be delivered. Also notice that some of the birds you see here have highly specialized equipment to help them feed. The long-billed curlew uses its long, narrow bill to probe deep into mud to find the clams and worms that other, shorter-billed probers cannot reach. And finally, see if you can spot birds that seem willing to feed only in certain parts of the estuary. For example, you won't see clappers hunting for food out in open water. Instead they'll be near areas of tall grass that offer good hiding places should danger arise.

In 0.4 mile, past the lagoon trail rimmed with pickleweed, cordgrass, and silverweed, you will arrive at a junction. Take a left here, heading toward Glenbrook Creek. The trail climbs up out of the *estero* and onto a broad, grassy area that offers fine views of Limantour Spit and the ocean beyond. In less than a mile you'll descend into a grassy drainage area and through a small but lovely pocket of alder forest. The alder is a commonly harvested hardwood in the northwestern United States, and its strong, durable wood is made into everything from tool handles to cabinets. For those with a limited amount of time or energy, this cool patch of forest makes a good turnaround point. Returning to the parking lot from here along the same path creates a walk of about 3 miles.

Steller's Sea Lion

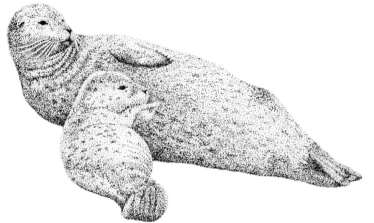

Harbor Seal

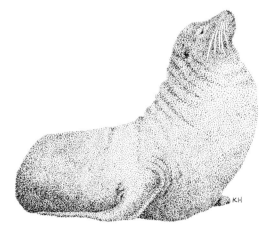

California Sea Lion

For those rested and raring to continue on into the great unknown, the trail climbs out of this drainage area and then heads back north on the shoulder of a broad, sloping ridge dappled with lupine, chaparral broom, and coyote bush.

To the west you'll be able to see the tip of Limantour Spit, separated from the east end of Drake's Beach by a small channel. Opening up to the north of the channel is Drake's Estero, which drains into the long, curved section of coast known as Drake's Bay. The shallow bay was so named to mark what some historians believe to be the 1579 landing site of Sir Francis Drake aboard the *Golden Hinde*—the first European to set foot on the peninsula.

Drake was essentially a cultured pirate in the service of his queen, Elizabeth I of England. Having sacked several small towns on the southern coast of South America for her, and then seizing a ship loaded with silver from Peru, he sailed to the north, reaching the central coast of California in the month of June. Here—some say at Drake's Bay, others say at San Francisco or Bodega Bay—Drake stopped for five weeks to make repairs to his sea-worn ship. Before leaving he tacked a plate of brass onto a wooden post that declared this land of the Coast Miwok Indians to be the property of the Queen of England. He and his crew then continued north, quite possibly in search of a passage that was rumored to exist around the top of North America known as the Strait of Anian. Strangely, they went no farther than the coast of Oregon, however, before turning around and heading back to England via the southern tip of Africa.

Up this shoulder 1.1 miles is the junction with a trail running west toward Drake's Estero. You continue north, following the signs for Muddy Hollow. Along this back stretch the trail follows an abandoned roadbed, first through open hillside, then east past a dark corridor of forest lining Glenbrook Creek, which is filled to the brim with songbirds. For 1.5 miles this easy-to-follow dirt roadbed becomes a carefree, yellow brick road, weaving past stunning ocean scenes and through rich, sun-baked aromas of wild earth gardens seasoned with a whiff of sea breeze.

This stretch is a good place to spot deer in the morning and evening hours, as well as raccoons, coyotes, and if you are lucky, a bobcat slipping through the tall grassy areas that surround the woodland corridors. Check the trunks of alder trees you come across for bobcat scratch marks, since this wild cat enjoys sharpening its claws on such surfaces as much as any household tabby.

The final trail junction occurs at a parking area just northwest of the Limantour Road (the highway you drove in on). From here you head southwest for a bit more than 1 mile, through a beautiful alder forest and along patches of blackberries and salmonberries. At 0.5 mile from the junction the stream running through Muddy Hollow splits into many different courses and then flows along the trail itself. This stretch requires a bit of fancy footwork to avoid getting wet, but in a hundred yards or so the stream again leaves the trail. This section is especially beautiful when lined with the flowers of spring. Keep in mind, however, that during that season Muddy Hollow can really live up to its name, so if you plan to hike the area you'll need appropriate footgear.

AÑO NUEVO RESERVE

Distance: 2 miles
Location: Northern boundary of Año Nuevo State Reserve, 3 or 4 miles north of the entrance station turnoff and south of Pigeon Point Lighthouse Hostel. You'll see a tree stump that looks like a fist on the west side of the Highway 1. Small parking area is here on the west side of road. You are entering along the northern boundary of the reserve.

Don Sebastián Vizcaíno first sighted this headland on January 3, 1603, and christened it Punta del Año Nuevo, "New Year's Point." Up until that time, and for more than a century later, this part of the California coast was the quiet, unruffled domain of the Ohlone Indians. The harvests of shellfish that the Ohlones made over the centuries along these beaches were incredible. Archaeologists have discovered midden piles of abalone, oyster, clam, and barnacle shells more than 30 feet deep and hundreds of yards across. Owing to this bounty, along with tons of smelt that were collected along this stretch of coast each season, the ravages of starvation were seldom felt in this part of California.

After having spent time as everything from a sand mine to a shipping center, today Año Nuevo is a 700-plus-acre nature preserve, particularly significant for the protection it offers to the magnificent northern elephant seal.

Because certain areas of the reserve are closed during parts of the year—in particular, December through March—you should plan to stop at the visitors' station on the main entrance road before proceeding with any walks. Keep in mind that even if you happen to be passing the reserve during the very restricted spring breeding season, you can still have a great on-foot experience by signing up for one of the 3-mile-long, ranger-guided walks that leave from the main parking area on the east side of the park.

This particular walk takes you to a set of lonely, windswept coastal dunes. The first 0.3 mile of trail flanks the northern border of Año Nuevo, winding through delightful grassland and marsh communities that are home to a variety of birds. An hour or so spent hidden among the tall vegetation will afford you splendid opportunities to see kestrels, hawks, and white-tailed kites soaring up and down this rich inland corridor. At the end of this grassy section you will reach a series of low dunes being reclaimed by willow, strawberry, coyote bush, and mock heather. Farther south along the coast is a rather large collection of dunes that are still drifting—one of the few active coastal dune fields to be found anywhere in the state. Those that are more stabilized, like those before you, will be quickly colonized by clusters of beautiful flowering plants such as sea rocket, sand verbena, and sea fig.

On the other side of these low sand hummocks is the beach itself, a quiet crescent cradled by flat headlands to the north and south. Follow the beach southward for about 200 yards, and then pick up one of several trails that climb up and across the promontory. As you work your way to the south, you'll be afforded fine views of the coast and reserve. There is a refreshing wildness here, totally unsuspected by those who never venture off the highway. Ducks, coots, and gulls are plentiful, and on the far side of the promontory, a series of small, unspoiled tidal pools await your discovery. Look for limpets, beautifully colored anemones, and peanut and red tube worms.

On a clear day you'll be able to see Año Nuevo Island to the south, which is a major breeding area for the northern elephant seal. These pinnipeds are enormous. The males can be more than 15 feet long and will often tip the scales at an unbelievable 6,000 pounds. The fights to establish breeding harems are much more than just an idle show; both winners and losers often end up bloody and battered from their efforts. This "pecking order," as opposed to a breeding system that depends on everyone establishing his own territories, definitely favors the strongest of the species. Studies conducted here at Año Nuevo revealed that only 4 percent of the male seals inseminated 85 percent of the females.

It's interesting to note that even after the female's egg has been fertilized, it does not become implanted in the wall of her uterus until ten to fourteen weeks later. This delay, when added to the eight-month gestation period, ensures that the single pups will be born here at the breeding grounds instead of out at sea, where they would certainly perish. The adult elephant seals will depart the rookeries in March, leaving their young behind to mature on their own.

Down the coast 0.7 mile is a small drainage crossed by a wooden bridge. About 70 yards past this bridge, after the path has turned slightly inland, a trail takes off to the right, climbing slightly upward and outward to a beautiful headland with a flat grassy bench. This is a superb place to lie back and let the magic of this unspoiled place roll over you like ocean waves. Notice the call of gulls, the wind through the tree lupine, the smell of salt mingling with the odor of vegetation at once dying and being born. Contemplating the natural rhythms that are cycling here on the edge of the continent is inexplicably soothing—providing a welcome respite for a busy mind.

South Central Coast

NORTH SHORE TRAIL—POINT LOBOS

Distance: 2 miles
Location: West of State Highway 1, 3 miles south of Carmel.
Take the first right past the main entrance station, which dead-ends on the west side of Whalers Cove. Follow signs for North Shore Trail.

It won't take many steps on the trail to see why Point Lobos, though relatively small in size, has been called the most beautiful coastal park in America. (All this beauty can, unfortunately, make it a busy place during spring and summer weekends. If you can come only during these times, a visit around 9:00 A.M. will provide you with the best opportunity for solitude.) When driving into Point Lobos, take the first right turn past the entrance station, following the paved road until it ends on the west side of Whalers Cove. Our walk begins on the west side of this parking area, following a pathway that has been designated the North Shore Trail. From here westward the sea has sculpted the rough headlands into long, gnarled fingers, which embrace striking inlets of clear, cobalt water. The rock on which you will be walking for the first 0.3 mile was born of fire more than 100 million years ago—congealed beneath the earth, uplifted, and then chiseled by nature's forces into the jigsaw of shapes you see before you.

On top of these offshore rocks a variety of birds can be seen nesting during spring and summer (take special note of Guillemot Island, visible from a point a bit more than 0.25 mile up the North Shore Trail). Among the most common are Pelagic and Brandt's cormorants, western gulls, and pigeon guillemots. This last bird,

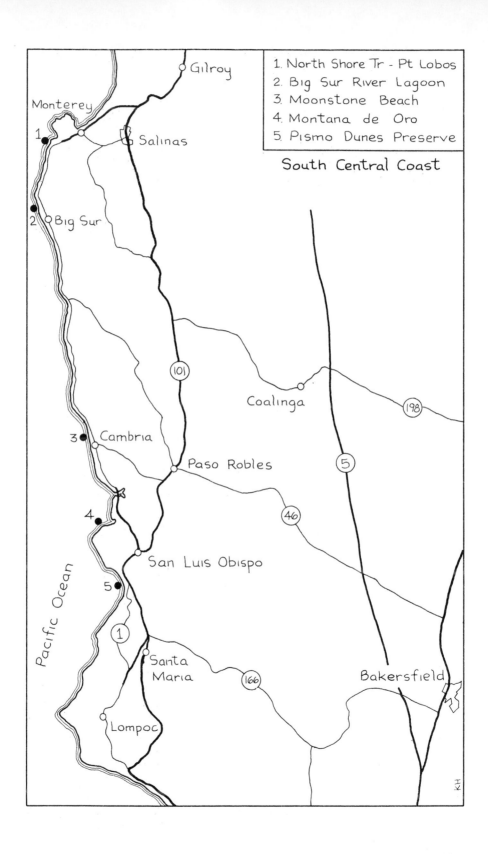

1. North Shore Tr - Pt Lobos
2. Big Sur River Lagoon
3. Moonstone Beach
4. Montana de Oro
5. Pismo Dunes Preserve

South Central Coast

Gilroy

Monterey

1

Salinas

2 Big Sur

101

Coalinga

198

3 Cambria

Paso Robles

5

46

San Luis Obispo

5

Pacific Ocean

1

Santa Maria

166

Bakersfield

Lompoc

KH

actually an auk, is not found in large numbers, each couple preferring to nest in relative isolation. Walkers with binoculars may be
lucky enough to see the birds diving for their supper, which consists of a variety of small fish. In addition, harbor seals can be seen
frolicking in the bays or resting on the rocks, as well as the smaller
sea otter, which will be found not on the shore, but floating hidden
among the thick beds of seaweed and kelp.

Towering over this rich web of life like veteran war senti-
nels are beautiful groves of Monterey cypress. These striking trees,
which were once widespread in the more temperate climate of
fifteen thousand years ago, have over the centuries been nudged
into smaller and smaller ranges. While you're likely to see many
areas along the coast where these trees have been planted, there
are actually only two native groves of Monterey cypress left in
California. It is the rarity of these trees that led to Point Lobos
being set aside as an area protected from future development.

These cypresses are among a group of trees sometimes
known as fire trees or fire pines, a term that refers to the fact that
the cones will open and disperse their seeds only during intense
heat. The cones you see on these cypresses may already have been
on the branches for several years. This after-the-fire planting
method ensures that young seedlings will become established before any other plants can fight them for sunlight.

If you look at the Monterey cypress trees growing back from
the ocean, you'll see that they lack the fantastic twisted shapes common to those growing on the sea cliff. The gnarled beauty of these
seaside trees is the result of years of fighting the terrific storm winds
that push and tear at them in their developmental years. Those who
have hiked in the Sierras may note the similarity of these twisted cypresses to the storm-worn bristlecone and whitebark pines that fly
their stout branches against the blue skies of the high country.

You'll be following the North Shore Trail for approximately
1.1 miles, coming out on the west side of the reserve at the parking
area for Sea Lion Point. Once you reach the parking area, walk
southeast *against* the one-way entrance road for about 0.15 mile. At
the point where the road becomes two-way again, on your left will
be a pathway marked Whaler's Knoll Trail. This is the path that
will form the return side of our loop walk.

113

From here the trail climbs through a stately Monterey pine forest for about 0.2 mile. Take note of the beautiful shrouds of lace lichen hanging from the dead branches of the pines. This unusual resident (lichen is actually a combination of a fungus and an alga plant) in no way harms the tree and provides valuable nest material for many birds of the forest. It can be found only in shaded areas that remain cool and humid throughout the year. These Monterey pines, by the way, are also quite rare. Like the cypress, they exist only thanks to the moisture-laden fogs that roll in during the summer, making up for the long months of dry weather prevalent on the California coast.

After reaching the top of the ridge in 0.2 mile, more-adventurous hikers may wish to climb northward to the top of Whaler's Knoll, which was actually a lookout used by commercial whaling fleets in the later 1800s. Spotters stationed on this hilltop would hoist flags on a tall wooden staff to signal an offshore ship that a whale had been seen; they would then rapidly raise and lower the flag to signal the captain when he had his ship headed in the right direction.

The Whalers Cove Trail rejoins the North Shore Trail less than 0.25 mile from the parking area that marked the beginning of our walk. Take time on the way back to study some of the other beautiful vegetation around these headlands. Here can be found the icy green of the sage and seaside daisy. Sticky monkeyflower and California lilac are two evergreen shrubs that add welcome splashes of color to the sometimes somber landscape, along with such wild flowers as lupine, California poppy, iris, asters, and lilies. Spring is especially stunning as far as wild flowers are concerned. There are, after all, more than three hundred species of bloomers at Point Lobos; the opening of their brightly colored faces provides vibrant accents to an already unforgettable coastal tapestry.

BIG SUR RIVER LAGOON—
ANDREW MOLERA STATE PARK

Distance: 2 miles
Location: South of Monterey on State Highway 1. Park at trail head no. 1, located on the west side of the highway opposite mile marker no. 52, at the extreme northern end of Andrew Molera State Park.

The environments available to you on the Big Sur River Lagoon walk are extremely diverse. Pockets of coastal prairie melt into a thick mixed-evergreen forest edged by a cheery river that has tumbled here from high in the Santa Lucia Mountains to a quiet, blue, seaside lagoon.

The walk begins in a grassland community replete with foxtail, rattlesnake grass, wild oats, ribgrass, and rye. In most years the fields are sprinkled with blue dicks, mariposa lilies, and blue-eyed grass. Though many of the grasses that now make up the coastal prairie were introduced by Europeans, the seeds from both native and imported species were an important food crop to Indians of the area. The gathering of seeds was nearly always done by squaws, who worked their way up and down the prairie, beating the ripe seeds of the plants into baskets with a small club-shaped device woven from sedge or rush.

If you look carefully at the seeds from this field grass, you'll note that most varieties are covered with tiny hairs, and some even have sharp points protruding from the ends. These were singed off by the Indians during a parching process, in which the seeds were lightly tossed in a basket filled with hot coals. Once dried, they could then be ground fine in a mortar, the end result being a meal or flour that the Spaniards called pinole. Oat grass in particular, though not likely native to the state, was a favorite for making pinole.

Into the walk 0.4 mile the path drops down onto a moist, low bench. Some years this trail receives so little use that trying to follow the path turns into somewhat of a jungle experience, as you pick your way through blackberries, laurel, thimbleberries, and—watch out!—the infamous, shiny, three-leaved poison oak. This very short stretch of lower prairie offers some excellent bird life, so

115

walkers wearing long pants will find the walk rewarding. If all this is too much of a Tarzan trip for you, you can return to high ground and head south (which would have been on your left as you walked down the trail on the outbound trip), and in a short while you'll come out on a dirt road that has been paralleling our course. Make a right here and in less than a hundred yards you will have rejoined our route. (The lower bench route also joins the same roadway, only a little bit farther to the west.)

It will be almost impossible for you to cover this stretch of grassland without hearing the "chuck," "buzz" and "ko-ka-ree" of red-winged blackbirds. These birds will almost always be found wherever there is an abundance of moist, grassy environments. These days they are perhaps the biggest devourers of the grass seeds mentioned earlier, a diet that is supplemented during part of the year by a variety of insects.

As previously mentioned, make a right turn at the point where the path comes out on an obvious dirt road. In a few short steps you'll enter a lovely, mixed-evergreen forest, where bright crescendos of bird song echo off the branches of sycamores, bigleaf maples, laurels, red alders, and tanoak. Sit for a while and enjoy this very special patch of woodland. During the late evening, if you have a little bit of luck and a pocket full of patience, you may spot a raccoon, rabbit, gray squirrel, opossum, or even a ringtail or weasel going about its business beneath this lush canopy.

If you were a nineteenth-century Indian well versed in the ways of the woods, you could hardly find a better place to be. Let's say that the position of the sun on the horizon, or a steady rumble in your stomach, or whatever you happened to be using as a clock, told you that it was definitely dinner time. Perhaps you'd start your meal with some tasty acorn mush made from the nuts of the tanoak. (If you were a trapper, you'd probably use the bark of this oak to make a concoction for tanning your animal skins—hence the common name of the tree.) But back to dinner. For the main course, a little deer meat might be nice. But—oh no!—you're out of arrows. No problem. Some of those young alders over there would be perfect for replenishing your supply. Blackberries would be good for dessert, and you could collect them in a fine basket made from the inner bark of the bigleaf maple. Later in the evening, when you discovered to your dismay that the Big Sur River water you had drunk earlier had given you diarrhea, you could reach for a nice decoction of alder bark. Eventually you would drift off to sleep on a full, settled stomach, knowing that if tomorrow the fleas or indigestion or even your rheumatism should flare up, there's a good crop of laurel leaves nearby to help you get through it all.

You will come to a couple of small forks in the next 0.5 mile. Stay along the north side of the Big Sur River, which will come out at a rocky beach bordering a lagoon. Just before the end of the trail is a signed fork, with the right branch heading uphill to a vista point atop the headlands to the north. You will want to take the left fork, which leads to the edge of the lagoon itself. This is a wonderful place just to sit back and soak in the quiet beauty of the Big Sur coast. Watch for egrets, willets, black oystercatchers, California and western gulls, surf scoters, and the busy black turnstones, which you'll see turning over the stones (hence their name) of this gravelly cove looking for crabs and sand fleas.

You can either return the way you came or else walk the dirt road straight east. If you take the road, when you reach a small cabin on your left, take the trail that leaves the road and runs northeast toward the highway. This will bring you out a short way from where you parked. (Continuing east on the dirt road will take you through a hike-in campground and out to the highway at a point about 0.3 mile south of the parking area.)

MOONSTONE BEACH

Distance: 0.5 mile
Location: North end of Moonstone Beach Drive at Vista Point.
Turn off to the left 1.5 miles south of San Simeon Creek Road, or 2.5 miles north of Cambria. (Moonstone Beach Drive runs for a bit more than 2 miles along the west side of State Highway 1 and has both a north and a south entrance.)

At 0.5 mile round trip, the walk above Moonstone Beach—so named for the moonstone agates that have been found there—is the shortest of any of our treks. It is included because the numerous side

117

trails leading to the edge of the ocean bluffs are surrounded by grassy perches, which are perfect for immersing yourself in the magic of the California coast. In December and January you may well spot gray whales on a southward journey to their calving grounds off Baja California. What must the sailors of nineteenth-century schooners have thought of this magnificent migration, as they piloted their cargo-ladened vessels among these gargantuan creatures on their way to make deliveries at Leffingwell Landing, just a few hundred yards south of where you now stand?

Head south from the Moonstone Beach Vista Point along a dirt path framed by Monterey cypresses and Monterey pines. Both of these species are part of a group of conifers that you may occasionally hear called fire trees or fire pines—the majority of the trees' seeds remain locked tightly in the cones until liberated by fire. Growing conditions are usually excellent after a fire has moved through a conifer forest; the heat not only releases nutrients from the soil but clears away thick undergrowth that would otherwise compete with the trees for sunlight and moisture. Those conifers that have viable seeds to drop on the burned floor will have a big advantage over other species in reestablishing themselves.

Before turning around at the Leffingwell Landing Picnic Area you may wish to take some time to watch brown pelicans, godwits, and surf scoters gliding up and down the coastline, as well as perhaps to catch a glimpse of the remarkable California sea otter. These are among the most engaging mammals in the world, and this stretch of coast is part of an extremely important reserve that has been established for their continued survival.

Sea otters, which are really the only true ocean-bound members of the weasel family, were first discovered in 1741 by the Danish explorer Vitas Bering (for whom the Bering Sea is named). These otters actually provided the majority of clothing and food that saved the lives of Bering and his crew when they were stranded for a winter on an island in the northern Pacific. Bering did not exactly return the favor when he finally got back to China, helping to stir up such a demand for the pelts that over the next century and a half, the poor sea otters were pushed to the very edge of extinction. (Some historians maintain that Russia sold Alaska to the United States in 1867 for a bargain basement price because it felt that the total depletion of the sea otter had rendered the land worthless.)

Caspian Tern

Willet

Black Oystercatcher

Killdeer

Marbled Godwit

Western Sandpiper

The sea otters' routine habits are fascinating to watch. Because they do not have the insulating blubber of many other sea creatures, they must eat fully one fourth of their total body weight each day to stay alive. This typically translates to about 15 pounds a day! Though the otters have their favorite foods, including sea urchins, abalone, clams, and crabs, they have been observed consuming more than forty different species of marine organisms. Shellfish are brought up from the ocean bottom, along with a good-size rock. An otter turns over on his back, places the rock in the center of his chest, and then hammers the shellfish on it until it breaks open, at which point he quickly gobbles up the goodies inside. The best time to watch otters feeding is during late afternoon and early morning. If at all possible you should bring a pair of binoculars. Otters spend most of their time in thick kelp beds, which have floating bladders that are difficult to tell apart from the heads of the animals.

You may also see frothy splashes in the kelp from otters rolling around in the water. They are doing this to trap insulating air bubbles in their fur, which will help keep them warm. Otters spend a great deal of their time grooming their coats for the same reason. The extreme importance of keeping their fur in good condition is why an oil spill in this area could mean death for hundreds of animals. A great deal of care must be exercised if we are to ensure that sea otters are to be around for generations to come. While their numbers slowly increased for half a century since about 1920, they now, unfortunately, seem to be losing ground again.

MONTANA DE ORO STATE PARK

Distance: 2.6 miles

Location: From U.S. Highway 101 near the southern edge of San Luis Obispo, head west toward Los Osos on the Los Osos Valley Road. This turns into Pecho Valley Road, which turns south near the coast and dead-ends in the state park. Our southbound trail takes off across the road from, and just south of, the ranger station and campground entrance road.

Montana de Oro State Park provides an absolutely stunning combination of land and sea. Great bowed lines of blue waves roll in from the west, licking long, dark fingers of 20-million-year-old volcanic rock. Just above the shoreline, headlands roll in gentle swales thick with chaparral, flushed in spring with mustard, brass buttons, paintbrush, tidy tips, and the bright orange heads of poppies, which inspired the Spaniards to christen these hills Montana de Oro, or "Mountain of Gold."

A short way into the walk an interpretive sign will inform you about an enterprising man named A. B. Spooner, who at the beginning of the twentieth century, used this small cove as a dock for cargo schooners hauling local butter, grain, and cheese to markets up and down the coast. Freight-hauling sailing vessels had by this time been on the wane for years, but Spooner took advantage of the fact that this section of coast was extremely remote, lacking reliable overland shipping of any kind. Local farmers were glad to pay Spooner's prices for his offer of quick delivery to some of the better California markets.

More than half a century earlier, at a time of heavy demand for goods by gold-rush immigrants, cargo-hauling ships along this coast enjoyed their few glory years. This was the era that produced the famous California clipper ships. It must have been a remarkable sight to watch these lean vessels running down the coast with the northwesterlies, great clusters of ivory-colored canvas pulling hard on the white pine masts. The fastest clippers made the long trip to New York around the southern tip of South America in a bit more than three months—half the average time for ship passage in the mid-nineteenth century. The beginning of the end for the clippers came in 1855, when a railroad line was completed through the Panamanian jungle, which reduced the passage time from New York to a blindingly quick thirty days.

On your right 0.3 mile into the walk you'll join a pathway that heads down to a rocky section of beach containing some small tidal pools. If this area is full of visitors, there's another fine collection of pools 0.35 mile farther down the trail. The tidal pools of this park are among the finest in the state, so you should plan enough time in your walk to explore them thoroughly. Gain a good feel of the distinct belts that different residents of the tidal zone tend to occupy. The spiral-shelled periwinkle, for example, will be found huddled on the rocks just above the tidal pools themselves,

121

while starfish, chitons, and gooseneck barnacles will be found down lower. The larger animals that are occasionally seen here, such as octopus and sculpin, will be found in the very deepest parts of the larger pools.

Though everyone is eager to see the action of animal organisms in a tidal pool, the plants themselves are extremely interesting. Wispy filaments of green algae are thought to be the organisms that gave rise to all the plants that today populate the land portions of the earth. There is a brown algae here that may have been the pioneer of chemical defenses in terrestrial plants such as poison oak. When the tissues of this algae are damaged, they release sulfuric acid. This acid can actually dissolve the surface cells of seaweeds lying beneath it, giving them a bleached pattern that has led to the plant being called the color changer. The beautiful sea palms you may spot here (they do look like palm trees) last only one year. The plant's final act is to release thousands of tiny spores, which course their way down the grooved leaves and fall to the rocks below; some of them will take hold and produce new plants the following season.

The rest of the walk is along a serene ocean landscape, your company provided primarily by pelicans, cormorants, and gulls. You will see cheerful-looking mats of fiddleneck, red maids, hummingbird sage, sea rockets, hottentot figs, tidy tips, beach lupine, and the familiar mustard and California poppy. Several of these plants had substantial value as food or medicine to Indians of the area. The fresh root of the poppy was used by some Indians to stop the pain of toothache, and a mild extract from the root was reportedly effective in the cure of headaches. Tidy tips, with their striking yellow and white petals, produced seeds that were greatly valued for the production of pinole, virtually any kind of meal that is made from parched seeds. The mustard you see along this walk was introduced into this area. Native peoples adopted the habit of eating mustard greens from settlers around the end of the nineteenth century.

About a mile into the walk you'll come to a path heading off to the left toward Pecho Valley Road. Stay right along the ocean bluffs. In a short way you will come to a fence, which marks the turnaround point for our walk. On the way back, note the 576-foot-high Morro Rock to the north, the so-called Gibraltar of the Pacific, first noted by the Spanish explorer Juan Cabrillo in 1542. This is the last of a series of volcanic plug domes that run in a line stretching northward from San Luis Obispo. (Morro Rock is at the north end of Morro Bay, a fantastically rich estuary, which some researchers think may produce four fifths of all the major harvestable ocean life found along the central coast.) Yet another interesting slice of nature north of here are the large groves of eucalyptus trees that line Hazard Canyon, which you passed driving in to this trail head. The trees are used as nesting sites from October through March by great congregations of monarch butterflies.

PISMO DUNES PRESERVE

Distance: 2 miles
Location: From State Highway 1 south of Grover City, turn west on Pier Avenue. The entrance station is just ahead. The beach itself is open to vehicles, and there are numbered signs from 1 to 8 running up and down the waterfront. Park next to marker no. 1. (If you prefer instead to park adjacent to the entrance station on Pier Avenue, this will add approximately 1 mile to the walk.)

From beach marker no. 1, located approximately 0.5 mile south of the Pier Avenue entrance station, walk east 40 yards to a fence that marks the boundary of the Pismo Dunes Preserve. Cross under this fence, and choose any of the many trails that make their way southward through the dunes. From this point a rather large ridge of sand forms a protective wall separating this beautiful dune community from the hustle and bustle of Pismo Beach. A surprising number of plants and animals are cradled in this folded sandscape, including the bright pinks and purples of sand verbena and sea fig and the delicate buzz and twitter of long-billed marsh wrens and Audubon warblers. The rolling golden hummocks of sand are split by narrow furrows, many of which are lined with the soft greens of willow, sage, and European beach grass. In such dense thickets

123

cottontail rabbits, valley quail, and even foxes and raccoons may be hiding from you.

The first white men to traverse the Pismo Dunes were part of a Spanish expedition in 1769 led by Don Gaspar de Portolá, the man who blazed the famous El Camino Real ("King's Highway") north through California in an effort to verify the existence of Monterey Bay. One hundred sixty years later, during the 1930s and 40s, these same dunes became home to a group of beat writers, artists, and mystics that called themselves the Dunites. After the first few people took up residence there, word began to spread that the dunes themselves were actually a powerful center for creative energy. Before long dozens of crude driftwood shacks had been built in the sand by freethinkers who had come there from all over California. At the height of their spontaneous community, the Dunites even published a small periodical of alternative thinking called *The Dune Forum*.

The Pismo Dunes are among the two or three largest coastal dunes in the state and perhaps the richest of all as far as plant life is concerned. It is not an easy task for a plant to set up shop in a sand dune. There are very few nutrients available, and water drains quickly out of reach. This lack of water is why you will see several types of succulents, which are able to store water for long periods of time in their fleshy tissues. There are also several dune plants like the beach grasses, which absorb moisture through their extensive root systems.

As you look at the vegetation of a dune community, it may seem that plants such as European beach grass, as well as certain kinds of flowers, have a strong preference for living on the tops of the sandy hummocks. In fact, these hummocks were created by the plants themselves, which are constantly pushing their stems above the dune surface at a rate just ahead of the rate at which sand accumulates around them. European beach grass was introduced here and in dunes throughout California for the express purpose of keeping the sand from being pushed inland by the onshore winds.

Take time to notice the difference that exposure makes in the types of dune plants that grow in any particular area. The beach (windward) side of the dunes is sparsely populated and has much smaller plants than those on the protected, leeward flank. Also determining where a certain plant will live is its exposure to the sun. Sand tends to reflect a great deal of heat. Many plants simply grow in a position where the sand slopes away from them. Others are protected by leaves covered with tiny white hairs, which reflect light away from them. (You can spot the same mechanism at work in many desert plants.)

Continue southward through the foredunes for about a mile (twenty to thirty minutes of walking), taking note of the many stories that are revealed in the dunes by the tracks of mice, skunks, and coyotes. Keep a special watch out for mouse tracks. If you see a line of them that suddenly disappears, look closely just beyond and outward on either side of the end point for faint signs of wing tips hitting the sand. Such evidence would suggest that a hungry hawk or owl, perhaps, brought a sudden end to the rodent's journey. Early morning is an especially good time to cover this stretch because bird life is then at its peak.

Once you've made your way a mile into the reserve, climb out of the foredunes and onto the crest of the fabulous large dunes that lie to the east. (You will only be able to go about a mile and a half southward in the reserve before running into an area that is open to off-road vehicles.) Though they look as though they'd be difficult to climb, these sandy giants are actually quite firm in most places. Going up is like walking in a dream—nothing but glaring blond sand rising before you like a yawning stretch of the Sahara.

Work your way back northward along the crest of the high dunes. If you don't want to cross back under the fence at the same spot that you entered the area, you can continue northward until you hit Arroyo Grande Creek, which forms the northern boundary of the preserve. Once back on the beach, you'll be only a few hundred yards north of marker post no. 1.

As you walk back along the beach, you'll see the shells of Pismo and gaper clams strewn about the sand. The Pismo clam is certainly one of the most popular shellfish in the area, although overharvesting in the past has reduced the population to only a tiny fraction of what it once was. Let it not be said that the Pismo clams don't do their part in trying to keep their own numbers up. A single adult will typically lay anywhere from 10 to 15 million eggs! Unfortunately, before these youngsters can settle into the sand and begin their main stage of growth, most of the lot is scooped up for dinner by marine predators. Pismo clams burrow themselves quite deep in the sand. They feed by means of small siphon tubes that extend upward from their hiding places to catch bits of food brought in by the ocean.

South Coast

CHERRY COVE (CATALINA ISLAND)

Distance: 3.5 miles

Location: From Isthmus Cove Beach, climb the obvious trail, which runs northwest up the hillside to intersect with a dirt road. You will skirt the northwestern lip of Isthmus Cove. Continue around Fourth of July Cove and finally reach the mouth of Cherry Cove in about 1.7 miles.

The Cherry Cove walk is a wonderful bayside stroll above a series of shimmering, crescent-shaped harbors. The entire Isthmus Cove area is a soothing blend of deep blue water framed by rugged headlands—a scene spiced with wind-tossed oak and cherry groves and rich, warm carpets of grass and chaparral. You could walk an entire day along this beautiful road, eventually coming out at the quiet, Parsons Landing Campground, 7 miles northwest of the starting point.

Standing at Isthmus Cove Beach, you can see a trail heading uphill for 50 or 60 yards to an intersection with a dirt road. Once on this road your walking will be on level ground, allowing lots of time for idle, seaside daydreams. It's hard to stroll above these quiet, blue harbors without giving some thought to the secretive comings and goings of smugglers, who have visited these very coves on a regular basis from the beginning of the nineteenth century. In the eighteenth and early nineteenth centuries the use of sailing schooners (and later the famous California clippers) to deliver cargo from the East Coast to the West Coast was an extremely lucrative business. At that time, however, the Spanish (later the Mexicans), who controlled California placed large customs tariffs on all Yankee

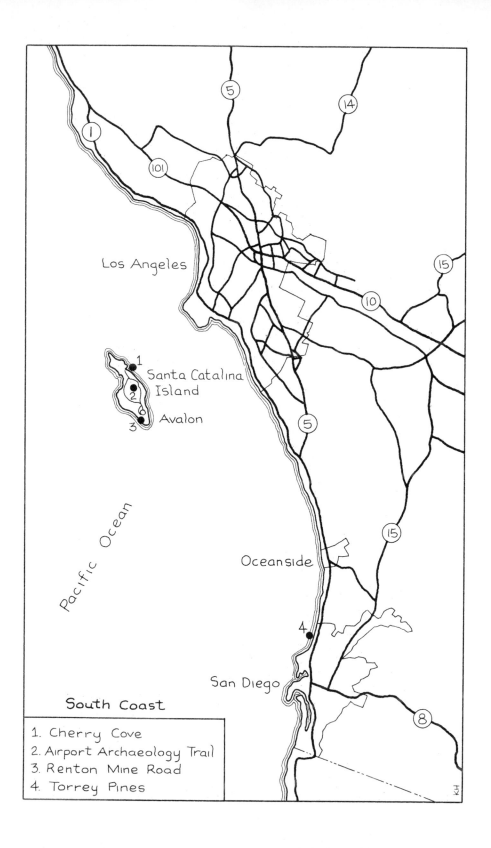

Los Angeles

Santa Catalina
Island

Avalon

Pacific Ocean

Oceanside

San Diego

South Coast

1. Cherry Cove
2. Airport Archaeology Trail
3. Renton Mine Road
4. Torrey Pines

traders doing business on the lower West Coast. A common scheme to escape these tariffs was first to unload a sizable portion of a ship's cargo on Catalina Island, head to the mainland and pay the assigned duty on what was left on board, and then return to the island to pick up the remainder of the goods and resume the northward journey. Throughout this period it was forbidden for a Yankee to touch ship at Catalina Island without special written orders from the Spanish governor.

Things did not always go smoothly for the sailors playing out this little subterfuge, and some captains docked on the mainland only to have their sails or even their cargo seized by the Spanish. Even in the face of such threats, a few were so bold as actually to erect warehouses on Catalina to protect their duty-free holdings. Such structures were, of course, immediately torn down as soon as authorities found out about them. Years later Catalina was used as a holding pen for Chinese slave labor, and it was an extremely well-used pickup point for alcohol during prohibition.

Off to your right just after beginning the walk you should see a large white rock dome. This is not some strange intrusion of white marble or granite but an ordinary rock covered with extrusions of sea-bird waste. It is called, appropriately, Bird Rock.

The jagged shoreline before you is a part of a massive block comprised largely of Catalina schist, that is, a type of fine-grained metamorphic rock. Taken as a whole, the geology of this island is an extremely involved puzzle, several parts of which have yet to be fully solved. Basically, 200 million years ago, the rocks that would one day make up part of Catalina Island were being carried slowly eastward on a block of ocean floor mantle known as the Falleron Plate. A hundred million years later, this eastward-moving plate began a terrific collision with the western edge of the North American continent.

Needing somewhere to go, the Falleron Plate began slowly to slip beneath the edge of the continental land mass, its solidifying mantle rock turning into liquid again as it sank back into the hot depths of the earth. (This hot magma would later rise to form many of California's interior mountain ranges.) As this mantle sank, much of the debris it carried was scraped off along the leading edge of the continent. The pressures brought about by this incredible colliding action, along with heat from magma inside of the earth, was so severe that it actually changed the composition of many rocks. It is the drastic effects of such heat and pressure that give rise to the geological term metamorphic.

After a period of violent volcanic activity, the submerged land mass holding what would eventually become Catalina Island began to drift northwest along a fault line, finally reaching this point, which is nearly 100 miles from the site it once occupied near the coast of northern Mexico. The landscape you see today is the result of centuries of weathering and erosion by the sea, each process slowly carving this block of metamorphic and volcanic rock into a wild frieze of bold headlands and crystal blue harbors.

In about 1.3 miles the roadway will join Cherry Cove, named for the beautiful groves of 40-to-50-foot-high Catalina cherry trees that grow in the mouth of this broad, V-shaped valley. This lovely, waxy-leafed tree produces large crops of tasty fruit, though the cherries consist of much more pit and skin than juicy flesh. Nevertheless, they were routinely harvested by Gabrielino Indians, and they are still considered well worth the effort by a variety of island birds, as well as the strikingly handsome Channel Island fox.

AIRPORT ARCHAEOLOGY TRAIL
(CATALINA ISLAND)

Distance: 0.5 mile

Location: Take Crescent Street in Avalon toward the large, round casino building. Turn left on Marilla, right on Vieudelou, and finally left again onto Stage Road. This will bring you to the airport terminal building. Walk out of the airport gate and take a dirt path located just outside the gate to the southeast.

The Airport Archaeology Trail is a short walk that is long on natural history and archaeology. One of the best features of this route is that you will see several things that will allow you to fine-tune your senses for treks on other parts of Catalina Island. Be sure to stay on the trail, since there are several native plants, such as sponge grass, that are doing their best to reestablish themselves here after more than a century of being mowed down by grazing animals.

It takes a little imagination to visualize what Catalina Island looked like before the introduction of domestic animals in the 1830s. A sound ecosystem is most often one that has evolved slowly over many thousands of years, prey balanced by predator, flora balanced by browser and grazer. When something is suddenly added to or taken away from the system, the results can be devastating. This occurred in many parts of the American West when horses and burros were abandoned by their owners and then multiplied to the point where they obliterated fragile desert ecosystems. On Catalina, much of the environment was destroyed by goats, pigs, sheep, deer, and bison.

This walk offers a fascinating lesson in the strange chain reactions that can occur from such introductions. As you walk down the path, notice that almost without exception, every large plant or bush growing here is surrounded by prickly pear cacti. Prickly pear did not use to be so widespread on Catalina. When overgrazing removed protective ground mats and grasses, it quickly spread and colonized, since in the freshly bared soil it no longer faced any competition for water and nutrients. The grazing animals themselves probably helped to bring prickly pear up to this area whenever the plant got caught in the fur of their legs. (Australia had an incredible problem with introduced prickly pear, which ultimately blanketed millions of acres of range land.)

As the prickly pear cacti grew, they tended to form protective enclosures. Those plants that were able to germinate within these "fences" were able to flourish because they were suddenly off limits to the hungry hordes. The larger plants you see here exist only because they have prickly bodyguards standing by their side. Now take what you see growing in these cactus enclosures, and imagine what the landscape would look like covered with such vegetation.

By the way, the cholla and prickly pear of this island too often provide us with another glimpse of how tragic the results can be of absent-mindedly altering a natural ecosystem. The goat population periodically explodes here, rapidly reaching numbers beyond what the available food supply can support. Some animals starve, while others die an excruciating death from trying to eat past the spiny armor of the prickly pear cacti.

About 0.2 mile into the walk on the right side of the trail you'll come to a rock outcropping that shows obvious signs of having been scraped and chipped. This is a coarse-grained metamorphic rock known as steatite, or soapstone, which the Gabrielino Indians used in the manufacture of cooking pots. (There is also a harder soapstone located on the island that was used in the manufacture of beads.) Soapstone is a superb material from which to fashion cooking ware. It is extremely easy to shape with abrading stones or crude knives, and the talc content results in a smooth-finished bowl that can withstand high levels of heat. These vessels, or ollas, became a major item of trade with peoples of the mainland. Such goods were carried across the channel in sleek canoes called *tomols*, which were constructed of narrow planks laced together through drilled holes and sealed with tar.

It is believed that Indians inhabited Catalina Island as long as four thousand years ago, though the arrival of the people known as Gabrielino is thought to have occurred about 500 B.C. It seems doubtful that the island ever held more than 1,500 or 2,000 residents at any one time, most of these concentrated in three or four main occupation sites. (There were, however, hundreds of smaller seasonal sites located near water sources.) The island was for the most part a place of plenty; the sea offered an abundance of shellfish, marine mammals, and offshore fish such as tuna that could be harvested by harpoon and net, while the island interior provided acorns and many kinds of wild plants.

Although it is probably never wise to speculate too seriously on the life-style of a culture that we have very little knowledge of, it's hard not to think that life on Catalina must have been a very special experience. How deep the rhythms of the tides and the cycles of fish and plant harvests must have seemed; how sweet the whispered music of the surf and the surge of new life running across the grasslands beneath the kiss of a spring rain.

Marsh Hawk

Brandt's Cormorant

Brown Pelican

Great Blue Heron

Great Egret

Surf Scoter

RENTON MINE ROAD
(CATALINA ISLAND)

Distance: 2.8 miles
Location: Head south along the coast on Pebbly Beach Road.
About 1.5 miles out of town the road makes a climbing hairpin
turn, becoming the Mount Ada Road. (Don't go straight or
you'll end up at the waste-water plant!) About 0.7 mile from
this hairpin turn you'll see a small dirt road heading off to the
left blocked by a locked gate. This is the Renton Mine Road.

Catalina Island is the kind of place that you know is going to get
under your skin even before your boat docks in Avalon. Crisp white
yachts and Mediterranean-style buildings perch on quiet curves of
clear blue ocean. Soft blond beaches cradle the waterfront, and
boulevards lined with palm and eucalyptus can be seen coursing up
the island's rugged eastern flank. But there is another, even more
intriguing world beyond the bustle of Avalon Bay. This island is
thick with natural wonders—a soaring, tranquil landscape sporting
more than six hundred species of plants, birds, and mammals,
some of which are found nowhere else on earth.

The Renton Mine Road, like so many on Catalina Island, is
inclined to slope. You will want to take the walk slow and easy,
which is not all that hard to do, since there should be enough
unfamiliar life forms along the road at least to make you stop and
scratch your head once in a while.

This is a particularly good road for your first walk on Catalina,
for the simple reason that it is one of the few easily reached areas
that can even begin to give you a sense of the great biological
diversity that is here. Many other interior zones, as you will see, are
not the same lush tapestries that they once were, having long been
at the mercy of scores of imported animals.

Significant altering of Catalina's environment is thought to
have began in the 1830s, when a boatload of goats was dumped on
the island, perhaps from one of the many smuggling ships that used
to frequent this area. In a surprisingly short amount of time there
was an extraordinarily large population of these creatures. In fact,
some researchers estimate their population level in 1900 to have
been an incredible 60,000. Next on the import list were cattle and

as many as 20,000 head of sheep, both of which were brought to the island for ranching during the 1860s. These were followed by a small herd of bison sixty years later, which arrived for the production of a movie called *The Vanishing American*. The film crew pulled out and left the bison to roam the range, and the herd was added to later by members of the Wrigley family. About a decade later came the final two members of the graze-browse-root brigade—deer and "wild boars," which weren't wild boars at all but domestic European pigs. Both of these latter species were added to create opportunities for hunting for sport.

The effect of all these imported species—none of which had any natural predators—was to turn Eden into 75 square miles of Armageddon. Overgrazing first eliminates vegetation that the animal most likes to eat. Unfortunately, the preferred munchies were often plants that occurred naturally only on Catalina. Only in the last ten to fifteen years, under the protective wing of the Catalina Conservancy, have a few of the hardest-hit plants begun to make a recovery. It is a painstakingly slow process, still halted now and then by wide fluctuations in the populations of the introduced species.

It is fortunate, then, that the Renton Mine Road is still swathed in thick cloaks of green Catalina countryside, though undoubtedly the exact proportions of the mix are substantially different from what they used to be. Plants here that might be new to you include the Catalina cherry, wild apple, and valley oak; there is no shortage of some old familiars, including sticky monkeyflower, fennel (a favorite of the bison), ceanothus, and lemonadeberry. This latter plant was used by Indians both on the island and on the mainland to make a tangy drink not at all unlike unsweetened lemonade. As you go a bit farther up, look down to your left at the lushness of the canyon bottom—a thick flush of life given to the land by a simple trickle of running water. The hardy explorer will find real magic down there, the place thick with tangles of clematis, elderberry, Catalina currant, island and valley oak, ferns, and wild grape.

Such quiet corridors are also good places for the patient stalker to try for a glimpse of some indigenous birds and mammals. Two of the easiest to spot are the Catalina quail and the Bewick's wren, both of which are found only in this tiny island world. Early-morning or late-evening walkers may well catch sight of the exquisite Channel Island fox, whose meals typically consist of small rodents, fruits, and even insects. It's fun to try to speculate just how this graceful little animal, the island's largest predator, came here in the first place. The question whether the Gabrielino Indians brought it centuries ago or it somehow crossed the channel on its own has been the subject of much speculation. Sadly, it has been documented that seeds from an introduced species of wild oat grass often end up in this little fox's eyes, too often leading to blindness.

The mining that took place in this particular canyon was for lead, zinc, and silver. A small gold rush had hit the island in the 1860s, long before the Renton Mine was in full swing. The resulting strikes, however, most of which were concentrated in the area of the isthmus, never did turn into a no-holes-barred bonanza.

Because this island has been under private ownership for most of the twentieth century it was completely passed over by biological and archaeological research efforts, which tended to spread from the coast of Southern California into the far reaches of the Pacific. It's odd to consider that we know a great deal more about remote atolls 2,500 miles to the southwest than we do about an island 22 miles from one of the biggest metropolitan centers in America. It is a lovely land, still awash with unsolved mysteries—a place to learn from and a place to nurture.

TORREY PINES

Distance: 2.6 miles

Location: Torrey Pines State Reserve. From Interstate 5 at the northern edge of San Diego, take Carmel Valley Road west 2 miles to the junction with North Torrey Pines Road. Turn left and follow this road up to the visitors' center parking area, which is located on the east side of the road. Our walk begins across from the visitor center.

If this is your first time heading up the coast on Interstate 5 out of San Diego, it may be more than a little difficult for you to believe that just north of the University of California at San Diego campus is a crisp, 1,000-acre pocket of unspoiled nature. Torrey Pines is, in fact, one of the finest coastal preserves in the state. Here are not only one of the rarest species of trees in the world but also more than three hundred species of native plants—fully half the number found in the entire 4,200 square miles of San Diego County. Keep in mind that to protect the rather fragile environment, Torrey Pines State Reserve keeps a tight lid on the numbers of people that can visit here at any one time. Early weekday mornings are the best time to do this walk.

Before heading out, spend a few minutes at the reserve's visitors' center, which is located right across the roadway from where our walk begins. Besides some good cultural displays, there is a small botanical area on the south side of the building that will introduce you to some of the more common plants you'll be seeing along our walk. You'll find the staff there to be particularly helpful in answering any questions that you might have.

Begin this trek on the Beach Trail, which takes off beside the rest rooms on the west side of the old highway. A short way down this rather busy path, take a right on a trail that heads toward Razor Point. Although this loop is not as liberally seasoned with Torrey pines as are the Guy Fleming and Parry Grove trails to the north, there are enough scattered members of this species for you at least to make a first acquaintance.

Early Spanish seamen made the first written record of this high huddle of pines 300 feet above the ocean, the grove showing up so distinctly along an otherwise scrub-covered coastline that it became an important landmark for sailing ships making their way along the coast in foggy weather. It was the plant specialist C. C. Parry who "officially" discovered the tree in 1850, naming it for his former professor and one of the most renown botanists of the day, John Torrey.

While the Torrey pine is not the rarest pine tree in the world, it is very uncommon. There are only a few thousand native Torrey pines in the world (up from a few hundred a century ago), and all grow within this reserve or in nearby scattered pockets, as well as on Santa Rosa Island across the Santa Barbara Channel. The tree bears its stiff, dark green needles on the ends of its branches in clusters of five. The 4-to-6-inch-long cones take three years to mature, and the rather large seeds they hold can either be released then or be locked inside the cone scales for ten or fifteen more years. Ground squirrels find Torrey pine seeds especially tasty and usually round up a good portion of the yearly crop for themselves. Like the redwoods, Torrey pines survive on these few bluffs because they are frequently wrapped in fog, a condition that increases moisture levels to a point where the trees can thrive in a place that would otherwise be too dry for them. (These trees are thought to have been fairly widespread 5 or 10 million years ago, when the climate was much wetter.)

A little less than 0.25 mile into the walk you'll come to a short spur path on the right, which leads to an overlook at the southern edge of Canyon of the Swifts. This is an exceptionally beautiful ravine, with rich golden walls of Torrey sandstone eroded by water and wind into a stunning collage of sculpted flutes and scarps. Most of the rock you'll see in this reserve is really a collection of sandstone layers, each deposited during successive rises and falls of the sea over the past 40 million years. In many places within the park it's easy to spot the different layers that distinguish between separate geologic events. The rusty red stone that sits on top of the beige-colored, fluted rock, for instance, is simply an iron-rich layer of sand and gravel that the sea deposited on top of the Torrey sandstone.

Continue to make your way westward down the trail through a fantastic variety of plant life. In early April there is a rich abundance of blooms here—the colors of lemonadeberry, red monkey flower, sea dahlia, primrose, and poppy flowing down the hills like bright spatters on an artist's drop cloth. Keep an eye peeled here for Beechey ground squirrels and black-tailed jackrabbits, and if it has rained recently, look in the soft dirt for tracks of the coyote and gray fox.

On your right about 0.4 mile into the walk is a spur trail to Razor Point. It's less than 0.1 mile to the point itself, and the trail affords outstanding views of the ocean and of the fluted Torrey sandstone so common to this section of the reserve. Return to the main trail and continue on past the Yucca Point turnoff to a junction with the Beach Trail, which you will take westward toward the beach. The path to the beach forks just before a series of steps marking the western terminus of the Broken Hill Trail. You will take a right here, drop down over a small ledge, and then work your way around a sandstone wall to a section of beach located just north of Flat Rock.

Notice that the upper portion of the beach is composed not of sand but of millions of tiny pebbles that let out long sighs with each receding wave. This kind of beach is common in narrow, rockbound coves and along stretches of coast framed by certain erosion-resistant rock. These beach stones have been rounded by the ocean waves, a process similar to what happens to pebbles lying in the bottom of a stream. Immediately behind you is a striking wall composed of thick layers of delmar siltstone and Torrey sandstone, capped by rusty-looking lindavista sandstone.

Our route back will be along the Broken Hill Trail, which begins at the steps located just south of where the Beach Trail veered west to Flat Rock. This is for the most part a drier section of the reserve, replete with tough, green chaparral. Look for black sage, laurel sumac, California buckwheat, ceanothus, manzanita, toyon, and scrub oak, along with a few cactus surprises along the way. There is a fork in this trail about 0.5 mile from the beach; stay to the left. You'll come out on a paved road now closed to vehicles (the old San Diego to Los Angeles highway). Take another left, and in less than 0.4 mile you'll be back at the visitors' center.

THE FOREST

The clearest way into the Universe," wrote the nineteenth-century wilderness lover John Muir, "is through a forest wilderness." Walking in the woods offers gifts of beauty and serenity to anyone who cares to receive them. It is a calm, nurturing encounter that strikes at the heart of the original meaning of the word recreation, "to restore." But beyond such a refreshing pause, there are times, as Muir suggested, when there seems to be even more there—a kind of fleeting magic that can sink beneath the most modern of minds, plucking strings inside the soul that have not been played for a thousand years. Perhaps it is some kind of distant déjà vu, flashed for a second in the pose of tree limbs against a pale sky, or in the sudden rhythmic movement of a hundred woodland birds, all prodded to flight by a common cue.

As Muir knew after having walked not only the American woodlands but those of Africa, New Zealand, and Brazil, the forests of California are among the most diverse and magnificent in all the world. The variety of climate and elevation there provides a melting pot of living conditions, or niches, in which different trees can establish themselves. Like birds or animals, trees do well only when they have access to the specific conditions for which they've evolved. Redwoods grow in only a few areas along the north coast, where summer fogs are frequent enough to provide them with the moisture they need to survive. Red firs thrive in the deep snows of the Sierras, yet do not do particularly well unless their feet are planted in well-drained soil. Ponderosa pines, which grow to magnificent proportions on sunny mountain slopes, begin to decline in vigor above 7,000 feet owing to the damage that heavy frosts inflict on the trees' growing shoots.

As you might have guessed, one of the things that helps to

143

create such a variety of niches in California—and therefore a variety of forests—is the state's great abundance of mountains. Temperature and moisture conditions change dramatically from the foothills of a high range to the summits, and from south-facing slopes to those that face north. In addition, the number and kinds of nutrients available to a tree depend a great deal on what kind of rock the mountain is made of.

One of the best ways to gain a feel for how mountains tend to be populated with predictable belts, or "life zones," of vegetation is to take a trip up the west side of the central Sierras. As we make this climb, however, keep in mind that nature is filled with scattered, unpredictable pockets where specific life forms flourish well outside of places where they are "supposed to." Assigning any type of zone or niche to a landscape is simply a crude way for man to understand general conditions in the environment. One other important point to keep in mind is, the farther north one goes, the lower the elevation at which the various plant zones occur. Another way to think of it is that going up 1,000 vertical feet is, as far as trees are concerned, equivalent to traveling north several hundred miles.

Let's start out in what is known as the Upper Sonoran Zone, which in the central part of the state lies between 800 and 4,000 feet. Here summers are long and dry, the thermometer often tickling the upper 90s during the months of May through August. Low elevation means a long growing season, but water is in such limited supply that only certain plants can take advantage of it. Here mixed with chaparral and toyon are live and interior oaks; there are digger pines and cottonwoods when groundwater is available.

As we move up into the Transition Zone between 2,500 and 6,000 feet, things begin to cool off a bit (temperatures typically drop 3 or 4 degrees for each thousand feet of elevation gained, as we have noted). The mountain forces clouds up into the cooler air, where they cannot hold as much moisture. Much of it falls to the ground as snow during the winter, and summer thunderstorms are a bit more common than they are down lower. This extra moisture and the slightly cooler temperatures are just what the trees need. Suddenly we are surrounded by beautiful big ponderosa pines (or yellow pines), as well as black oak, Douglas-fir, incense-cedar, sugar pine, and white fir, to name but a few.

The next higher step is into the Canadian Zone (as you remember, going up is like going north), located roughly between 6,500 and 8,000 feet. Here we experience a big change in both temperature and annual moisture. Summer days rarely rise above 82 degrees, while winters are cold with heavy snows, at some locations 300 or 400 inches a year. A few more thunderstorms fall during the summer, and what does hit the ground stays there longer because of the cooler weather. At this point we reach the trees for which severe winters pose no problem. These include aspen, lodgepole pine, western white pine, red fir, and Jeffrey pine.

There is yet one more zone of trees to reach—the Subalpine Zone, generally located between 7,500 and 10,000 feet. Within this belt we are at what for most trees is the point of diminishing returns. There is certainly abundant moisture here in the form of snowfall and occasional summer rains, but conditions are too cold for tree growth and reproduction to be carried on at optimum levels. The growing season is a scant two months long, and damaging frosts can occur at any time of the year. Here are the true survivors: whitebark pine, mountain hemlock, Sierra juniper, lodgepole pine, and foxtail pine. Trees that appear very small may actually be quite old. In fact, were you to climb just above this belt into the Alpine Zone, you'd find that the few trees that can exist there do so in what amounts to a prone position. Exploring in the Sierras near Cathedral Peak, John Muir found a mature whitebark pine growing at 10,700 feet that was only 3 feet high and had a trunk just 6 inches in diameter. When he counted the growth rings, he found it to be an astonishing 426 years old. A small branch of this whitebark, only ⅛ inch across, had been weathering the seasons of the high Sierras for 75 years!

You may have noticed on our trip up the west side of the Sierra Nevada that all but the lowest life zone was dominated by pines or firs, as distinguished from broadleaf trees such as oak, alder, or cottonwood. The weather pattern we found on our quick climb—hot, dry summers down low and short, cool ones above—is a pattern that prevails for much of the state. Such conditions are not

145

particularly appropriate for deciduous trees, such as maple, beech, sycamore, birch, or dozens of others that thrive in the East. These trees lose too much moisture through their broad leaves to survive the droughts of California, and they spend too much time growing a new crop of foliage each year to do very well at high elevations, where moisture is high but growing seasons are short. And so we find the tree that thrives in the West, the conifer.

Conifers, which have probably been around for more than 300 million years, have turned both water conservation and quick growth into fine arts. Take a close look at a pine needle and notice its waxy coating. This is important not only in insulating the cells from temperature extremes, but it is also very effective in reducing moisture loss from transpiration. (You can see similar waxy coatings on many desert plants.) This tough coating is one of the reasons you see pine needles lying on the ground intact long after they have fallen from the tree; such coatings do not yield easily to the processes of decomposition.

The conifer also has a few other survival tricks up its branches. The sticky resin that a crushed needle leaves on your fingers freezes well below the temperature that water does. It is, in effect, nature's equivalent to antifreeze. Also, take a close look at the shape and suppleness of a pine tree. Snow loads tend not to accumulate, or if they do, they can be shed without harm to the tree. You'll notice that this specialized shape is more and more pronounced the higher you go. Firs growing at the edges of high mountain meadows are often shaped like narrow lances.

Conifers also tend to have some interesting strategies when it comes to propagating their own kind. Those trees known as fire pines, such as Monterey cypress and knobcone pine, keep their precious seeds locked up tightly within heat-resistant cones until after a fire happens to rage through the area. Heat from the flames melts the gluelike resin holding the cone scales together, allowing them at last to fall to the ground and get down to the business of growing. Though it may seem like a very destructive event, fires actually release a number of valuable nutrients being held in the duff layer (decayed matter on the forest floor). Any tree that can sprout rapidly after a fire will be assured of getting its fair share of both sunlight and moisture. The coastal redwood, another of the

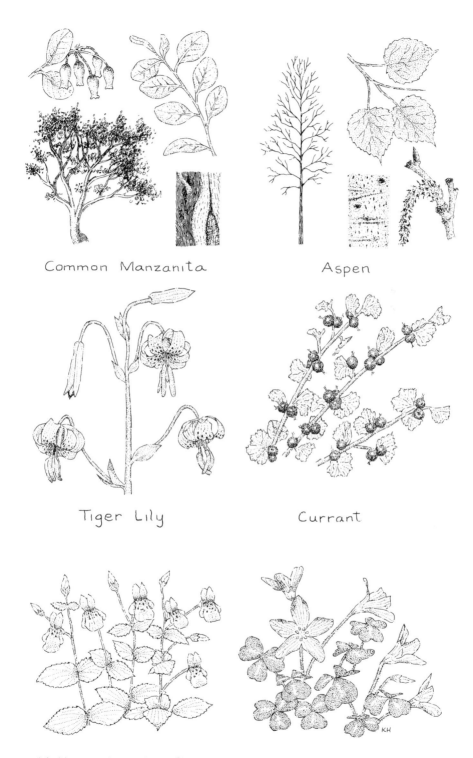

Common Manzanita

Aspen

Tiger Lily

Currant

Yellow Monkeyflower

Redwood Sorrel

fire pines, not only has seeds that do well on burned soil but also has the ability to propagate itself by sprouting entirely new trees from the roots or trunk.

Like everything in nature, forests are hardly static environments. The majority of wooded areas you'll be walking through are undergoing some stage of change that will eventually lead to what is known as a climax forest. This is the "ultimate" plant community for a particular environmental niche and consists of trees that thrive so well under the existing conditions that were it not for disturbances such as fire, logging, or disease interrupting the status quo, they would persist indefinitely. When the trees and understory vegetation are wiped out by, say, a fire, the process of reclaiming the land according to a particular series of plant communities begins almost immediately. First come grasses and small plants such as fireweed, which are well suited for growth on burned soil. Some of these will then yield to quick-growing shrubs, which may in turn be followed by a grove of deciduous trees. High in the mountains this plant community might consist of aspen. Then finally, under the shaded canopy of the quaking aspen come the young members of the climax forest, which in this case is likely to be a species of fir. These steps are fairly easy to identify, but don't get the idea that a fir forest that has burned down will grow into a new fir forest again in a short time; the entire process may take three or four hundred years. Of course nature is, above all else, very, very patient.

California not only has the biggest species of tree (giant sequoia) but also the tallest (redwood) and the oldest (bristlecone pine). More than 75 percent of the seventy-four known species of conifers can be found here, as well as a rich tapestry of madrone, oak, laurel, alder, and willow. If, as the poet W. H. Auden once said, a culture is no better than its woods, then California would appear to be in better shape than any of us might have imagined.

148

North Coast Forest

BOY SCOUT TREE TRAIL

Distance: 3.6 miles

Location: Located on the Howland Hill Road, east of Crescent City in Jedediah Smith Redwoods State Park. From downtown Crescent City, take U.S. Highway 101 south to Elk Valley Road and turn left. Howland Hill Road (County Road 417) takes off to the right (east) in approximately 1.5 miles. Continue east on Howland Hill Road for about 3.1 miles to the signed trail head, located on the north side of the road.

From the Hiouchi area on U.S. Highway 199, turn south 1 mile east of Jedediah Smith Redwoods State Park on County Road 427, following signs for the South Fork of the Smith River. At 0.5 mile after leaving 199 the road will split. Take the right fork—this is Howland Hill Road. It is approximately 4.4 miles to the signed trail head, located on the north side of the road. It is also just under 1 mile west of a metal bridge crossing Mill Creek. (Note: The Howland Hill Road is quite narrow and inappropriate for vehicles pulling large trailers.)

Stopping after an initial climb of about 0.25 mile, the walker on the Boy Scout Tree Trail feels his pulse and breathing slacken, and then, ever so slowly, the hushed beauty of the mature redwood forest rolls over him like a mist of eiderdown. Lady ferns and narrow spikes of deer ferns huddle along the trail, and redwood sorrel plants fill the open spaces with what appear to be rich green carpets of shamrock.

Because this forest is so still and quiet, slight eruptions of bird movement and song, though there are relatively few contributors, are rather easy to spot. Nuthatches and chickadees flit here and there looking for insects, offering only a muffled "peep" or

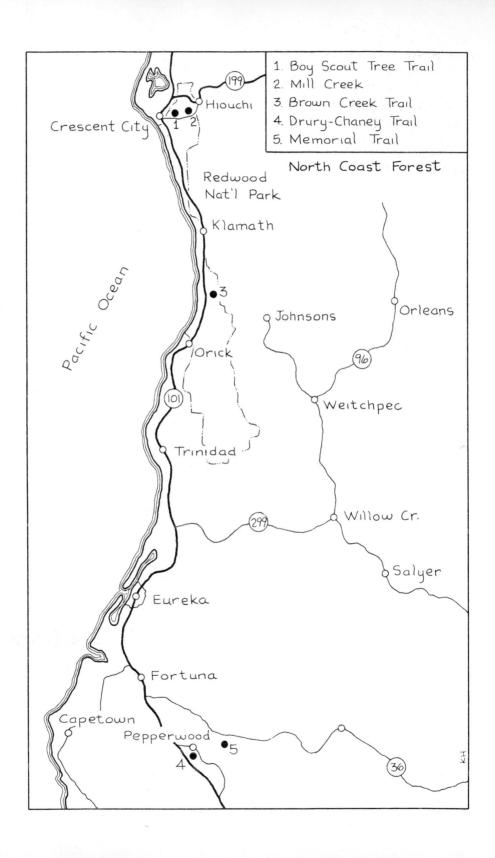

1. Boy Scout Tree Trail
2. Mill Creek
3. Brown Creek Trail
4. Drury-Chaney Trail
5. Memorial Trail

North Coast Forest

199

Hiouchi

Crescent City

1 2

Redwood
Nat'l Park

Klamath

Pacific Ocean

3

Johnsons

Orleans

Orick

96

101

Weitchpec

Trinidad

Willow Cr.

299

Salyer

Eureka

Fortuna

Capetown

Pepperwood

5

4

36

KH

"tee dee." Occasionally, this rather somber mood will be broken by the piercing "shaack! shaack!" of the Steller's jay, who, except when near her nest, seems compelled to announce her presence to the entire world.

About 1 mile down the Boy Scout Trail, the path begins to wind along the top of a small ridge with mature redwoods on either side. Such ridge-top walking affords you a wonderful degree of visual depth that would otherwise be impossible to obtain, since the sword ferns and lady ferns are so tall here that they would block the view if the terrain were flat. Take time along this stretch to notice the patterns of the forest. Certain hardpan, or clay, soils sustain only groundcovers, making holes that look like sunshine spotlights in the otherwise solid forest of trees. At the edge of these magic circles are black oak, California bay oak, and chinquapin, as well as lesser trees such as dogwood and hazelnut, all craning their necks for a chance at the light.

It is a difficult proposition for redwood seeds to take root and mature in an old-growth forest. Instead, redwoods tend to sprout new trees from their own root system, which is the reason why you may see younger trees growing either in straight lines along a single root stem or in a circle around the parent tree. (The giant sequoia of the Sierras, sister to the coast redwood, can reproduce only by seed.)

If a young redwood forest is cut down, it quickly replaces itself by this root-sprouting method. For some reason, however, old trees do not seem to have the vitality needed to sprout a complete replacement crop. Lumber companies that clear-cut old-growth stands instead of merely thinning them (as is happening right now around Humboldt Redwoods State Park) and then make no attempt to reforest the area artificially are essentially destroying their own most important resource.

Standing in the midst of one of these forests, try to imagine the sweat and toil that would have been necessary to harvest one of these enormous trees with the rather elementary tools of the nineteenth century. Standing on staging boards driven into the tree several feet above its thick base, two men might labor with 14-foot-long cross-cut saws, wedges, and double-bit axes twelve hours a day for six days in order to bring down a single tree.

151

If the tree was not felled properly and the brittle wood splintered, the entire week's work was for nothing. But even in the absence of such catastrophe, the real work had only begun. All the tree's branches had to be cut off and the trunk cut into 30-foot lengths. This often meant an additional nine or ten cuts, though the task was sometimes aided by the use of blasting powder. One could hardly just drag these sections of the tree to their destination across the forest floor, since each piece may well have weighed in at a hefty 100 tons. Instead, teams of men had to construct a series of "skid roads." Wide pathways were hacked out in the forest, which were then paved with smaller logs that had been cut flat on one side with a sharp hand tool called an adz. By keeping the surfaces of these wooden roadways well oiled, a team of ten oxen could pull out several pieces of a redwood tree at one time. Owing to the amount of work such road building involved, the more remote parts of the redwood empire remained untouched until the arrival of the machine.

At 1.7 miles the trail begins a descent over a series of wooden steps, crossing a beautiful forest stream about 0.1 mile farther on. Before turning around here for the trip back, spend some time walking down along the stream, noting the plants that thrive in this wetter environment. Since redwoods rarely grow along the very edges of streams or rivers, often enough life-giving light filters down to enable a wider variety of plant life to exist. Lady ferns are very fond of stream sides, and you may spot violets, lilies, dogwoods, and buttercups.

MILL CREEK

Distance: 4 miles
Location: Located on Howland Hill Road, east of Crescent City, in Jedediah Smith Redwoods State Park. From downtown Crescent City, take U.S. Highway 101 south to Elk Valley Road and turn left. Howland Hill Road (County Road 417) takes off to the right (east) in approximately 1.5 miles. Continue east on Howland Hill Road for about 4 miles to a metal bridge crossing Mill Creek. Park on the east side of the bridge; the trail takes off from the west side.

152

From the Hiouchi area on U.S. Highway 199, turn south
1 mile east of Jedediah Smith Redwoods State Park on County
Road 427, following signs for the South Fork of the Smith
River. At 0.5 mile after leaving 199 the road will split. Take the
right fork—this is Howland Hill Road. It is approximately 3.5
miles to a metal bridge crossing Mill Creek. Park on the east
side; the trail takes off from the west side. (Note: The Howland
Hill Road is quite narrow and inappropriate for vehicles pulling
large trailers.)

A brilliant, sparkling watercourse dancing its way through the most
magnificent trees ever to spring from the earth—if that is your
fantasy, then this is your trail. The Mill Creek walk begins with a
short climb, just enough to work off the chilly morning mist that so
often wraps itself around the coastal redwood forests. Keep an eye
out here for the graceful trillium and the soft yellow petals of the
evergreen violet, so named because the plant's rounded, heart-
shaped leaves are visible throughout the year.

A hundred yards or so into the walk, another path joins the
Mill Creek Trail from the left. Stay right. In less than 0.5 mile,
after winding through beautiful patches of sword ferns, the trail
enters the hushed, primeval world of an old-growth redwood forest.
Many of these trees have been around for eight hundred to twelve
hundred years. Several were already many times man's height when
Richard the Lionheart took the English throne in 1189; they were
stout and flushed with fine, feathery branches by the time Marco
Polo first set foot in the Chinese court of Kublai Khan.

Despite the fact that redwoods are the tallest trees in the
world, they are surprisingly quick to establish themselves in this
very competitive environment. New trees come more often from
sprouts than from seedlings. If the area is logged, for instance, new
root sprouts will be established in a matter of weeks; at the end of
the first year the tree may already be more than 6 feet high. The
reason for such rapid growth is to ensure the tree a place in the sun.
If an area is logged over, the redwood will likely be competing with
hemlocks and Douglas-firs in the race to establish a canopy of
needles before it is totally shaded by its competitors. The dense
shade of these forests is one reason why you see relatively few
flowers or shrubby plants growing on the forest floor.

153

The redwood has a distinct growth advantage in that while as a young tree it will not thrive in the shade, it is at least fairly tolerant of it. (Seedlings, however, require at least partial sun.) While most trees need a constant source of light, the redwood can wait in "suspended adolescence" for several centuries until an opening in the forest canopy occurs. Furthermore, a redwood that loses its own canopy to fire or lightning will immediately grow another one, thus keeping potential competitors from getting the daylight they need to establish themselves.

The beautiful green carpets of shamrocklike leaves (with star-shaped pink flowers from March through September) are made up of a plant known as redwood sorrel, which can grow profusely in redwood forests up to about 3,000 feet of elevation. Sorrel, along with maidenhair fern, sword fern, and five-finger fern, forms a delicate contrast to the otherwise solemn mood of the redwoods.

If you are here in July or August, you may wonder how such huge trees manage to survive the rather hot, dry summers of the northern coast. To make matters worse, redwoods do not have the moisture-absorbing root hairs typical of so many species of trees, leaving them very susceptible to conditions of drought. The answer is that these grand fellows owe their continued existence to fog. Fog "thick as pea soup" is so common in the swath of country where the redwoods occur that most years it accounts for the equivalent of at least 6 to 12 inches of rain. By the time the fogs lighten in late fall, the winter storm systems roll in and drop all the moisture the great trees could need.

Although today northern California contains the only native coastal redwood forest in the world, this was certainly not always true. Fossil records show that a good dozen species of the genus *Sequoia* were spearing the sky in many areas as long as 100 million years ago. (By the way, while both the Sierra "big tree" and the coastal redwood are sequoias, they are nonetheless two different trees.) Fifty million years ago the sequoias actually dominated the forests in the northern part of the continent, stretching all the way from the far West to Pennsylvania. It was the gradual change to a colder, drier climate that ultimately spelled the end for nearly all the world's sequoia groves. The populations of two Sequoia species—the coastal redwoods (*Sequoia sempervirens*) and the giant sequoias or big trees (*Sequoiadendron giganteum*) of the Sierras appear today to be stabilized. The latter was able to adapt to the colder conditions, while the redwoods in front of you happened to be in an environment that, because of the moderating effects of the ocean, changed comparatively little.

A little less than 2 miles into the walk, in the middle of a wonderful, old-growth forest, listen for the sound of a small waterfall up ahead. The first right fork you come to off the main trail will lead you to an overlook of the cascade. Although modest in proportion, this is nevertheless a lovely fountain of cool, clear water, flowing over rocks covered with a thick, lush carpet of fine, green moss. The falls serve as our turnaround point.

Wandering through the middle of these old-growth redwoods, you might wonder how they came by the genus name *Sequoia*. A Hungarian botanist named them, presumably to honor the great Chief Sequoya of the Cherokees. Though the chief probably never set eyes on one of these huge trees, the honor was nonetheless appropriate if it was given on the basis of pure accomplishment. Sequoya was the only person in recorded history to invent an entire alphabet for a living language. He perfected his eighty-six-character alphabet in twelve years, and it proved to be so logical and easy to learn that the majority of the Cherokee nation became completely literate in a matter of months. The English alphabet, by comparison, took more than three thousand years to reach its final form.

BROWN CREEK TRAIL

Distance: 3 miles

Location: On the east side of U.S. Highway 101, about 8 miles north of the town of Orick. The trail takes off near mile marker no. 129.09, across the highway from a signpost marking an access point for Prairie Creek Trail.

The Brown Creek Trail is for the jungle explorer in you. The trail is not maintained to the normal width that most walking paths are, and the resulting experience of rubbing legs and elbows with neck-high ferns in a grove of gargantuan redwoods is like taking a stroll into the primeval. Here, unlike in some other areas of Redwood National Park, there seems little doubt that as much as 120 inches of rain can fall on these groves every year. This, along with between 6 and 12 additional inches of moisture from summer fogs, makes life spring forth from this acidic soil in overwhelming profusion.

Less than 0.1 mile into the walk you'll come upon a trail branching off to the right. This is the pathway by which you'll return, but for now stay to the left.

Even by themselves a grove of redwoods constitutes one of the largest volumes of living matter per acre of land of any environment on earth. But then add to this a thick carpet of bracken, sword, and lady ferns, and beneath sunlit rips in the tree canopy throw in a garden or two of azaleas, huckleberries, dogwoods, tanoaks, silk tassel, and blackberries, and you end up with a volume of life that all other places are measured against.

One of the frustrating things about redwoods is that the height of their foliage makes it very difficult to study any part of them but their trunks. Some people use binoculars to observe life among the high branches—a technique that works especially well if you search for trees at the edge of clearings, where sunlight will illuminate your subject. If you are lucky enough to stumble across a recently fallen tree, or even a large branch or two, take time for a close look at the foliage. Redwood cones grow at the tips of the branches and are only about 1 inch long. Perhaps even more surprising is the size of the seeds themselves, which are only about three to four times the size of a pinhead! It takes 120,000 of them to make a single pound of seed. August and September are the months to look for cones with seeds ready to be released.

Quiet walks through redwood forests will likely sooner or later offer you a glimpse of the graceful, black-tailed deer or Roosevelt elk feasting on the plants that grow in the sunlit openings. Before this land was sliced into private parcels and prior to the introduction of cattle, Roosevelt elk roamed these woods in great numbers. (These animals are, by the way, named after President Theodore Roosevelt.) Their meat was prized by local Indians and later provided food for many a hungry settler.

156

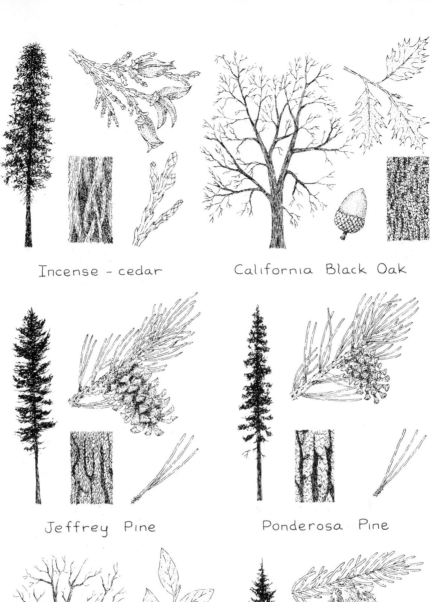

Incense - cedar

California Black Oak

Jeffrey Pine

Ponderosa Pine

Canyon Live Oak

Douglas-fir

Should you happen to spot one of the larger males of this species, you'll understand why early Spanish missionaries considered them to be terrifying beasts. The biggest and best weigh in at half a ton and stand as high as a horse. Frightening or not, it took the white man only a few decades nearly to wipe the animals from the face of California. So great was the slaughter that in the 1870s, a law was passed that made it a felony to kill an elk.

Just about 0.9 mile from the first trail junction you'll reach the point were Brown Creek Trail intersects with the generally south-to-north running Rhododendron Trail. Take a right here, and begin working your way uphill past beautiful collections of rhododendrons toward an elevated plateau deep in the redwoods. From this point you can look toward the west into a landscape rich with the shadows and smells of the coastal redwood ecosystem. This is a particularly good place to watch for bird activity in the canopies below.

One mile along the Rhododendron Trail will bring you to a junction with the final leg of our triangular walk, the rapidly descending South Fork Trail. In 0.6 mile you'll reach a T intersection with the Foothill Trail. Take a right, cross a small footbridge, and in a few yards you'll be back near the starting point at the junction of Brown Creek Trail, less than 0.1 mile east of U.S. Highway 101.

After such a walk it is easy to understand how these dark, shadowed forests have given rise to such a rich crop of myth and fantasy. Nearly all coastal Indian tribes attributed some sort of spiritual significance to the great redwoods, whether it was as a rich source of personal power or a belief that the trees were fashioned from the spirits of mighty warriors killed in battle. Later the Spanish unleashed a flood of tales relating the existence of gnomes and elves living secret lives in the nooks and crannies of the great trees. Years later Irish gold-rush immigrants breathed life into the first of the redwood leprechauns. Fresh in our own memories are the grand abodes of the ewoks in the branches of the trees, made famous in the successful *Star Wars* movie saga. While the very young among you may have been under the impression that such scenes were shot on location in the great forests of the planet Endor, they were, in fact, captured a short way north of here along the Smith River drainage, in the magical world of the coast redwoods.

DRURY-CHANEY TRAIL

Distance: 2.7 miles
Location: At the northern end of the Avenue of the Giants,
which is located off U.S. Highway 101 approximately 30 miles
south of Eureka. The path takes off directly across from the
Pepperwood city boundary sign, located on the south side of
Pepperwood. (This sign is on the east side of the Avenue of the
Giants and is visible to traffic heading north.)

I needed barely a dozen steps down this pathway before being
struck with the feeling that I had stumbled into the very heart of
redwood magic. The understory here at the beginning of the walk
is a wonderful blend of ferns and cloverlike sorrel, spreading from
either side of the trail like a soft carpet laid to cushion the gnarly
feet of the giant trees.

In 30 or 40 yards you will reach a fork in the trail; the left
branch takes you back to the highway, so stay right. Take note of
how the occasional bright columns of sunlight coming in through
rips in the forest canopy spotlight a very different group of life
forms. Instead of shade-loving ferns and sorrel, you will find tanoak,
alder, and madrone struggling against one another for a precious
beam of sunshine. (The tanoak, by the way, is so named because
the bark produces what was once a widely used agent for tanning
hides. During the 1920s and 1930s, many tons of tanoak bark left
this area by rail bound for commercial tanning factories in Sausalito.)

These sunlit openings, which also sport various types of
grasses and shrubbery, are what coax black-tailed deer out from the
dark depths of the redwood grove to browse. So what may seem
like a rather insignificant event—a large redwood toppling over in
a windstorm—may well open the canopy and create a new kind of
environmental niche, where an entirely different plant community
will quickly lay claim to the land.

As you make your way deeper into the forest, cock an ear for
bird song. While birds are not as prevalent in a redwood forest as in
many other types of woodland, there are nevertheless enough
feathered residents here to catch the attention of the observant
walker. The raucous cries of the Steller's jay are in sharp contrast
to the quieter behavior of the pygmy nuthatches and chickadees,

159

who are usually too busy searching for insects to give much more than a brief "peep" or "tee dee" between bites. Watch the ground closely here and you'll probably see the robin-size varied thrush, which is distinguished by an orange throat with a dark gray band across the breast. The thrush's meals come primarily from insects, along with an occasional worm found in open spaces on the forest floor.

You are actually walking in what was once the domain of the Sinkyone Indians, a small but widespread population of people that occupied more than 100 square miles of redwood country until they were pushed out by settlers in the 1860s. Though they were a hunting-gathering society, there was little need for them to make the great treks for food and clothing materials that Indians of more arid regions were forced to do. Acorns (from the tanoak) and salmon were mainstays, with deer, rabbit, game birds, and various types of berries filling out the fare. The great redwoods themselves were very important to the Sinkyones. They fashioned canoes from large sections and used smaller slabs as a building material. They wove fiber from the roots of the great trees into storage and cooking baskets. These people could actually fell a redwood by maintaining a carefully controlled fire at the base of the tree. Once down, they used crude wedges and hammers to split the tree into planks, or if a canoe was desired, they typically carved it out by means of a mussel-shell blade lashed to a stone handle.

Notice on the return side of the loop portion of the walk, just beyond the Irving bench, how thick and healthy the ferns are. Can you come up with any theories as to why this particular location seems so perfect for their growth?

About 80 yards past the Irving bench, on the right side of the trail, is a huge redwood stump that has a lesson to teach about decomposition. Thanks to mild temperatures and ample rainfall (about 65 inches per year) the process of turning plant cells back into soil that can then sprout and nourish new plants is fairly rapid. Not only is there a healthy carpet of sorrel on this island in the sky but a small collection of lady ferns and even a few small trees.

If you look closely at this stump, you'll see the broken ends of boards that have been driven into its sides. These are the remains of staging boards, which loggers stood on to reach a higher, slimmer part of the trunk so that they would not have to cut through the extra thickness at the very base of the tree. From these perches two men might pull a crosscut saw back and forth for seventy hours or more, stopping occasionally to hammer wooden wedges into their cut so that the saw blade would not bend under the great weight of the tree. Sometimes the fragile trees would splinter upon hitting the ground, which made them all but useless to the harvesters. Nevertheless, a redwood forest yielded twenty times the amount of timber obtainable from a typical acre of eastern hardwood forest, so the splintering of a tree here and there was hardly viewed as a catastrophe.

Looking at a healthy redwood tree that has recently fallen from natural causes, you might suspect that it could only be at the hand of a hurricane that such a knockdown could occur. But the root system of a redwood is actually quite shallow, rarely sinking more than 6 feet beneath the surface of the ground. Instead it opts for a system of shallow runners, which is a very effective means of gathering nutrients. A good glimpse of a partial redwood root system can be found on the return part of this walk, to your left about 60 yards from where the loop part of the trail rejoins the single pathway leading back to the highway.

MEMORIAL TRAIL

Distance: 1.6 miles

Location: From U.S. Highway 101 near Alton, head east 18 miles on State Highway 36. Grizzly Creek Redwoods State Park entrance is on the south side of the road. Turn right past the entrance station and park. Walk west through the picnic area, cross the Van Duzen River on a summer bridge, and follow a gravel road south for about 40 yards. The trail takes off into a wooded area on your left.

Grizzly Creek Redwoods State Park contains the most inland grove of *Sequoia sempervirens* to be found anywhere in the state. Given the rather high moisture requirements of redwoods, it's more than a little surprising to find this grove shooting toward the sky 30 miles east of the ocean.

161

Grizzly Creek was once the high-noon stage stop for coaches jolting their way from Strong's Station to Bridgeville, along what was at the time the main route connecting Eureka to San Francisco. The campground lies in the same place where weary horses and passengers once found much needed respite in the tall grass and cool water of the Van Duzen River.

The creek flowing in from the north, as well as the park itself, was named for the grizzly bear, which was at one time very common here. *Ursus horribilis* could be spotted almost anywhere, gathering berries and acorns or flipping out tasty salmon and steelhead along the banks of the river. Incredibly, the great beast was totally wiped out from Humboldt County just two short decades after the first tidal wave of white settlers burst across the Sierras in search of gold.

Just a few yards along the Memorial Trail you'll come upon a fine stand of scouring rush (also sometimes called horsetail, probably because horses and cattle were often seen eating it during the spring). For many children the scouring rush was considered to be "nature's Tinkertoys," since they can easily be separated at the joints and then put back together again. (Remember, though, no picking of plants in any state park.) The particularly "scouring" part of scouring rush is the stem itself, which was used by many Indian tribes to put a fine finish on arrows or other woodwork, much like we use sandpaper today. It's also been recorded that medicine men could obtain wonderful effects at healing ceremonies by tossing scouring rush stems into the fire, where they would explode with an amazing variety of pops and crackles.

You may notice that although this is indeed redwood territory, this forest is somewhat drier than many woodland areas that you may have walked through along the coast. Shade- and moisture-loving plants, such as ferns and redwood sorrel, are a bit more scattered here, although you will have no trouble finding the tiny white bells of the salal and the soft yellow petals of the Oregon grape, both of which are also fairly common nearer the coast.

The pathway climbs for 0.2 mile, at which point the trail splits into a loop. Take a right here, following the circle around in a counterclockwise direction. The trail winds through fairly dense vegetation, much of it marked by tanoak, firs, bay laurel, and bigleaf maple. The combination of trees here makes this an especially beautiful place to visit when the warm colors of autumn are being painted across the faces of the hills.

It is not until the far eastern side of the Memorial Trail, about 0.6 mile into the walk, that you join the Bard Trail, which heads downhill into a virgin grove of redwoods. Though the grove is quite small, it has a charm all its own, standing tall and stately on the banks of the Van Duzen. (The Van Duzen, by the way, was named for a member of an 1850 prospecting expedition led by Dr. Josiah Gregg. The Gregg party named several of the rivers in this region.) There are fine places at the riverside edge of this grove just to sit and take in the sparkling peace and quiet. The more ambitious may want to walk the riverbanks in search of the tracks of raccoon, black-tailed deer, or even bobcat.

If you're lucky, you may see a river otter doing a wonderful water dance in the currents of this river. While most people are aware that otters are champions when it comes to sliding down mud banks, their bent for creative play actually goes much further. For instance, a few people have observed otters actually throwing small rocks into the water and then retrieving them again, time after time. River otters have their favorite foods—among them trout and crayfish—though they will eat many other goodies, including frogs, insects, plants, and if need be, an occasional snake.

When you are done with your riverside explorations, return to the Memorial Trail and continue around the loop, finishing your walk back at the picnic grounds where you began.

North Sierras—
South Cascades

McARTHUR-BURNEY FALLS STATE PARK
(PACIFIC CREST TRAIL)

Distance: 2.4 miles
Location: From State Highway 89, just south of the main entrance to McArthur-Burney Falls State Park, head northwest on Clark Creek Road. The parking area for the walk is about 2 miles in on the right side of the road.

The pathway leading from the parking area of McArthur-Burney Falls State Park crosses the Pacific Crest Trail a short distance from Clark Creek Road. Our walk turns left here, following the Pacific Crest Trail, a major recreation path that runs 2,600 miles from Canada to Mexico, in a northwesterly direction. Before beginning the actual walk, however, you may want to continue straight on the original pathway 200 feet to a bridge, which crosses Burney Creek. This stream is as beautiful as any in the area—a rocky ribbon of snowmelt and spring water dancing in the summer sun. From here it flows north for 0.2 mile before leaping over an eroded basalt cliff, forming a waterfall so magnificent that President Theodore Roosevelt once called it the eighth wonder of the world. (A trail follows along the west edge of the creek to an observation area adjacent to the falls.)

Back on the Pacific Crest Trail, you'll be walking through a beautiful forest of ponderosa pine, incense cedar, black oak, and to a lesser extent, white oak. White oak is most easily recognized by its light-colored, checkerboard-pattern bark and long, pointed acorns; black oak has very dark bark, and the deeply cut leaves have tiny points at the ends of the lobes.

164

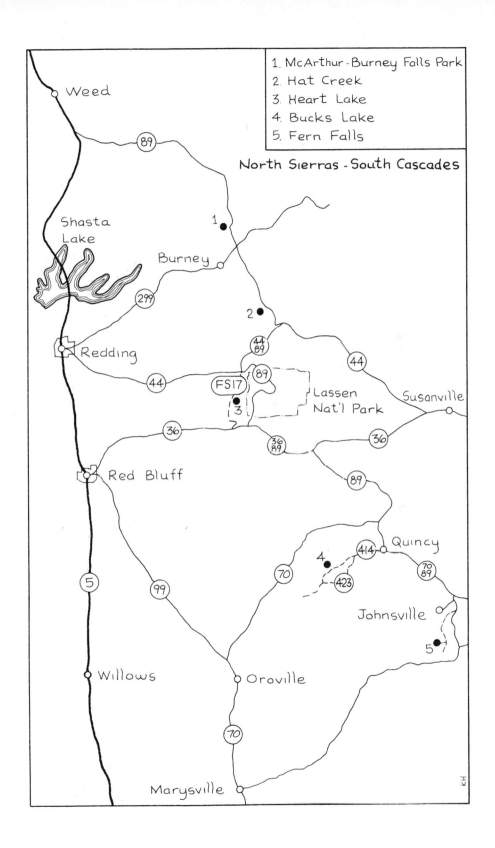

1. McArthur-Burney Falls Park
2. Hat Creek
3. Heart Lake
4. Bucks Lake
5. Fern Falls

North Sierras - South Cascades

Weed

Shasta Lake

89

Burney

299

Redding

44

FS17

89

44/89

2

1

44

Susanville

Lassen Nat'l Park

36

36/89

36

Red Bluff

89

5

99

70

4

414

423

Quincy

70/89

Johnsville

5

Willows

Oroville

70

Marysville

KH

Oaks were an extremely important food source to local Indian tribes, with a single family often consuming 500 pounds of acorns in a year. Acorns from white oaks are the largest of any oak in the state, and most trees produce large numbers of them every other year. Black oak acorns, while not as plentiful, tend to be very rich in oil, a characteristic that made them ideal for making breads, mush, and soups.

Another tree that you'll see along the path here is the Douglas-fir, which is not really a fir at all but is instead in an obscure category all its own known as the false hemlocks. There are two good clues for identifying a Douglas-fir. The first is the bark of the young trees, which is a smooth gray color laced with blister lines. (These blisters, filled with pitch, are also a characteristic of young true firs.) The other, even better clue to identifying Douglas-fir is its cone, which is typically about 3 inches in length and has fork-shaped bracts sticking out from between the scales.

Douglas-fir is an extremely important commercial timber tree; in fact, in the United States it ranks first in total production of lumber. The needles, picked fresh from the tree, have been used as a coffee substitute for more than a century. Interestingly, the mature Douglas-fir has a number of small, ropelike roots that may run 8 to 10 feet in length with no noticeable change in diameter. Yuki Indians, who lived southwest of here near the coast, harvested these root sections and then used them to create beautiful baskets.

You will cross a dirt road about 0.5 mile in, where the landscape becomes more and more dominated by oaks. Up until this point you may have noticed that with the exception of the hollylike squaw carpet, there is really very little understory vegetation here. The reason is not lack of moisture but rather what happens to this moisture once it reaches the ground. This entire region of the state was once dominated by volcanic activity; in the fairly recent geologic past layer after layer of lava poured out of the ground and spread like thick, black pudding over hundreds of square miles of land. When this lava cooled into what is called basalt rock, it trapped an abundance of gas bubbles inside. (Pick up one of the pockmarked rocks along the trail here and feel how light it is.) This very porous rock is what underlies all of the forests that surround you. When moisture does fall here it simply percolates deep into the ground, making it unavailable to many of the plants that would otherwise be growing beneath the trees.

More than a hundred bird species have been recorded in McArthur-Burney Falls State Park, including such beauties as the bald eagle, the great blue heron, various grebes, the kingfisher, and the great horned owl. In these woods keep a close eye out for the dark gray head and light-colored underparts of the Oregon junco, which can usually be seen in open areas or in the lower branches of trees. Look also for the beautiful evening grosbeak, with its thick, conical bill and dark golden body and black tail and wings with a white wing patch; and for the red-shafted flicker (actually a wood-pecker), who has a dappled ivory chest and whose expert woodpecking ability provides nesting holes for a variety of other birds.

At 1.2 miles into the walk you will reach a second dirt road. This is our turnaround point. The Pacific Crest Trail continues on to the northwest, crossing the splendid Pit River at the Lake Britton Dam. The Pit River was named by Hudson's Bay Company fur trappers for the Indians along the banks who dug deep pits in the ground to trap big game.

HAT CREEK

Distance: 2 miles
Location: Park at Rocky Campground, located on the west side of State Highway 89 about 17 miles north of Lassen National Park. (This is the first camping area south of Bridge Campground.) Our walk crosses Hat Creek on a wooden bridge, then turns right and heads downstream.

Hat Creek is easily one of the most beautiful watercourses in the entire state of California. It runs fast and full of spirit, white veils of bubbly water pouring over the smooth faces of the rocks, dashing through a green tunnel of trees like a runaway train. Hat Creek begins in the snowy high country of Lassen National Park, 22 miles south of here. It runs to the north until it meets the Pit River on the east side of Lake Britton; the combined watercourses then flow west into Shasta Lake and the Sacramento River. Much of the

Sacramento supplies irrigation and drinking water for the more-populated areas to the south. To this end Lassen National Forest contributes more than 600 million gallons of water.

Cross the wooden bridge located in the center of Rocky Campground, and then begin to make your way slowly downstream. This mile will pass all too quickly, so take your time to explore this most magic of all environments. Life is full and rich here, the stands of ponderosa and Jeffrey pine, oak, white fir, incense-cedar, and Douglas-fir joined by dogwood, elderberry, willow, twinberry, and cottonwood. These thick tree canopies are extremely important where the stream forms shallow pools, because their shade protects the water from becoming too warm to support life. Birds are also more plentiful here—flycatchers, woodpeckers, western bluebirds, wrens, and warblers filling the sunlit canopy with clear song and quick flashes of wings.

Only about 0.1 mile into the walk is a parched black talus slope on the left side of the trail, a reminder that the corridor of shrubs and wild flowers basking in the cool spray of Hat Creek is the exception, not the rule. All of this area is underlain by hardened lava, most of it coming from a collection of fissures and spattercones a few miles to the south of where you now stand. Such material is very porous, and what moisture does fall on the ground quickly sinks away. If you walk away from the streamside environment, you'll see that because of drainage there is little ground vegetation beneath the conifers.

The currents of Hat Creek are extremely strong, as you will find out if you try to wade across to the other side. Every organism that lives or feeds in this watercourse must be prepared to deal with this situation. While it is virtually impossible for permanently rooted plants to do so, there are many other organisms that have met the challenge. Turn over a rock and you'll likely see various kinds of fly larvae stuck to the bottom. Most of these small creatures, which are among the favorite foods of trout, are able to hold fast in the current by anchoring themselves to surfaces by means of an adhesive disk located at the back end of their bodies.

Another common way of surviving strong stream currents is through body shape. Fish are oblong because this shape offers them the least resistance to the water—an adaptation that you will also see in river otters and even in the birds known as water ouzels, who are able to streamline themselves when poking under submerged rocks for food. Even with this adaptation, as any stream fisherman knows, fish spend the vast majority of their time in quiet pools, where they do not have to fight so hard to stay in one place.

There are many small organisms for which any kind of travel in strong currents would be perilous. They spend their lives beneath the protection of rocks, and a few actually make shelters from tiny pieces of stone. Instead of going after food, the vast majority of such creatures simply wait for it to come to them. One type of caddis fly spins a silklike net, which it then places out in the current to catch whatever plankton happens to be floating by. Yet even with all these precautions, the mortality rate for tiny, bottom-dwelling organisms is extremely high.

There is a beautiful sandy beach located 0.75 mile downstream from the Rocky Campground bridge, which makes an ideal spot to picnic or for younger children to explore the water environment under fairly safe conditions. Below this beach 0.25 mile you will come to our turnaround point at Bridge Campground.

HEART LAKE

Distance: 5 miles

Location: About 1 mile north of a summit crossed by Forest Road 17. This is a dirt road that connects State Highways 44 and 36, located due west of Lassen National Park. The signed trail head is on the east side of the road and follows along the north side of Digger Creek. (Note: A Lassen National Forest map will be a big help to you in locating this trail head. Be careful, though; the red "Scenic Trail" that is shown just south of Digger Creek does not exist.)

The trail along Digger Creek to Heart Lake is scheduled to become part of the National Scenic Trail system, a network of walking trails developed to provide the American people with additional opportunities for outdoor recreation. Unfortunately, while the intent was a noble one, repeated refusals to fund much-needed trail maintenance in the national forests has already left many such paths in miserable shape. This particular candidate for scenic status is, fortunately, in relatively good condition.

The walk to this delightful little lake begins in a thick garden of tobacco brush (ceanothus), a shrub with dark, serrated leaves and, from June through August, profusions of beautiful white flower clusters. This plant has a rather interesting relationship with another resident of the area, the tortoiseshell butterfly. Every so often the population of this insect absolutely explodes, bringing almost total defoliation to hundreds of acres of ceanothus. (Look for pupae hanging from the branches.) These massive butterfly swarms can be surprisingly widespread, and high-country hikers sometimes come upon hundreds of dead butterflies strewn across remote snowfields high in the Sierras.

The trail winds alongside Digger Creek for about 0.2 mile, climbing quickly for about half that distance. (Digger, by the way, was the name given to many California Indian tribes by gold-rush immigrants. It was hardly a complimentary term, suggesting that the Indians were ignorant savages who could survive only by digging up roots and bulbs.) This beautiful stream, clear and cold, is born of the snowy high forest that flanks the western side of Lassen National Park. Note that in many places along the watercourse there are fine collections of wild flowers, shrubs, and grasses, while only a few yards away the ground may be almost completely bare. As in other walks in this region, this lack of ground cover is the result not so much of drought as of a thick underlying layer of porous basalt rock, which allows rain and snowmelt to percolate too far down and out of reach to be of any use to many plants.

The one brilliant exception to a dry, drab, coniferous-forest understory is the snow plant, a member of the heath family, which is fairly typical along the first mile of this walk. Every part of this fleshy plant, from stem to flowers, is a stunning red, made even more noticeable by the fact that it is usually found growing alone in a patch of pine duff, where almost nothing else can survive. The snow plant is among a group of organisms known as saprophytes, a term that means that they are able to live on decayed organic matter.

The trail continues eastward, making its way through some

Western Ground Squirrel

Black-tailed Deer

Marten

Gray Fox

California Ground Squirrel

Ringtail

beautiful incense-cedar and Jeffrey pine. At just under 2 miles you will pass a small aspen grove on the right side of the trail. Aspen tend to propagate by means of root suckers. If a fire wipes out a section of forest, new trees will spring up quickly from undamaged underground roots.

Aspen can be very good storytellers. Look on the smooth white bark for claw marks left by black bears. Lower branches often show fresh chew marks from where deer have been browsing on the leaves. Rabbits occasionally get into the act by chewing on the bark around the base of the tree, and during the winter quail will munch on the tender buds.

Even though aspen can establish themselves quickly, their reign is not forever, as the pines and firs of a climax forest eventually move in and overtake them. Barring any fires or other major disturbances, this small grove of aspen will also one day yield to the climax forest.

After crossing a delightful stream gushing with snowmelt, continuing 0.2 mile, you will reach Heart Lake. Although small, it is very attractive, rimmed by white fir, willows, manzanita, and pine, as well as a fine collection of one of the loveliest of the high-country wild flowers, the shooting star. These lavender beauties are found only where ground moisture is plentiful; more often than not they serve as the perfect warning flag that you have entered the heart of mosquito country.

Immediately behind Heart Lake is Rocky Peak. As you face this mountain, on the other side of the ridge lying to your left is the wild, volcanic high country of Lassen National Park. At the park's timberline the snow may linger for nine months of the year, reaching depths of more than 25 feet by late winter.

BUCK'S LAKE

Distance: 1.7 miles

Location: From Quincy, head west on Buck's Lake Road to the southeastern edge of Buck's Lake. The trail leaves from the north side of the road at the Mill Creek trail head. (This is about 0.2 mile past Whitehorse Campground, which is located on the south side of the roadway.) Park on the north side of Buck's Lake Road, just east of a large white sign advertising Buck's Lake Lodge and Marina.

Crescent-shaped Buck's Lake, managed by Pacific Gas & Electric, is an exceptionally beautiful, high-country recreation area. It is virtually surrounded by the Plumas National Forest, with the wild, untrammeled Buck's Lake Wilderness spreading north toward the Feather River from the eastern shore of the lake. You are more than 1,600 feet higher here than you were in the town of Quincy. While it is fairly rare for winter snows to accumulate in the town, here they can pile up in considerable quantities. This condition, along with the cooler temperatures that occur with the gain in elevation, is what enables trees such as white fir and Douglas-fir to grow here and bumper crops of wild flowers to sprout. Take special note of the red columbine and penstemon splashing colors at your feet.

Some of the names in this region—Gold Lake, Silver Lake, Rush Creek, Rich Bar—leave little doubt that this was high-pitched, gold-fever country. In fact, the Buck's Lake region was near the northern tip of an oblong stretch of land running down to Mariposa (near Yosemite Park), which by the spring of 1850 was awash with more than forty thousand miners engaged in a desperate search for "color."

The area had its share of success stories. Seven friends from Monterey extracted nearly 275 pounds of gold in eight weeks; ranchers washed fifteen thousand dollars worth of the precious metal from nearby streams in less than a month; and of course John Bidwell, southwest of here on the Middle Fork of the Feather River, staked a claim that eventually earned more than 300 million dollars.

But far more often those who had made the great overland trip from the East ended their mining days with little more than a

173

pocketful of memories. Some stayed on in California, becoming merchants, restaurateurs, carpenters, and ranchers. But a good many also returned to the farms and families they had left behind in Michigan, New York, North Carolina—so glad to be home but happy, too, that they had heeded the wild, romantic call of California.

Several areas near where you are now walking have respectable populations of that largest and most amazing of rodents, the beaver. Beavers, as everyone knows, spend a good deal of their time in the dam-construction business. They begin by carrying broken pieces of trees and various other debris and placing them at the narrowest point in a stream. They add more and more sticks, and even stones, until the structure reaches substantial proportions, after which they cover it with mud found along the banks and at the bottom of the stream.

Building a lodge is the next order of business. It is constructed in much the same way somewhere near the deepest part of the pond. This dome-shaped fortress of sticks and mud is an impressive affair, with partitioned sleeping quarters and one or more tunnels that connect it with the outside water. Here a couple (mated for life) will raise their broods of one to six youngsters, who stay under the parental roof until they reach the age of two, when they will go out and start families of their own.

Beavers store their winter supply of food underwater, which in climates where it freezes must be beneath the level at which ice forms on the ponds. This larder consists primarily of shrubs and various types of trees, including aspen, willow, and alder, which, as far as beavers are concerned, have absolutely delicious bark. When the winter winds and snows are howling outside, the beaver has only to swim down to the bottom of the pond, chew off a branch or two from his pantry's supplies, and bring it back to dine on in the comfort of his lodge.

The creation of a beaver pond means a radical change for the stream environment. As a result of the dam, some wildlife will be pushed out of the area, but far more will come in, including fish, wading birds, ducks and geese, and many types of insects that would not have been present otherwise. As the years go by, the pond will fill in with sediment, turning first to marsh, and then later into rich green meadows filled with forage that other types of wild-life will use to stay alive.

This trail was once maintained by the Boy Scouts, but when I walked it, it appeared that the Scouts had perhaps abandoned the project for other pursuits. There are places beginning at the 0.5-mile point where it is easy to lose the path. This is not a real problem, since you simply want to continue following the lakeshore. If you are having a bad time of it, however, you can walk away from the lake a distance of about 50 yards, where you'll join an old logging road that also parallels the shore. Once past this wet area you can descend again and rejoin the footpath.

At 0.8 mile you'll come upon a small headland covered with giant boulders and slabs of beautiful, crystal-flecked granite. Such rock is common in this region, and much of it, such as that which makes up the sheer cliffs and deep canyons to the west, is of magnificent proportion. Long ago this granite existed as molten magma underneath a group of large volcanoes; later it cooled and hardened beneath the surface of the earth. The volcanic rock was eventually eroded away by wind, rain, and ice, leaving the sturdier, more erosion-resistant granite behind.

FERN FALLS

Distance: 2.5 miles

Location: From State Highway 89, approximately 2 miles southeast of Graeagle, head south on Forest Road 519 (follow-ing signs for Gold Lake). In about 6 miles you'll come to a dirt road heading west, marked by a sign for Gray Eagle Lodge. Turn onto this road, and take a right at a trail sign for Smith Lake and Gray Eagle Creek. A short distance down this road are two trail heads; ours is the more westerly, which eventually leads to Gold Lake.

The Fern Falls walk represents all that is unforgettable about the California high country—the smells are crisp, the streams run like liquid crystal, and the dark green forests drape across the broad, granite shoulders of the Sierra like a threadbare shawl.

There is a very short climb about 0.25 mile into this trail,

175

after which you will be afforded a flat walk through paradise. The first part of the pathway is framed in red fir, lodgepole pine, Jeffrey pine, and Douglas-fir, with the open areas claimed by manzanita and currant bushes. Mule ears wave their sunshine-yellow heads in the drier exposed areas, while tiger lilies and shooting stars color the wetter meadows and the banks of streams.

Despite the rather close proximity to Gray Eagle Lodge, this is actually a very good trail to take during the early morning or late evening hours to observe the bird and animal life of the area. Among birds, there is the striking black-and-white body plumage and golden chest feathers of the Williamson's sapsucker, the mottled brown fox sparrow, the husky goshawk, the tiny, green-tailed towhee wearing his rust-colored cap, and a myriad of flycatchers, chickadees, and wood warblers. (The Plumas National Forest actually contains more than 220 species of birds.)

The mammals of the area are scarcely less varied or interesting. One of the most skilled hunters here, which you will see only with a bit of quiet, patience, and luck, is the weasellike pine marten. This creature hunts both by night and by day, moving mile after mile through the tree tops or quietly scuttling along the ground checking the nests of squirrels, chipmunks, rabbits, and rats. Except for mating season the pine marten runs a totally solo act and tends to become absolutely outraged at any kind of contact with other small mammals.

Even the ravages of winter are not enough to slow down this ball of fury. Wrapped in a thick coat of luxurious fur, he will continue to hunt in the harshest of conditions; special tufts of hair on the soles of his feet allow him to walk across the snow. As if the animal's unbelievable grace, speed, and bad temper weren't enough to discourage all but the boldest of predators, the marten even sports a set of glands that can emit a fluid only slightly less noxious than that of a skunk.

Not surprisingly, this walk is also where you'll find some of the marten's favorite four-legged dishes. One that would almost certainly win the award for giving the boldest show of authority with nothing to back it up, is the small tree squirrel known as the chickaree. Like its enemy the marten, there seems to be no end to the energy that this little packet of gray fur can muster. During the late summer and into the fall the forest is riddled with the sound of pine and fir cones being cut from the tops of trees by chickarees and toppling to the ground. Some of these seeds are eaten on the spot, but the vast majority are buried for use over the long winter (chickarees do not hibernate). Of course many of the thousands of seeds that the chickaree stores are not dug up again, and in this way the little squirrel is an extremely important tree planter. Unfortunately for the chickaree, he is an appetizing meal to more than just the marten. Weasels, fishers, and foxes are always on the lookout for this nut-stuffed tidbit, and occasionally, one will even fall victim to the claws of a lucky bird of prey.

Ringtails, skunks, mink, and even an occasional badger can also be found in this area. Look for their tracks in the soft mud that surrounds many of the streams and spring-fed meadows near the trail.

Besides being immersed in the natural magic of the Sierras, you happen to be on ground that was once covered with the footsteps of men who were players in one of the most fantastic episodes of history that California has ever known. This was gold country, and on quiet evenings you can almost make out the sounds of pickaxes singing against the stone and stream gravel rolling across the bottoms of wooden rockers. A short distance to the east lies Beckwourth Pass, a low, easily negotiated route across the northern Sierras that was discovered by Jim Beckwourth (or Beckwith) in April 1851. Over this route hundreds of gold seekers made their way to the northern mines. And, if the truth were known, it would probably be safe to say that a few of those first immigrants over Beckwourth Pass were burning the soles off their shoes to get there, still mesmerized by the 1850 tales of "Gold Lake."

The most widely accepted version of the Gold Lake story has as its star a man named Stoddard, who came into the gold country during late autumn of 1849. Having just crossed the Sierras, he and a companion became lost while out hunting for food. Lo and behold they came upon a lake. It was not just any lake, mind you, but one that was littered with gold. There were gold nuggets covering the shoreline, and gigantic gold chunks could be seen shimmering on the sandy bottom. Unfortunately, before they could load their pack saddles with some of this bounty, the two men were

177

attacked by Indians. Only Stoddard escaped to tell the tale. Forced by bad weather to wait to relocate the lake, the following spring Stoddard, with the entire town of Marysville on his heels, set out for the very hills you are now walking through.

In the meantime, the Gold Lake stories were becoming more and more incredible. Indians, it was said, fashioned crude chairs and couches from giant slabs of gold taken from the lake. The precious metal, reported one miner, could be "scraped by the pound." In the end, of course, no such lake was ever found, and Stoddard was written off as a crazy old man. The tale did open this area to exploration, however, and there were indeed some who found plenty of "color" in these streams. Perhaps as a kind of tongue-in-cheek tribute to the entire mad affair, the lake 3 miles south of here was given the name Gold Lake.

In 1 mile you'll come to a trail junction. Take a left here, following the signs toward Fern Falls and Hawlsey Falls. It is only a short distance from this point to Gray Eagle Creek, and just upstream from where the path meets the water you'll see a sign for Fern Falls nailed to a tree. Make your way up along the west side of the creek a few yards until you come to the falls. The water here cascades down a small box canyon, lined with a collection of beautiful ferns and wild flowers drinking in the cool spray. This is not a spectacular waterfall, but it is typical of the charming surprises that lie wrapped in a thousand rocky folds of the Sierra Nevada.

Central Sierras

CALAVERAS BIG TREES—SOUTH GROVE

Distance: 4.2 miles (with side spur up to Agassiz Tree)
Location: South side of State Highway 4 at Calaveras Big Trees State Park, approximately 25 miles northeast of Angels Camp. The South Grove is located on the extreme southern end of the park, 0.5 mile before the end of the paved road. The parking area is well marked. (Note: Be sure to pick up a trail guide to the South Grove at the contact station or visitors' center near the entrance to the park.)

"There is something wonderfully attractive in this king tree that draws us to it with indescribable enthusiasm," wrote John Muir of the giant sequoia. "And when one of the oldest attains full stature on some commanding ridge, it seems the very god of the woods."

It was in 1852, while hunting meat for a nearby mining operation, that Augustus T. Dowd stumbled onto the trees that now make up the North Grove of Calaveras Big Trees State Park. Though a party of army explorers under Joseph Walker had actually run across *Sequoiadendron giganteum* (big tree) nineteen years earlier, it was Dowd's discovery that ultimately resulted in the trees being introduced to the world. In practically no time throngs of journalists, botanists, and tourists were making their way to Calaveras County to see these primeval marvels with their own eyes.

As might be expected, the discovery of so stunning an attraction did not slip past the attention of those with a mind for money. Promoters removed the bark in numbered sections from two sequoias (one was felled first, the other died on its feet years

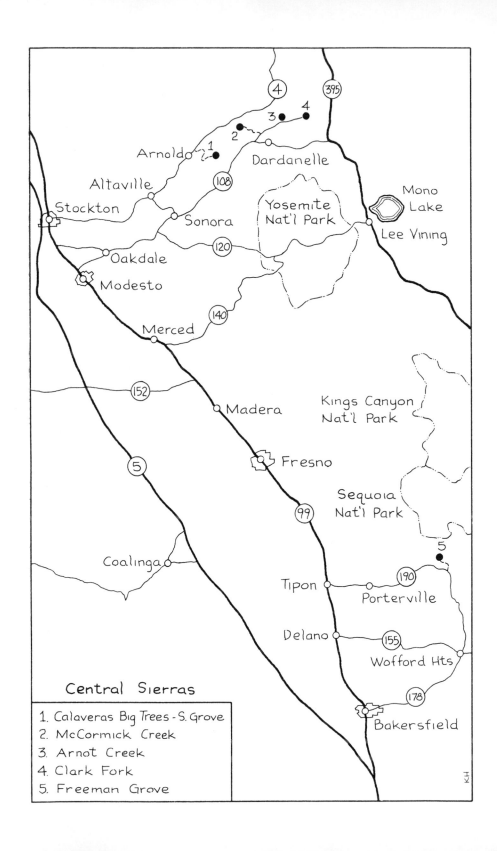

④ 395

3 ● 4 ●

1 Arnoldo 2 ●
● Dardanelle

108

Altaville

Stockton

Sonora

Yosemite
Nat'l Park

Mono
Lake

Lee Vining

120

Oakdale

Modesto

140

Merced

152

Madera

Kings Canyon
Nat'l Park

5

Fresno

99

Sequoia
Nat'l Park

5 ●

Coalinga

Tipon 190

Porterville

Delano 155

Wofford Hts

178

Bakersfield

Central Sierras

1. Calaveras Big Trees - S. Grove
2. McCormick Creek
3. Arnot Creek
4. Clark Fork
5. Freeman Grove

KH

later) and "reassembled" the trees in exhibit halls around the world. The stump of the fallen tree was later chiseled smooth and used both as a dance floor and a theatrical stage. The trunk, believe it or not, was carved where it lay into a two-lane bowling alley. The region's Miwok Indians, their world already crumbling under the advance of the gold rush, must have found such treatment of the sacred sequoias strange indeed.

While the North Grove at Calaveras Big Trees State Park has been visited by millions of people, the South Grove, reached by a mile-long walk, offers an exquisite chance for solitude among these ancient giants. So pleasant is the trek to the grove itself, along dancing streams and past enormous sugar and ponderosa pines, that this would be a place ideal for loitering, lingering, daydreaming, and other soul-worthy pursuits even without the presence of the great sequoias.

But indeed the sequoias are here, as you will see for yourself after climbing gently for about 0.5 mile, then leveling off for another 0.4 mile to where you will cross a fire road, and finally taking a short 0.1-mile stroll across Big Trees Creek into the western edge of the grove. This last section, by the way, is especially beautiful during the spring, when dogwood bracts dress the forest with delicate spatters of ivory.

Stretching to the east from the Big Trees Creek crossing are nearly one thousand mighty giant sequoias of various ages, comprising the largest grove north of the King's River, which is located about 150 miles to the south. It would be hard to find a sequoia forest more beautiful than this one. During the afternoons, shafts of sunlight filter down through the sky-high sequoia canopies and the thick arms of the red firs, bathing the forest with light every bit as serene and unworldly as that which pierces the stained glass windows of Gothic cathedrals.

If you have visited the redwoods of the California coast, you may recognize a couple of differences between these two kings of the forest. The cones of the giant sequoia of the Sierra are about twice the size of those of its redwood sister, and instead of the foliage being flat like that of a fir, it is composed of tiny bracts arranged in a spiral pattern along the twig. While the old coastal redwoods tend to be taller, the veterans of the Sierra are much broader at the base. A diameter of 25 to 30 feet is fairly common, which is roughly twice the size of the coastal redwoods.

As a matter of interest, a Sierra sequoia also happens to live longer—two thousand to three thousand years—compared to a typical life span of seven hundred to twelve hundred years for the coastal redwood. It is absolutely uncanny to consider what was going on in the world when California's senior sequoias were youngsters: Buddhism was being founded in India in the fifth century B.C. about the same time that the Greeks were defeating the Persians in the battle of Marathon. The early books of the Old Testament were in the process of being written down. By the time that Mayan culture reached its peak in Mexico in A.D. 465, some of the trees in this grove were already more than 12 feet thick. Hold your body against one of the big trees for a moment, and feel your heart beat across a span of twenty-five centuries.

The trail reaches a junction a short distance after recrossing Big Trees Creek at the site of a fallen sequoia. A left will take you around the north side of the loop and back to the trail head. First, however, walk up the path on the right for about 0.6 mile to where it dead-ends at the Louis Agassiz Tree, the largest giant sequoia in the park. This senior citizen is 250 feet high and 25 feet across when measured at a point 6 feet above the ground. During your walk back toward the trail head you'll pass several trees that are not as broad as the Agassiz but that actually exceed it in height by more than 50 feet. If it helps to have a frame of reference, we're talking about roughly the same height that the Statue of Liberty reaches when standing on her 150-foot-high pedestal.

McCORMICK CREEK

Distance: 3.2 miles

Location: From the town of Sonora head east on State Highway 108 into the Stanislaus National Forest. Several miles past
Donnell Vista is a junction with another paved road (Clark Fork
Road) heading off to the left. Turn onto this, and in about 1
mile you will come to dirt Forest Road 6N06, also taking off to
the left. Follow this for about 7 miles to where it ends in a large
parking lot. There is an obvious trail heading due north from
this parking area. Our path, however, is along an old roadway
heading east.

On weekends during midsummer the number of cars at the
McCormick Creek trail head parking lot might shock you. Most of
these hikers, however, are bound for the exquisite Sword Lake,
Lost Lake, or the Bull Run Creek area, all of which lie a short
distance to the north. Our walk heads east from the parking area
along a faint roadway that most hikers never set foot on. The
beginning of the trek is through a delightful, mixed-conifer forest,
which eventually opens up to frame lush meadow lands spotted
with granite swales and towering volcanic plugs.

During the first 0.2 mile you'll be able to catch occasional
glimpses of some triangular-shaped, snow-capped peaks just off to
the right (southeast) in the far distance. These are mountains in the
northern part of the Emigrant Wilderness, a spectacular collection
of high-country streams, meadows, and glacial lakes. It was in this
general vicinity that during the spring of 1827, mountain man
Jedediah Strong Smith struggled eastward on his way to a rendezvous northeast of Salt Lake, becoming in the process the first
American ever to cross the High Sierras.

Smith and a party of trappers had entered Southern California several months before along the Mojave River, searching, as
always, for promising new beaver country. When the Spanish governor in San Diego heard about this little uninvited foray into
Spanish territory, he gave explicit orders for the party to leave by
the same route that they had come. Once out of sight of the San
Gabriel Mission, however, the explorers turned northward toward
the San Joaquin Valley, along the way poking their heads up various tributaries that might hold beaver. The men did in fact try to

183

cross the Sierras twice, once at the Kings River and again at the American, but winter still held too firm a grip on the high country.

The weary travelers turned around and headed south again to the Stanislaus River, where Smith and two others left the main portion of the party and headed east into the mountains along a route just south of where you now stand. The three arrived at the Utah rendezvous site six weeks later with one bedraggled horse and one mule out of nine remaining, three having perished in the Sierras and the rest having been eaten by the starving men. "My arrival caused a considerable bustle in camp," wrote Smith in his diary, "for my self and my party had been given up as lost. A small Cannon from Saint Louis was loaded and fired for a salute."

A little more than 1 mile into this walk you will come to a small grove of quaking aspen, their leaves trembling even in the slightest whisper of air movement. Most aspen groves are not collections of individual seedlings but rather "clones," which have sprouted from a single root system. If you happen to be here during autumn, notice how all the trees in a particular clone group turn the same color at about the same time.

This site is typical of the conditions relished by aspen—an ample water supply and plenty of sunlight. Though aspen is the most widely distributed tree in North America, it will typically live only about sixty to seventy years. In many places in the Sierras aspen make up what is known as a transition forest, eventually yielding the ground to firs or other shade-tolerant conifers of a climax forest. It's fun to study the smooth white trunks of aspen, for either the vertical lines of claw marks left by bears or the swollen signatures of passing cowboys or sheepherders who roamed these meadows long ago. (It is no longer appropriate to "autograph" any tree, both for aesthetic reasons and because such cuts in the bark provide easy access for invading insects and disease.)

After about another 0.5 mile of walking through fantastic, open high country, you'll come to our turnaround point at McCormick Creek. This small watercourse, which is born about 3.5 miles north of here in the heart of the Dardanelles, is a fine stream to have long talks with on sunny summer afternoons. It's a most patient listener, and some surprising insights tend to rise from beneath the gurgling song it sings on the way to the Stanislaus River.

184

Although McCormick Creek is our turnaround point, before you head back, take a short trip of about 100 yards past the creek to an enormous field of corn lilies, which are also known as false hellebore. This amazing plant (which is sometimes mistakenly called skunk cabbage) is quite poisonous to stock and even game, though it is rarely eaten by either. Some California Indian tribes took advantage of chemicals in corn lilies that are very effective in lowering blood pressure and heart rate. (Too large a dose, however, could prove fatal.) If you're a gardener, you may recognize the name hellebore as a type of insecticide sold in many nurseries and garden shops. This plant, dried and ground, is the source.

ARNOT CREEK

Distance: 2 miles
Location: From the town of Sonora, head east on State Highway 108 into the Stanislaus National Forest. Several miles past the Donnell Vista is a junction of two paved roads. Take a left, following the Clark Fork. You'll find the trail head on the north side of the road next to a steel bridge, approximately 5.5 miles after turning off Highway 108. This bridge is 3.2 miles west of where the Clark Fork Road ends at Iceberg Meadow.

In some ways the Arnot Creek Trail is more of a meander than a walk; it is best suited for those who simply enjoy poking around the watery nooks and crannies of a clear mountain stream. (This is an ideal environment to explore with children.) The actual trail, which follows along the creek the entire way, receives so little use that in places it can be hard to find. This is hardly a problem, though, since the forest is open and spacious enough for you to make your way along quite nicely with no guidelines whatsoever.

There are a couple of options for routes along the lower part of Arnot Creek. My favorite is to proceed up the west side of the stream (the side with the small parking area) for about 0.2 mile, and then cross over to the other side via a large tree that has fallen across the creek.

You are walking in one of the more common types of California montane forests and one of the most beautiful. It is known as a mixed-conifer forest, and the mix is primarily made up of Jeffrey pine, red fir, incense-cedar, and an occasional white fir. If you can take this path after a rain or during the late spring just after the snow has melted off, you'll be amazed at the delicious pine smells that this particular blend of trees produces. It's rather like sticking your head in a cedar chest filled with pine boughs and a dash of pineapple-vanilla. (The pineapple-vanilla comes from the Jeffrey pine. Those interested in a more substantial whiff should proceed immediately to the nearest Jeffrey and place their nose against the bark of the trunk.)

About 0.5 mile up on the east side of the creek is an excellent stand of the jointed, asparagus-resembling plant known as horsetail, or scouring rush. This latter name refers to the presence of a mildly abrasive silica in parts of the stem, which nineteenth-century Americans found ideal for scrubbing dirty pots and pans. The plant was also useful to many California Indian tribes in the manufacture of perforated clam-shell disks called wampum (short for wampumpeag), which was used as a type of money. After the shells were shaped, horsetail stems were used to polish them to a clean shine.

For those with a bit of patience, this section of Arnot Creek is a good place to look for one of the most amazing birds to be found anywhere in the world, the dipper, or water ouzel. The dipper is a dark bluish gray, robin-size bird with a sharp call that sounds like "seeet." (His actual singing, however, is an exceptionally sweet, melodious production that bubbles and flows like the stream itself.) The place to find this fellow is not on the stream bank or in nearby pine and fir branches but rather *in* Arnot Creek, and in the fastest whitewater, at that!

The dipper, you see, feeds on insects and insect larvae found on the bottoms of mountain streams. He plants his head under the water and, like a man crouching against a ferocious windstorm, walks upstream along the bottom, turning over leaves and pebbles in his search for such tasty tidbits as mosquito larvae. Though he doesn't necessarily prefer the deep, fast water found in the middle of the stream, he can sometimes be found there. In such conditions he opens his wings about one third of the way and

Pygmy Nuthatch

Red-shafted Flicker

Chestnut-backed
Chickadee

Steller's Jay

Western Flycatcher

Western Tanager

KH

uses them like ailerons on an airplane, flowing in and out of the violent, frothy current with amazing ease.

John Muir reported that during the winter, when streams were covered with snow or their waters cloudy from undissolved ice particles, the dipper would sometimes set up shop in an open lake. Here he fed at depths of 15 or 20 feet, using his wings to swim gracefully back and forth between the algae-covered bottom and the surface. Muir never saw a single stormy or dreary day but that the dipper did not break out his best song. During raging snowstorms, while other birds seemed to be huddled for dear life in the north end of Yosemite Valley, the dipper stood by his cold, frothy feeding grounds and made melodies. If you spend much time with the dipper, you'll find it almost impossible not to develop a special liking for him. "Among all the mountain birds," wrote Muir, "none has cheered me so much in my lonely wanderings—none so unfailingly."

I recommend turning around at a point about 1 mile up Arnot Creek, at the southern edge of the Carson-Iceberg Wilderness. (This would be about thirty minutes of slow walking.) The more adventurous can continue on through a second-growth forest until 1.4 miles from the trail head, where the trees become larger and the country takes on a much wilder flair. At 2 miles in you will intersect Woods Gulch coming in from the left. There are beautiful pockets of meadow in this area, and the region forms the junction for several fast-flowing water courses. Here is prime country for nook-and-cranny exploration, with neither solitude nor surprises in short supply.

CLARK FORK

Distance: 3.2 miles
Location: From the town of Sonora, head east into the Stanislaus National Forest on State Highway 108. Several miles past the Donnell Vista, you'll come to a junction with the Clark Fork Road. Take a left here, and follow this paved roadway to its end at Iceberg Meadow. There is a small parking area here, and the path takes off from the south side.

If you're a lover of wild mountain rivers, the Clark Fork walk is the one for you. The Clark Fork is born of the icy high country that cradles Sonora Pass, located less than 10 miles southeast of here as the hawk flies. Well into summer the river is fed by numerous springs and steely snowmelt streams, and by the time it reaches this point it is slip-sliding through the conifer forest like a bear on rollerskates.

Into the walk 0.3 mile you'll cross up and over a rugged outcropping of rock that borders the north side of the stream. This area is really a geological grab bag. There are large loaves of granite that have been split across hundreds of yards by an erosional process known as jointing. This breakdown is caused primarily by the freezing and thawing of water in rock fractures; it results in a landscape of giant blocks and sheer cliffs. Twenty million years ago, this area was also the sight of some fantastic volcanic mud flows. The Dardanelles, located just a few miles west of here, more than likely looked like a series of wide open faucets, pouring a boiling mixture of lava and mud across the landscape.

Once past the rock outcroppings your attention can turn to the beauty of this mixed-conifer forest—Jeffrey pine (smell the pineapple-vanilla bark), manzanita, chinquapin, Western white and lodgepole pine, and near the stream corridor, healthy populations of rugged red fir. For the most part, the existence of a red-fir forest is a good indication that you've entered a world where mild weather is only about a five-month proposition. Snowfalls here, and especially closer to the headwaters of the Clark Fork, can amount to 200 or even 300 inches per year. Red firs also tend to grow close together. This means that they are very effective at shielding the ground from sunlight, so you're likely to find small snowfields lying beneath the branches well into the month of June.

As is true in an old-growth redwood forest, the lack of sunlight reaching the forest floor results in a scarcity of ground plants, so the birds and animals living in the immediate area will have to take much of their sustenance from what the red fir itself can provide. Thus you'll find such birds as kinglets, nuthatches, chickadees, and woodpeckers, who can live on insects found along the trunk and in the needles, and chickarees and gray squirrels, who can dine on the cones.

Throughout this walk you'll be moving along the southern border of the Carson-Iceberg Wilderness—a 160,000-acre tapestry of light-footed streams, soaring peaks, and lush mountain forests. While the Stanislaus National Forest is one of the busiest in the country, the remote trails of the Carson-Iceberg area open many doors to peace and solitude.

If you came into this area from the west, more than likely you drove through the charming little town of Sonora. In the 1860s, the people of this town were distressed by the fact that they were being left out of a rush of business-producing mining activity on the other side of the Sierra divide. They figured that in order to cash in on the action they would need to construct an eastbound road right over the top of the mountains. The first route they tried was along the trail that you're now walking. As you'd easily see if you continued up the Clark Fork far enough, this is mighty tough country to hack a road out of.

Defeated along the Clark Fork, the citizens of Sonora eventually selected the route that now forms Highway 108, crossing the divide at Sonora Pass. The Bartleson-Bidwell party had, with heroic struggle, worked themselves and their mules and horses across this route in the autumn of 1841, becoming the first American settlers ever to immigrate to California by crossing the forbidding Sierra Nevada. Many more would use Sonora Pass in the years ahead, few of whom did not suffer some kind of hardship in the process. After making his way across the pass in 1854, Grizzly Adams reported that the route was littered with broken wagon parts, "melancholy evidence of the last season's disasters."

Construction of a toll road over the pass began in the summer of 1863 and was not completed until two years later. The road served its purpose, although traversing it was far from a stroll through the park. To make the 200-mile round trip from Sonora to Bridgeport, located on the other side of the Sierras north of Mono Lake, a six-horse team needed a full three weeks.

For those who are up for a hearty walk, the point at which the trail joins Boulder Creek on the north, 1.6 miles up, is a fine turnaround spot. If you're not interested in this long a trek, there are more picnic and fishing holes between mile 1 and mile 2 of the river than you'd care to count. Shortening the trip to match your interests and energy level will still leave you well satisfied.

FREEMAN CREEK GROVE

Distance: 3 miles

Location: Heading east from Porterville on State Highway 190, climb up into the Sequoia National Forest. Just before Highway 190 comes to an end, take a left on paved Forest Road 21S50. Take the first available right turn onto a dirt road, which will immediately bring you to a Y intersection. Take a left onto Forest Road 21S99, and drive past a closed Forest Service gate. The trail head is just beyond this gate.

The Freeman Creek Grove of giant sequoias is a relatively unvisited place compared to many of the more famous groves in and around Sequoia National Park. Besides the glory of the big trees themselves, the trail to the grove winds through a striking, mixed-conifer forest laced with cool streams, lush meadow lands, and, well into summer, a showy collection of Sierra wild flowers.

Just after leaving the parking area, the Freeman Creek Trail (more commonly known as the Lloyd Meadows Trail) makes a short horseshoe turn to the right. Do not accidentally go straight on a faint pathway that takes off from this turn. A short distance from this point you will be on the north side of a fine meadow drained by Freeman Creek. Here grow many of the best and brightest of the high-country flowers—shooting stars, buttercups, yellow monkeyflowers, swamp onions, and penstemon. In addition there are some moisture-loving shrubs such as the western blueberry and red elderberry, which provide fruit relished not only by several species of birds but also by coyotes, rodents, martens, and bears. While walking this portion of the trail in July, I happened to startle a fine young black bear, who was sampling a few blueberry branches in the upper reaches of this very meadow.

Black bears, by the way, are fairly common throughout this area and northward into Sequoia and King's Canyon National Parks. A black bear is a most intriguing animal, "a happy fellow," as John Muir said, "whom no famine can reach while one of his thousand kinds of food is spared him." On this point Muir could not have been more correct. In addition to the bulbs of various lilies and the fruit of blueberries, elderberries, wild cherries, manzanita, and service berries, this shaggy eating machine will also consume acorns, mice, fish, grasshoppers, ants, chipmunks, pocket gophers, and ground squirrels, to name but a few of his "thousand." Cubs are born in the den during midwinter. So sleepy is mom during this big event that, for the most part, the little blind bruins rely on instinct to locate her milk. The youngsters will spend the summer with her learning important bear lessons, den with her for yet another winter, and strike out on their own by the following fall.

Keep an eye out for fine collections of tall, purple lupine, as well as the gray-green, elliptical leaves of the bush chinquapin growing in the open spaces between the red and white firs and Jeffrey pines. The nuts of the related golden-leaf chinquapin, also spiny like these of the bush variety, were used as a food source by several Indian tribes along the north coast.

Less than 0.5 mile into the walk you'll meet the first young giant sequoias, or big trees, of the Freeman Creek Grove. It would seem logical that a tree that typically reaches such a ripe old age would grow at a very slow, determined rate. In fact, not only do these young sequoias grow more than a half inch of new wood each season, but they will continue this growth rate for the rest of their lives, which may stretch over two thousand years! They do not really grow old and sick but more often simply topple over one day at the strong hand of a Sierra windstorm.

The cones of the big trees are rarely more than 2 inches long and have seeds so small that it takes more than 90,000 of them to make a pound (compared to 4,000 a pound for Jeffrey pine and 2,100 a pound for sugar pine). Under ideal climate conditions and with a fire to help open the cones, a pure stand of big trees can release an amazing 14 million seeds per acre in a single year. These seeds are the only chance the tree has to reproduce, however, since, unlike the coastal redwoods, the big tree has no ability to produce youngsters through root suckers.

Although the giant sequoia may not be quite as tall as the coast redwood, it is much bigger at the base. The trees in this grove are typically 12 to 16 feet in diameter, but the largest known big trees are nearly 30 feet thick when measured 5 feet above the ground. Members of the 1864 Whitney geological survey party found a hollow fallen sequoia north of here into which they rode horseback for 76 feet and then "turned around easily."

Basically this trail begins a gentle descent at about 0.3 mile, goes down at a sharper rate for a short distance, and then levels out a bit before the turnaround point. During this first descent Freeman Creek is especially beautiful, its banks lined with lady ferns, monkeyflowers, and an occasional red columbine. Freeman Creek continues to flow eastward for about 3 miles, makes a turn toward the southeast, and in 4 more miles joins the Kern River directly east of the Needles Fire Lookout.

At 1.3 miles the forest will open up considerably, with the dominant vegetation shifting to black oaks, chinquapins, and various types of shrubs. Shortly after this you will come to our turnaround point at a collection of large boulders. There are good views from here of the mountainous country to the east, which frames the southwestern border of the Golden Trout Wilderness. This is a wild area of more than 300,000 acres, particularly well known for the scattering of beautiful, dry meadows that have served as pillows for many a weary hiker's head.

San Bernardino National Forest

HEAPS PEAK ARBORETUM

Distance: 0.7 mile
Location: State Highway 18 (Rim-of-the-World Highway), east of Santa's Village, northwest of Running Springs, on the north side of the road.

The Heaps Peak Arboretum offers you one of the most enjoyable means of learning about local flora that you'll find anywhere in the San Bernardino Mountains. The 0.7-mile circular path is usually not overcrowded on mornings during the week; however, traffic can be heavy on virtually any summer or early autumn weekend. Although the vast majority of walks that I've been steering you toward are along trails that offer at least some respite from the madding crowds, the Heaps Peak Arboretum walk is included because I'm convinced that anyone who spends thirty minutes here will reap ten times that amount of time in additional enjoyment on his other treks throughout these mountains.

The numbered stops along the arboretum path are keyed to a well-written brochure, produced by the Rim-of-the-World Interpretive Association, which can be picked up at the trail head. Rather than adding additional stops to what is already a packed agenda, we can take some of the existing discussions found in this guide and explore them further. Keep in mind that while most of the discussions here are in fact aligned with specific stops on the interpretive brochure, they are identified not by number, but by subject matter. This is done so that it won't cause mass confusion for us if the arboretum assigns new numbers to their stops.

194

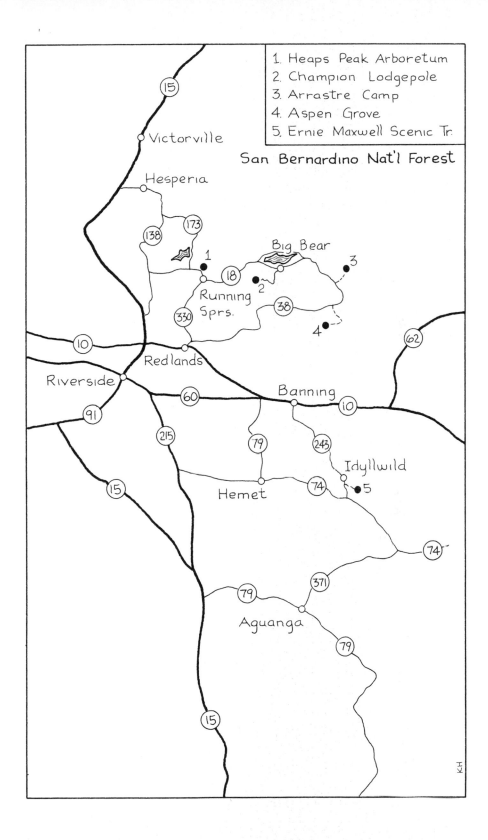

San Bernardino Nat'l Forest

1. Heaps Peak Arboretum
2. Champion Lodgepole
3. Arrastre Camp
4. Aspen Grove
5. Ernie Maxwell Scenic Tr.

Coulter Pine. Just before the path makes a large horseshoe turn to the right, there is a fine example of the tree that bears the world's largest pine cones. It was discovered by the Irish botanist Thomas Coulter in 1831. The large seeds were relished by Serrano (Spanish for "mountaineer") Indians. In fact, the harvest of all seasonal nut crops, particularly acorns and, where available, pin-yons, was an activity that had great spiritual significance for these people. After all, there were some tribes for which such crops made up more than 50 percent of their diet. Nuts could be eaten by themselves, but they were more commonly made into breads and mush or added to soups and stews. (As important as pine and oak nuts were to both foothill and desert Indians, it's a mistake to think that life was a dreary slide from one bowl of mush to the next. These people probably had at least seventy or eighty types of plants and animals available for their consumption in any given year.)

California Black Oak. A short way down the back side of the nature loop are fine examples of the California black oak, which is the most widespread variety of mountain oak in the western United States. Black oaks are fairly easy to distinguish from other types of oak because their deeply cut leaves have distinct spiny tips on the ends of their lobes.

If we can turn back for a moment to our discussion of nuts as a food crop for Indians, the black oak deserves special attention as perhaps the most widely harvested nut crop of them all. Indians would walk great distances to gather the nuts of this tree, even if other types of acorns were much closer at hand. Even though the black oak typically produces a nut crop only every other year, those harvests sometimes exceeded 200 pounds per tree. But what seems to be especially significant about this particular acorn, besides its good taste, is its firm consistency when cooked, which was very important to the production of good acorn mush. In fact, although mush was made from various kinds of acorns, nuts from the black oak were almost always added in order to achieve proper texture in the final product.

Incidentally, were you to pick an acorn off the tree and eat it raw you'd find it to be very bitter, a result of high levels of tannic acid in the nuts. This was removed by a rather lengthy process known as leaching, which usually involved placing ground meal in a woven basket or a shallow pit in the sand and running great quantities of water through it, a process that took about two hours.

The nuts from black oak groves were important trade items, and in some instances these trees actually served as the center point for the organization of tribal families. Some anthropologists have suggested that there was a direct correlation between the abundance of oak groves in any particular territory and the complexity of a tribe's social system. The people here in the oak-rich San Bernardinos tended to have more elaborate lineage structures than did the people, say, of the Mojave Desert.

Ponderosa Pine. Just past a small footbridge on the return side of the loop trail is a fine example of the stately ponderosa pine, or yellow pine. This stately tree, the most widely distributed pine in North America, has come to be thought of as one of the classic threads in the rich, wild tapestry of the American West. It will be one of the very first of the grand pines to greet you as you make your way up from the desert floor into the mountains. (This tree prefers a longer growing season than the Jeffrey pine, and therefore is found at lower elevations.)

You will undoubtedly come upon forests in these mountains that contain both Jeffrey pine and ponderosa pine. The easiest way to tell them apart is by their cones. Those of the Jeffrey will be rather large with spines that point down, while ponderosa cones will be small and have sharp spines pointing outward.

Knobcone Pine. Located on the final stretch of the arboretum loop, the knobcone is the most proficient of several western trees that have evolved to hold their seeds tightly within the cones until the occurrence of fire. There was a time when lightning-caused burns worked their way through the forests of the West on a fairly regular basis. The fire pines, as they've been called, were able to take advantage of the altered environment by immediately dropping healthy, fast-growing seeds onto the freshly burned ground, giving them a major jump on other species whose seeds would have been destroyed by the heat.

Contrary to what you might think, freshly burned soil can be ideal for new pine growth. The flames release nutrients from the soil as well as kill a host of harmful parasites. Perhaps most important of all, however, is the fact that the removal of the existing vegetation eliminates competition for sunlight, which is an extremely important ingredient for the healthy growth of most young pine seedlings.

CHAMPION LODGEPOLE

Distance: 1 mile
Location: From State Highway 18 turn south on Tulip Lane from the west end of Big Bear Lake Village. A short way past Coldbrook Campground on the right, make a right turn, following the signs for champion lodgepole pine. The trail head is 5 miles back off the pavement on Forest Road 2N11.

Although short, the Champion Lodgepole walk is very pleasant and can easily be extended to include more of the forested high country surrounding Siberia Creek. There are, by the way, interpretive brochures with natural history information keyed to the numbered sign posts you'll see between the trail head and the champion lodgepole pines. Unfortunately, you can't always be assured of finding one in the rack located near the parking area. Those who are planning to pass by the ranger station on the north side of Big Bear Lake may want to pick up a brochure there, instead.

If you've been walking in some of the drier parts of the San Bernardino Mountains, this trek will be a good opportunity for you to see what a little bit of water can do. The first section of trail follows a delightful little stream that dances quietly northward in the soft sunlight of the mixed-conifer forest. The tall, cornstalk-looking plants that you'll see lining this watercourse are known, appropriately, as corn lilies. In the spring it is very easy to confuse them with another rich green wetland resident known as skunk cabbage. The skunk cabbage is edible (the roots are dried and roasted), while the corn lily definitely is not. It is extremely poisonous to sheep and cattle, and limited doses to humans have the effect of slowing the heart rate and lowering blood pressure.

Along this stream corridor you'll likely see beautiful collections of red paintbrush—a plant that also does quite well in much sunnier, drier conditions. All the credit for being able to live in such a wide range of ecological niches cannot go to this plant alone. The lovely paintbrush has evolved into a rather extraordinary opportunist. Typically it will send root stems down just far enough to make contact with the roots of another plant. (In dry country, this will often be either sagebrush or bitterbrush.) It then proceeds to connect itself to the other plant's root tissues, drawing both food and water as needed. While the paintbrush does have the ability to manufacture its own food, in many places it can be difficult to find one that isn't raiding at least a little of its neighbor's pantry.

In some of the grassier areas surrounding this path, keep your eye out for oval depressions where the grass has been laid flat. Such a spot was likely the recent resting place of a mule deer. These graceful animals are most easily spotted during feeding, typically early in the morning or, even more commonly, late in the evening. The rest of the time they rest in grassy areas like this or beneath the low branches of shrubs and trees. Far better, you might think, if deer had dens or caves to hide in for protection from their predators. But the sector of the deer population that is most vulnerable to predation, young fawns, inadvertently foil bobcats and coyotes because they do not develop their strong "deer smell" until they are older and fairly fleet of foot.

At just under 0.5 mile you will come to a split in the trail. The right fork heads to the champion lodgepole pines, just a few yards to the north, while the path you were on climbs past Gunsight Notch, eventually reaching the beautiful backcountry surrounding Bear Creek, one of the main inlets supplying water for 8-mile-long Big Bear Lake.

The sheer size of the champion lodgepole is indeed impressive—110 feet tall with a circumference of about 20 feet. What is even more intriguing is that this four-hundred-year-old giant, as well as the many other large lodgepoles in this area, are growing at an elevation that is fully 500 feet lower than that at which nearly all other Southern California lodgepoles are found.

Some historians think that it was the explorers Meriwether Lewis and William Clark who actually gave the name lodgepole to this pine. On their fantastic westward journey in the early nine-

199

teenth century, they came across Indian tribes living east of the northern Rockies who made forays to the high country to cut these trees for use as tepee (or lodge) poles. Perhaps I should clarify. The lodgepoles of the Rocky Mountains are rather small, 40-to-50-foot-high trees with a straight, slender trunk typically 6 to 12 inches in diameter. Had all lodgepoles been the size of this champion, or even the 2-to-4-feet-thick specimens found in the high Sierras, you can rest assured that Lewis and Clark would never have found Indians dragging them off the mountains to build tepees.

ARRASTRE CAMP

Distance: 2.25 miles

Location: State Highway 38 east of Big Bear Lake, north of Onyx Summit. Head east on FS 2N01, which is about 1.2 miles south of the Balky Canyon Road (FS 2N04). A short way down this dirt road in the bottom of a ravine is a Pacific Crest Trail sign on the right. The trail is just past this sign on the left, on the east side of the stream bed, not, as the Forest Service map shows, on the west side. You can park adjacent to the dirt road just above the trail sign. (Note: If you don't want to go on this fairly rutted dirt section, park up on the pavement and walk the additional 0.4 mile to the trail head and back. It will help a great deal to have a forest map with you.)

Although only a short distance from the highway, the Arrastre Camp walk is one of those totally overlooked, no-particular-destination-in-mind rambles through the forest that will really allow you to leave cares and crowds far behind. Noble old Jeffrey pines and an occasional ponderosa mingle with fir and willow to form a quintessential, southwestern high-country forest—a magnificent last stand before the San Bernardino Mountains tumble eastward onto the hot, dry skin of the Mojave Desert.

The limited use that this stretch of the Pacific Crest Trail receives, along with the abundance of trees and thick streambed cover, makes this walk a particularly good one for observing a wonderful variety of bird and small-mammal life. Say's phoebes, Steller's jays, and Cassin's finches are all found here, as is the tiny, brown creeper, who can be seen tracing spiral circles up the trunks of pine trees in his never-ending search for insects. Also nearby are a number of woodpeckers, like the beautiful red-shafted flicker, and soaring above the soft green needle canopies, golden eagles and red-tailed and Cooper's hawks.

As for mammals, you should have little trouble spotting both California ground squirrels and gray squirrels, although rabbits, mule deer, striped skunks, and deer and meadow mice may be a bit more secretive. In soft, muddy areas along the stream bed (in the summer you will have to wait until reaching our turnaround point), look for tracks of the badger, bobcat, kit fox, and ringtail.

The traits of this last animal, one that some people spend years trying to spot, could probably use a little clarification. You may often hear the ringtail referred to as a miner's cat, banded-tail cat, coon cat, civet cat, or ring-tailed cat. The strange thing is that it is not a cat at all, nor does it particularly look like one; it resembles instead an unlikely hodgepodge of weasel, rodent, and raccoon. (The raccoon part, by the way, is the long tail ringed with bands of black fur.) As if the poor animal doesn't have identity problems enough, its scientific name, *Bassariscus astutus*, translates into "clever little fox."

The ringtail has a wide range of selections for his daily menu but seems to have a distinct preference for small rodents such as chipmunks, ground squirrels, and mice. Being an able climber, he will occasionally take to the trees for a bit of bird, and he has also been known to eat insects and fruit. (If you are here in late summer when the manzanita berries are ripe, you may see places where the fruit has been chewed off, perhaps by this fellow.) Young ringtails are born in early summer in litters of three or four, and by autumn they have been taught the ropes of "ringtailing" well enough to strike out on their own.

One of the plants you will see growing in fair abundance along the stream channel is willow—good evidence that even when this rocky bed is completely dry, water is probably not far underground. Willows have always been important plants to Indians. The wood was pliable enough to make fine bows, and the tough strings of the inner bark could be woven together and used as a crude substitute for rope. A pithy, semisweet tissue just inside the bark was in some areas considered to be a fine substitute for chewing tobacco. Teas were made from the bark itself to cure colds and fever, and water in which bark had been soaked for several days was supposedly quite effective for treating diarrhea. Both beavers and rabbits consider the outer covering of willow shoots to be excellent fare, while mule deer tend to concentrate on leaves and small twigs. If you look carefully at these willows, you will almost surely see evidence of such recent dining activity.

Half way to the Arrastre Camp you'll pass a beautiful cover of wild roses. Their fragrance, especially when mingled with a hint of pine, produces one of those extraordinarily fresh scents that you know would be powerful enough to transport you back to this very spot if only you could bottle the stuff and take it home with you. It was, in fact, simple grafting of wild roses that enabled man to produce flowers with petals that could be pressed to make fine perfumes.

The cool, flowing water at Arrastre Camp can be a welcome surprise on a hot summer day. An *arrastre*, incidentally, is a rather crude horse-, mule-, or man-powered device used to crush rock in order to recover whatever precious metal it contained. The name hints at the flurry of gold fever that washed across the San Bernardino Mountains, first in the form of placer mining during the 1860s and later as quartz, or "hard rock," mines. One of the greatest mines in this latter category was E. S. "Lucky" Baldwin's Doble Mine, located just 10 miles northwest of here at a place known, appropriately, as Gold Mountain.

Baldwin was not called Lucky for nothing. For one thing, he made a cool 3.6 million dollars selling his shares of a mine in the Comstock Lode, which not long afterward was found worthless. Another tale relates the time that, just before leaving on a South Pacific vacation, Lucky instructed his broker immediately to unload all of his stock in the Consolidated Virginia and California mines. The only problem was that the broker could not sell the certificates because Baldwin had absent-mindedly set sail without endorsing them, which was not really a problem at all, since when he returned the stock was worth about eighty times what it was on the day he left.

ASPEN GROVE

Distance: 2.3 miles
Location: Northeastern corner of the San Gorgonio Wilderness. Take State Highway 38 from Redlands, head south on the entrance road (FS 1N02) to Heart Bar State Park. Do not turn into the state park campground but instead keep following FS 1N02 to a fork at 1.2 miles. Take the right branch (1N05), following the sign for Fish Creek. It is just a bit more than 1.5 miles from this fork to the Fish Creek trail head sign, located on the right side of the road. The trail number is 2E05.

The walk to the Fish Creek Aspen Grove, as well as the remaining 0.8-mile trek up the stream itself to monkeyflower flats, is a wonderfully rich, mellow saunter, perfect for late-evening forays with a special friend and a bottle of chilled wine.

On your way down the small dirt road from the parking area are wonderful views into the San Gorgonio Wilderness. Here are huddled the summits of the highest mountain range in Southern California. Grinnell Mountain lies to the southwest, and directly to the south is the high and mighty Ten Thousand Foot Ridge, birthplace of light-footed Fish Creek you see flowing below. In just a couple of hundred yards you will arrive at the crossing for the creek, which also serves as the entrance point for the wilderness itself. Immediately before you on the west side of the stream is our aspen grove—modest, to be sure, but nevertheless the largest grove of these trees in Southern California.

Aspen trees are in fact the most widely distributed tree on the continent, and comments about their brilliant, whitewashed trunks and dancing leaves can be found laced throughout the earliest diaries of the American West. Early French-Canadian trappers working west across the Canadian Rockies told the tale that aspen wood was used to build the cross upon which Christ was crucified— an event that has caused the leaves of the tree to tremble ever since. In fact, if you look closely at the stems you'll see that they are flattened at the point where they join the leaves. This makes them quiver in the slightest of breezes, a fact that some scientists have suggested may increase the leaf's total exposure to the sun.

To the fur traders who passed down the crucifixion story, as well as to generations of trappers after them, the aspen also had some extremely important practical applications. Scanning the broad flanks of mountain ranges, you can quite easily pick out the groves of aspen from among the dominant cover of conifers, especially late in the season when the trees are flying their brilliantly colored flags in the autumn sunshine. And, where there are aspen, there are likely to be beaver. The aspen is one of the beaver's favorite foods. He not only nibbles on the tender bark throughout the summer but stores great quantities of aspen branches under the ice of his pond for winter dining, as well. Once a trapper located a colony of beaver, it was with a juicy aspen branch that he lured the animal into a steel trap, starting the process of turning a furry engineer into a hat to be worn on some urban gentleman's head. So well did the system work that were it not for a sudden change in fashion, the beaver would likely be extinct today.

The majority of the aspen trees you see in the West have not grown from seeds but are "clone groves" that have sprouted from a common root system. Such "clone groves" can be very large, and one way to tell the extent of any single collection is to watch which trees turn the same color at the same rate during the fall. This type of growth is very convenient after a forest fire, since new trees can sprout up almost immediately from undamaged root systems. The aspen is, in fact, one of the first trees to reclaim land damaged by fire, although under ideal conditions they are eventually replaced by pines or firs.

As you walk up Fish Creek, take notice of the great diversity of plants growing along this watercourse, almost none of which are found even a short distance away in the understory of the mixed-conifer forest. A little water, along with some added sunlight, can work magic. Here truly is the artist's palette, stained with rich splashes of paintbrush, lily, lupine, red columbine, geranium, and monkeyflower, as well as with an abundance of green grasses, willows, and flowering shrubs. Incidentally, the leaves of the monkeyflower you see here were occasionally eaten by Indians, and settlers found it a fine substitute for lettuce. They are not at all disagreeable in taste and contain many times the vitamins of the iceburg lettuce that we eat today.

A word here about collecting wild plants for food. In an area like the San Bernardino National Forest, which receives more use than almost any other public land in the country, it is really inappropriate to pick any plant. A single weekend of even restrained picking along a watercourse like this one could leave the place looking as if it had been grazed by a hundred head of longhorns. Save your wild-food forays for less heavily visited areas, and even then, be sure to take only one or two plants from each healthy colony.

The trail winds slightly away from the creek, through fine, open forests of incense-cedar, Douglas-fir, and ponderosa and Jeffrey pine. About 0.5 mile into the walk is a veteran incense-cedar that was the grounding staff for a bolt of lightning. This kind of fiery blow can actually burn many types of trees right to the ground. The incense-cedar, however, is able to withstand much from both fire and disease, thanks to the thick layer of bark protecting the heartwood. This fibrous coating, which may reach a thickness of 6 inches, was popular with many early California settlers for use as roof shingles on their log cabins.

About 0.15 mile past a drainage area which comes into the trail from the right, is monkeyflower flats—a lovely garden containing all our previously spotted flowers, along with beautiful clumps of wild rose. This park is a wonderful place to lie back late in the day and feel the evening shadows roll over the land. The smell of pine and roses and the gurgles of Fish Creek, can make you feel totally relaxed, rather like the last fallen leaf of the forest sinking into the soft mantle of the first snow.

ERNIE MAXWELL SCENIC TRAIL

Distance: 3.4 miles

Location: From downtown Idyllwild head south on the Idyllwild-Hemet Highway, then left on Saunders Meadow Road. Take another left on Pine Avenue (0.9 mile from the highway), then a right at a T intersection onto Tahquitz View Drive. Drive past the South Fork Trail road junction, and about 0.7 mile from where you turned onto Tahquitz View Drive you'll see a small sign on the right marking the Ernie Maxwell Scenic Trail. You may have to park at a turnout slightly past the trail head. Be careful that you do not block traffic.

The Ernie Maxwell Scenic Trail, dedicated to an editor and publisher of the *Idyllwild Town Crier* and a president of the local chapter of the Izaak Walton League, is as pleasant a wooded walk as you'll find anywhere in California. The soothing effect of this forest is immediate; stately incense-cedar, ponderosa pine, Jeffrey pine, white fir, and Coulter pine wrap you in a fine cloak of prime green conifer. Shafts of afternoon sunlight pour down through the canopy, spotlighting the easy flutter of black oak and alder leaves. Only occasionally do these warm fingers of sunshine reach down far enough to touch the scattered huddles of bracken fern growing on the forest floor.

The mild weather and the variety of vegetation make this area a haven for birds; more than 185 species were identified in a study that surveyed the land upward from Lake Hemet. On this particular walk you're likely to see several feathered residents, including the Steller's jay, white-headed woodpecker, western bluebird, Cassin's finch, mountain chickadee, and white-breasted nuthatch, while common summer visitors include the western tanager, olive-sided flycatcher, and western wood pewee.

Some birds are easy to recognize from appearance alone. The brilliant yellow breast and orange head and throat of the western tanager are great distinguishing marks, as is the feathered head crest of the Steller's jay. Other birds, however, are not so easy to tell by sight alone, especially in a dark forest where subtle markings may not show up. At that point it comes in handy to know something about the particular habits of the birds, which will at least help you to identify the family, if not the actual species. Nuthatches, for instance, will invariably be seen looking for insects by walking head first down the side of a tree. Woodpeckers tend to have short legs and long toes and claws for clinging to tree trunks, as well as sturdy, pointed beaks for digging insects out of their hiding places. Knowing such characteristics can be especially helpful when looking for a woodpecker such as the white-headed variety, since he is a quiet fellow who rarely drums at all, preferring instead to tear pieces of bark from the tree to reach the insects underneath.

These rich forests were popular summer destinations for Cahuilla Indians, who are thought to have obtained roughly 15 percent of their yearly food supply from this type of environment. Most sought after were acorns from the California black oak. You can recognize these by the deep lobes on the leaves that are tipped with small spines. The black oak produces acorn crops only every other year, but crops tend to be quite large—in a favorable season 200 to 300 pounds of nuts per tree. In addition, a greater percentage of the individual nut is made up of edible material. Another important aspect of this species is that the ground nuts assumed a very desirable custardlike consistency when they were boiled with water to make mush, a mainstay of the Cahuilla diet. Though it's doubtful that the Indians were aware of the exact nutritional value of acorns, it so happens that levels of fats, carbohydrates, and proteins were higher in black oak acorns than in the nuts of almost any other species.

One final fact about acorns. As has been noted, the bitter-tasting tannic acid in them has to be leached out before they can be consumed—this was usually achieved by pouring a great deal of water through the ground meal. One Cahuilla myth states that at one time the acorns of all oak trees were naturally sweet. But the creator of the Cahuilla, a god known as Mukat, became displeased with the behavior of his people and as punishment turned the acorns bitter.

Into the walk 0.3 mile you'll come to a massive granite boulder, the same type of rock that forms the soaring, rugged highline known as Marion Ridge, which is visible just across the stream-eroded valley to the north. Ninety-five million years ago this rock was part of an enormous underground pool of hot magma, which rose up through the existing surface rock to create what is known as a batholith (which literally means "deep rock.") When magma cools very slowly deep within the earth, it tends to form slabs of coarse rock whose individual grains can be seen with the naked eye. One of the ways such slabs weather is by forming vertical and horizontal joints, a process that results in the rugged, pinnaclelike topography of Marion Ridge.

You will cross a tiny, spring-fed watercourse about 1.2 miles into the walk. Past this 40 yards notice the thick layer of pine needles covering the hillside to the right of the trail. You would not see such deep accumulations of needle duff in the forests of the

207

east and northwest, where a greater amount of summer moisture is available to water the bacteria that break down organic matter and turn it back into soil. Pine needles also contain large amounts of a woodlike material known as lignon, which is highly resistant to decay. In addition, the needles are covered by a tough, waxy coating that helps to regulate water loss in the tree. There are indeed vast threaded networks of fungus present in this soil, excreting enzymes that will eventually digest these needles. But it is a painstakingly slow process.

Our turnaround point comes 1.6 miles into the walk, where the trail makes a left turn past rocky Strawberry Creek. Notice the difference in vegetation in this area—the greater abundance of plants such as twinberry, alder, and bracken fern—as well as the birds you see here, which were not present elsewhere along the path.

THE MOUNTAINS

In the spring of 1868, a genial, thirty-year-old wanderer arrived in San Francisco aboard a Panama Steamer, bound, as he himself recalls, for "any place that is wild." Sixty miles southeast of San José he reached a low pass over the Diablo Mountains. From this 1,386-foot-high perch he was afforded his first glimpse of a land that would change him forever and, in the process, change the way that Americans would come to think of the rich wilderness heritage cradled in the arms of California.

Looking eastward from the summit of the Pacheco Pass one shining morning, a landscape was displayed that after all my wanderings still appears as the most beautiful I have ever beheld. At my feet lay the Great Central Valley of California, level and flowery, like a lake of pure sunshine, forty or fifty miles wide, five hundred miles long, one rich furred garden of yellow compositae. And from the eastern boundary of this vast golden flowerbed rose the mighty Sierra, miles in height, and so gloriously colored and so radiant, it seemed not clothed with light, but wholly composed of it, like the wall of some celestial city. Along the top and extending a good way down, was a rich pearl-gray belt of snow; below it a belt of blue and dark purple, marking the extension of the forest; and stretching along the base of the range a broad belt of rose-purple; all these colors, from the blue sky to the yellow valley smoothly blending as they do in a rainbow, making a wall of light ineffably fine. Then it seemed to me that the Sierra should be called, not the Nevada or Snowy Range, but the Range of Light. And after ten years of wandering and wondering in the heart of it, rejoicing in its glorious floods of light, the white beams of the morning streaming through the passes, the noonday radiance on the crystal rocks, the flush of the alpenglow, and the irised spray of countless waterfalls, it still seems above all others the range of light. (From John Muir's essay "The Yosemite")

213

And so John Muir began his courtship with the mountains of California, an affair that lasted nearly a half century, until his death in 1914. There had been others, however, to whom the state's mountains had dealt lessons so difficult that any appreciation for their beauty and mystery was lost beneath an enduring bitterness. Twenty-five springs earlier, the California high country offered the explorer John C. Frémont a landscape that was "steep and slippery with snow and ice; the tough evergreens of the mountain impeded our way, tore our skins, exhausted our patience." For John Bartleson, one of the very first settlers to make the trip overland into the state, the hardships of merely crossing the mountains were enough to evoke some rather charged responses. "If I ever get back to Missouri," he said in 1841, "I would gladly eat out of the trough with my pigs."

Since these early days, millions have found their way to these hills. Some have come for the inspiration offered by the high ranges that parallel the coast, some for the quiet solitude of the thick-forested peaks of the Northwest, and still others for a chance at a piece of the gold that still waits at the cool granite feet of the Sierras.

The mountains of California are striking evidence that, geologically speaking, the area has not been a dull place. The Klamath Mountains in the northern part of the state tore away from the Sierras about 140 million years ago, and they have put about 60 miles of land between the two ranges since. Granite blocks in the Coast Ranges appear to match up perfectly with the southern hook of the Sierras, indicating that they too have been shuffling northward along the San Andreas Fault at a rather impressive rate. Twenty million years ago the Los Angeles basin was spouting lava all over what would turn into Burbank, while a world away, runny, black basalt was pouring out of gaping fissures to form a 200-foot-deep blanket over what would one day rise into the mighty Cascades.

Most of us don't tend to think about long-term, ongoing processes, although movements along the Southern California fault lines happen regularly enough to remind us that the process of rearranging the earth is not yet completely dead. But there are other, more subtle examples of large-scale landscape architecture waiting for us when we visit the mountains. When you're walking in a canyon formed by a river or stream, stop and consider how much material had to be moved to carve such a vast space out of solid rock. Note what happens to the color of watercourses during spring snowmelts or after heavy rainstorms. The thick, cloudy liquid is really a mountain in suspension, running particle by particle back toward the sea from whence it came. Perhaps this meditation on erosion will even make you a bit more appreciative of the earthquake aspect of restructuring the landscapes. After all, if the land is not uplifted and rearranged at the same rate that the rains and winds tear down the mountains, before you know it California would be as flat and featureless as a pancake.

Since these peaks will more than likely be a dominant part of our landscape for a long, long time to come, let's turn our attention to learning how mountains manage to call many of the tunes that plants, animals, and people have danced to for thousands of years.

The geological formation of mountains aside, we can distill many of their most dynamic properties into one simple word: water. Mountains push air masses higher into the atmosphere, where temperatures are cooler. Since cool air cannot hold as much moisture as warm air, all or a portion of whatever water cargo the air is carrying ends up being dumped onto the high country in the form of rain or snow. This additional water, most of which would not be here at all if the terrain were flat, is responsible for an amazing variety of things. First of all, it forms a large winter snowpack—in some places 20 or more feet deep—that is slowly released in the form of streams and rivers that eventually end up as irrigation for a lettuce patch or water for our sun tea. It is almost certain that California could not support a population a tenth its current size without mountain-generated water.

This water also has a lot to do with the type of terrain that greets you on your forays into the high country. The beautiful, polished granite canyons of the Sierras, the sheer green faces of the Trinity Alps, the rugged rock channels of the San Bernardinos—all are the result of flowing water whose source is the mountains themselves. When moisture enters rock joints and then freezes, it can pry giant slabs from the faces of mountains as if they were blisters of dried paint; sometimes it creates jagged pinnacles like the Devil's Postpile, other times it sculpts graceful domes like those of Yosemite. The particular shape left by water's magic wand depends on what type of rock it is working with.

The water-sculpture concept can be taken even further, if you consider that it was the high country snagging great blankets of snow during the ice ages that allowed glaciers to form. These glaciers scoured the mountains into stunning tapestries of U-shaped valleys, plunging waterfalls, and cobalt-colored cirque lakes.

So as we climb the mountains, we feel the continuing drop in temperature, which produces the steady increase in waterfall, which produces belt after unique belt of plants—each having evolved to take advantage of the climatic conditions found in that particular stretch of mountainside. These plants in turn give rise to rich communities of birds, insects, and mammals, some of which, like the chickaree, or pika, never stray from their home zone, while others scramble up and down the flanks of the peaks a step ahead of the shifting seasons. It is difficult to comprehend the complexity of biological systems that have evolved from the mere presence of large rock masses sticking out of the ground. But this is one environment whose total has always seemed far more than the sum of its parts. We return to the mountains again and again, awed by their unwavering power, soothed by the life that lies cradled in their arms.

Throughout most of his mountain wanderings John Muir never failed to carry one book with him, volume one of *The Prose Works of Ralph Waldo Emerson*. These pages he not only read but took to heart, agreeing or dissenting with Emerson by way of scores of penciled comments in the margins of the book. At one point Emerson makes the claim that in nature there is a "certain enticement and flattery, together with a failure to yield a present satisfaction." Adjacent to this comment Muir wrote "No—always we find more than we expect." To anyone who wanders a lifetime through the mountains of California, it seems impossible to feel any other way.

Shasta-Trinity National Forest

DEADFALL LAKES

Distance: 6 miles

Location: Take the Stewart Springs Road exit west off Interstate 5, just north of Weed. Follow this road (which becomes Forest Road 17) up into the forest approximately 15 miles to a pass where you'll find the well-marked Parks Creek trail head. Our path—part of the Pacific Crest Trail—takes off to the south. (Note: Stewart Springs Road forks to the left off the main road only about a mile from Interstate 5; the sign may be missing. Half of the distance on this road is dirt.)

The Pacific Crest Trail from the Parks Creek trail head to Deadfall Lakes is a true slice of high-country heaven—lush meadows, yawning vistas, and deep rock basins filled with azure water. Although the walk is longer than most, 6 miles round trip, it is for the most part flat, and it offers enough beauty and natural diversity to make the miles fly by more quickly than you may have thought possible.

During the first 0.3 mile you will be afforded excellent views to the west of the Trinity Alps country, one of the most rugged, inaccessible mountain ranges in America. Geologists know less about this region than any other in the state, one reason being that there are very few visible rock outcroppings poking above the dense vegetation. Though they are thought to contain sizable reserves of gold, manganese, and chromium, the extreme ruggedness and remoteness of the Trinities have prevented such resources from ever being developed to any great extent. When a rancher found "color" along the Trinity River in 1848, Sierra gold fever leaped 200 miles northward in a single bound. But beyond the river

217

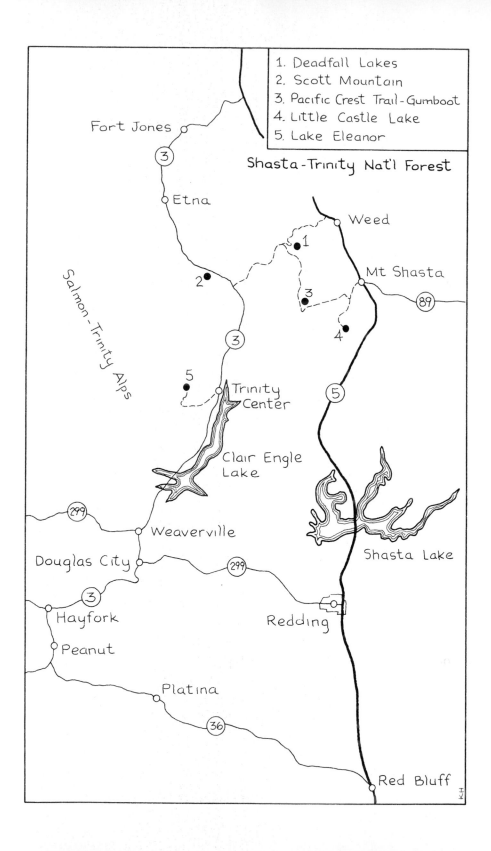

1. Deadfall Lakes
2. Scott Mountain
3. Pacific Crest Trail-Gumboot
4. Little Castle Lake
5. Lake Eleanor

Shasta-Trinity Nat'l Forest

Fort Jones

③

Etna

Weed

①

②

Mt Shasta

③

⑧⑨

③

④

Salmon-Trinity Alps

5

Trinity Center

⑤

Clair Engle Lake

②⑨⑨

Weaverville

Douglas City

②⑨⑨

Shasta Lake

③

Hayfork

Redding

Peanut

Platina

③⑥

Red Bluff

K.H

in the rugged Trinity Alps, what gold was extracted flowed much more quietly, one leather saddlebag at a time.

It was on the south side of these mountains, along the South Fork of the Trinity River, that in the spring of 1828 Jedediah Strong Smith struggled toward the coast on a trapping expedition with seventeen men and three hundred wild horses and mules. So rugged and dangerous was the trail along the high cliffs that many of the animals fell to their deaths. There were times when making a single mile of progress took an entire day.

Stately Jeffrey pines rise from either side of the trail, lending to the land a kind of sterling beauty that is unmistakably the American West. Ahead of you and far below the trail, a band of plush green meadow frames the dancing waters of Deadfall Creek. Like most of the streams along this side of the divide, it is bound for the Trinity River, located some 2 miles to the west.

About 2.6 miles in, note the long runs of broken rock on your left running down from the high cliffs above. Freezing water has wrenched sections of rock from the face of these cliffs as effectively as any hammer and chisel could ever do. These giant slabs are then broken down into rocks called talus, the size that you see here, which will be broken down to an even smaller size known as scree. Eventually these rocks will be reduced to so many grains of sand, pushed ever closer to Deadfall Creek by rain and snowmelt. Today's sand grains no longer continue their journey to the Pacific Ocean but are instead stopped only 30 miles from here, in the slack waters behind Trinity Dam.

A short distance past the talus runs is a trail junction. The left fork goes to the largest of the Deadfall Lakes, while the Pacific Crest Trail heads west. Take a left here and head toward the large mountain immediately in front of you. A short walk will bring you to the shore of the lake. Like many of the true alpine lakes, this one is a turquoise jewel, a strange, tinted snapshot of the high-country sky. Water that rarely warms beyond 50 degrees, along with a severe shortage of nutrients being washed into the water, keeps the lake from ever developing the populations of microorganisms and plants that would change its cool, sterile blue to the greenish color of life. By the way, while there are exceptions, the unproductiveness of most high alpine lakes means that they cannot

219

offer predictably good fishing unless they are stocked on a regular basis.

Another smaller, but equally beautiful lake lies just to the northwest of this one. It has a fine collection of granite slabs that are perfect for picnicking or just relaxing in the warm mountain sunshine.

When you reach a point about 1 mile up the trail on your way back to the parking area, stop and take a look at the difference between the north-facing mountain slopes behind you and the south-facing ones ahead. If it's not past midsummer, you'll likely see traces of snow on the north faces, while the south faces will already look dry and parched. Notice the differences in ground cover and the number of trees present on each side. North-facing slopes are protected from the rays of the sun, meaning that what water is available to them does not evaporate as quickly. Generally speaking, snow is deeper on a north face, rock is broken down into soil at a faster rate, and a wider variety of alpine trees and plants can take hold and survive there. Use this information to your advantage. Plan your spring walks in the high country to follow along exposed south faces. Then, on hot days during the summer, try to stick to north faces, where there may be more trees to offer you shade.

SCOTT MOUNTAIN

Distance: 3.4 miles
Location: West side of State Highway 3 at Scott Mountain Summit, about 25 miles north of Trinity Center.

The Scott Mountain walk is basically a steady climb on the first part of the trip, leading in 1.7 miles to a magnificent view of the wild Siskiyou Mountain country to the northeast. Most of the walk is through a beautiful, mixed-conifer forest, which, it is hoped, will divert your attention from the uphill task.

Begin your trek from a large, dirt parking area on top of the divide, adjacent to the Scott Mountain Campground. (You'll be heading north on the Pacific Crest Trail, so look for wooden "PCT" posts to guide you.) The landscape of this region is blanketed by stately conifers with a healthy understory of currant, bear grass, ceanothus, and manzanita.

You may well be confused when trying to determine the difference between two of the area's most striking conifers—the ponderosa (or yellow pine) and the Jeffrey pine. Here are some pointers that you can put to use on this walk. The easiest way to distinguish between the two trees is by their cones. Those from the Jeffrey pine will be 6 or 7 inches long and 5 inches across with spines on the scales that point down toward the base of the cone. The ponderosa's pine cones, on the other hand, are rarely more than 4 inches long and have spines on the cone scales that point straight out. (The ponderosa cone would prick you if you squeezed it in your hand, while the Jeffrey cone would not.) The other easy test is to sniff the bark. Jeffrey pines have a delightful pineapple-vanilla smell, while ponderosas have a odor that is fairly indistinguishable from that of other conifers in the forest.

Both ponderosa and Jeffrey pine produce excellent lumber. In addition, the pitch of the Jeffrey contains a chemical with nearly pure concentrations of a hydrocarbon known as heptane, a substance found also in petroleum. Heptane from Jeffrey pine pitch was the first substance used to develop a grading system for gasoline, which later came to be known as the octane rating.

At 0.2 mile the trail meets a dirt road. Continue across this road on the path you're on, climbing steadily. At 1.5 miles the trail reaches a vista point on the left. To the southeast is the wild Salmon-Trinity Alps Primitive Area. Straight ahead, however, is a view of another kind.

This is logging country. A great deal of the land before you was acquired by the early railroad companies, who were granted alternate sections of ground as part of their charter agreements to build rail lines throughout the West. This incredible giveaway of natural resources was what enabled the old railroad corporations to turn into today's most powerful timber companies. (These deals were occasionally made even sweeter, such as when an 1880s government surveyor in the pay of timber companies was caught expanding company-alloted sections of land from the usual 640 acres each into pieces that measured more than 1,300 acres!)

On a distant mountain slope directly in front of you are the scars from a massive timber-harvesting operation that entailed removing all the trees from an area at once, a process known as clear-cutting. In certain circumstances clear-cutting may actually be beneficial, since it allows various grasses and shrubs that are eaten by wildlife to flourish in the new-found sunlight. For a clear-cut really to be utilized in this way, however, the logging company must clean up most of the residue branches and logs (called slash), since a littered ground severely reduces new plant growth. Also, clear-cutting for the benefit of wildlife is ideally done in small patches, because deer and elk don't often stray very far from the protection of the forest corridor.

When a large clear-cut is made on a steep slope like the one before you, there is very little good to say for it. In the first place, the total removal of vegetation from a hillside means that there will be very little left to stop the forces of water from washing away precious topsoil. Taking all the trees from a hillside can increase water runoff by 40 percent. It has been estimated that in this type of country it takes several hundred years to build a single inch of topsoil. And where there is no topsoil, there are, for all practical purposes, no plants. What soil is left on these hillsides after the clear-cut is eventually washed into area creeks, filling them with silt and severely reducing the survival rate for the fish that live there. The heavy damage caused to mountain slopes during certain nineteenth-century gold-mining operations caused erosion that killed enormous numbers of trout and choked off many of the best salmon and steelhead runs in the state.

In the second place, even if the mountainside is not being terribly eroded, the extra water runoff increases the rate by which minerals are leached from the ground and carried out of the ecosystem. Nitrogen in particular, which is a critical element in plant growth, can be reduced to dangerously low levels.

Finally, it's important to realize that the forests before you actually regulate the rate of water flow into streams and rivers, thereby determining if there will be a steady supply of irrigation and drinking water or if the majority of it will run off too fast to be of practical use. While much of this forest is privately owned, similar mismanagement is happening on our public lands, as we forego the enforcement of environmental regulations in an effort to cut "unnecessary" government spending.

About 0.2 mile farther you'll come to a low saddle, which is most obvious if you look toward the right side of the path. The north vista is blocked by a small, rocky hummock, but you can climb this in a matter of seconds by heading up it at right angles to the trail. This is our turnaround point, and it is a spectacular spot for a picnic lunch. The sweeping view to the north is of the Siskiyous, a wild, lonely mountain corridor leading into southern Oregon. The name Siskiyou, by the way, was first used to denote a single mountain pass where a Hudson's Bay Company trapper lost a trusty packhorse while making a crossing in 1828. *Siskiyou* is a Cree Indian word for "bob-tailed horse."

PACIFIC CREST TRAIL—GUMBOOT

Distance: 5 miles
Location: Take Lake Road west out of the town of Mount Shasta toward Siskiyou Lake. Continue on around Siskiyou Lake on Forest Road 26, which turns to dirt in about 12 miles. A short distance past the point where the pavement ends, there is a left fork heading to Gumboot Lake. You stay on Forest Road 26, making two climbing horseshoe turns until you reach a pass, only about 2 miles from the Gumboot Lake turnoff. There is a well-marked sign here for Gumboot trail head. Walk north, following the Pacific Crest Trail markers.

The Gumboot walk is a delightful ridge path along the Pacific Crest Trail, offering immediate views west toward the Klamath National forest and, farther to the south, into the rugged, glaciated peaks of the Salmon-Trinity Alps Primitive Area. After you round a small shoulder of land that runs north for about 0.2 mile from the trail head, a grand vista opens up in the other direction, toward Gray Butte and mighty Mount Shasta to the northeast.

Shasta, named after a group of Indians living in the region north of here, was a source of both inspiration and orientation for thousands of nineteenth-century travelers. Few explorers—from

Fray Narcisco Duran in 1817 to John C. Frémont thirty years later—failed to mention the striking effect of this 14,161-foot, snow-capped volcano rising unchallenged out of the pine-covered flatlands.

Shasta is a gigantic peak, measuring about 80 cubic miles in size. It has erupted with heavy lava flows several times during the last million years, and has thereby built itself layer by layer into a graceful cone that was later gouged and slashed by ice-age glaciers. The last eruption of the volcano is thought to have occurred in 1786.

Mount Shasta was very special to John Muir. He ascended the peak for the first time in the fall of 1874, and again in April of 1875, this time pathfinding for a government survey party. No sooner had he come down from the summit on this latter trip than he made a rendezvous at timberline with the local mountaineer and guide Jerome Fay, determined to climb up yet again the next day for the purpose of making barometric studies. It was on this trek that Shasta came very close to claiming the life of "John of the Mountains."

Muir and Fay reached the top of Shasta with little trouble, leaving at 2:00 in the morning in order to be able to walk on top of the ice-crusted snow. When they reached the summit, they looked down to see giant cumulus clouds massing in Shasta Valley, and before long, the gray swells had totally obscured their view of the lowlands. "We stood solitary in the sunshine between two skies," wrote Muir, "—a sky of spotless blue above, a sky of glittering cloud beneath."

Muir was so busy with his studies that he ignored the ominous weather that began to show its face about noon. When the men finally began their descent, it was in the midst of violent volleys of hail and snow, followed by raging winds and temperatures falling to below zero in a matter of minutes. Lightning began to flash in the gray darkness, with thunder making "an almost continuous roar, stroke following stroke in quick passionate succession, as though the mountain were being rent to its foundations and the old volcano were breaking forth again."

The two men spent the long, bitter night high on the mountain, laying against a pool of hot sludge fired by a series of volcanic

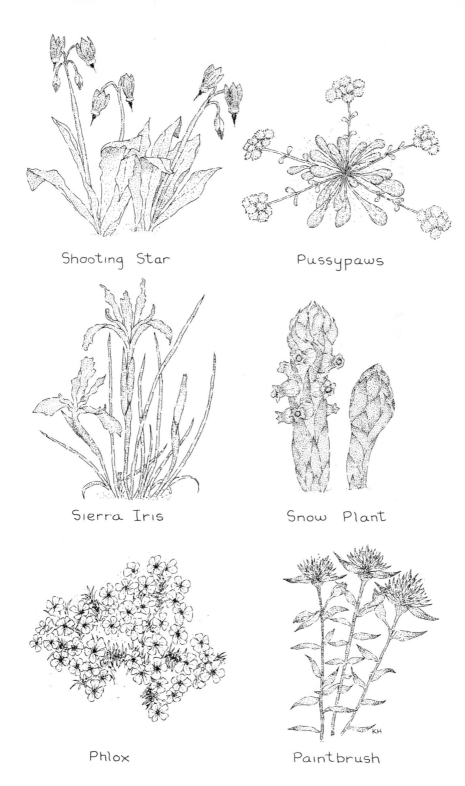

Shooting Star

Pussypaws

Sierra Iris

Snow Plant

Phlox

Paintbrush

steam vents, part of their bodies boiling, part freezing, not daring to sleep for fear that carbonic acid from the vents would bring death. When at last they rose to continue their descent the next morning, they were covered with ice, their pants frozen so stiff they could hardly be made to bend, their feet riddled with frostbite. Down they waded through several feet of new snow, finally reaching their timberline camp about 10:00 A.M. on the first day of May—thoroughly exhausted, yet alive to climb another mountain, another day.

As is true throughout California, much of the water used for drinking and irrigation comes from high peaks that trap great quantities of snow during the winter and then release it in the form of streams and rivers throughout the hot, dry summers. Mount Shasta happens to be the source of the Sacramento River, one of the most important watercourses in the northern part of the state.

In 0.75 mile you will come upon a dirt road that crosses the range from east to west. The Pacific Crest Trail continues heading north on the other side. In another 0.15 mile is a fine view of Gumboot Lake below you to the right, and in another 0.4 mile you can look down the left side of the ridge into Picayune Lake.

The mountains that you see lying off to the east are the result of volcanics, their peaks of andesite and basalt actually quite young. The ranges you are walking on, however, as well as those to the west, are composed of much older rocks. Most of this area consists of dark-colored igneous rocks that were once part of the ocean floor. In the stretches of trail past Picayune Lake, however, you can see stones that are made up of pink and white feldspar mixed with tiny kernels of clear quartz. This is simple granite, a substance that has boiled up through the rocks of the old sea floor to form some of the higher, more spectacular peaks of the area.

After going through a beautiful wooded corridor of fir and pine for 0.3 mile, the trail meets another pathway heading off to the left, which eventually joins Little Picayune Creek. This junction is our turnaround point. The Pacific Crest Trail continues to make its way north, passing above Porcupine Lake and then Toad Lake, about 2 and 3 miles respectively. For anyone who has the time and energy, Toad Lake in particular is a superb destination.

LITTLE CASTLE LAKE

Distance: 1.8 miles
Location: Follow Lake Road west from the town of Mount
Shasta. Past Siskiyou Lake is a marked turnoff to the left for
Castle Lake. From the parking area at Castle Lake walk up an
old gravel roadbed, which runs east along the north side of the
lake. Our trail begins at the northeast corner of the lake and
climbs up along the east side.

The Little Castle Lake walk begins at Castle Lake, an alpine jewel
set in a polished granite basin that seems to become more beautiful
the longer you linger. A sheer wall of rock, part of a glacial cirque,
plunges into the lake from the south side, while the rest of the
water is framed by a few scattered patches of grass and rounded
slabs of granite that continue to be thrust up from inside the earth
by the freezing and thawing cycles of the north country winters.

The trail up to Little Castle Lake begins at the northeast
corner of the big lake. Though less than a mile, it is a fairly steep
climb. Frequent rest stops on the way up allow you to study Castle
Lake from a new angle, to peer down through the clear cobalt
waters at the features only visible from this high perspective. Castle Lake, by the way, is clear for a reason. A lake that is surrounded
by layers of soil tends to be nourished by organic debris continually
washed into the water. This nourishment provides food for the
development of algae populations, the tiny organisms that tend to
give lake water a cloudy appearance. But the rocks and scree at
Castle Lake offer little nourishment, a condition that, along with
cold temperatures, tends to keep algal populations to a minimum.

Take note of the changes that occur as you climb higher on
this pathway. As is typical with any mountain environment, areas
exposed to harsher conditions may have familiar species of plants
growing in a stunted form. Shrubs become smaller and stem flowers
shorter. This size reduction is not only due to the fact that short
growing seasons mean less growth, but it is a very practical method
of protecting the plant against the drying, tissue-damaging effects
of strong winds. Notice the way the trees growing on the exposed
ridges here are not only smaller than their counterparts down lower
but also tend to become very twisted.

227

The hardy larkspur—not a favorite of ranchers, as it is noxious to cattle—can be seen both high and low along this trail. Also look for currant bushes, pussy paws, and red columbine. As you climb the final crest before reaching Little Castle Lake itself, you can find small heathers growing among the smooth granite boulders. If you were intending to take a dip in Little Castle Lake, you will be disappointed, since you could probably let out all your breath, lie with your back on the bottom of the lake, and find your face still out of the water.

Though Little Castle Lake was never as big or as deep as its big sister below, things used to be different. This is a perfect example of lake succession, where over the years, bodies of water tend to turn into terra firma, one day sprouting wild flowers instead of water bugs. Unlike Castle Lake below, Little Castle Lake has had a fairly steady stream of nutrients entering it from the surrounding soil. Algae populations developed, and seeds from water plants sprouted in whatever areas were shallow enough to allow their growth. As plants died each year, they sank and became part of the bottom of the lake. These sediment layers built up year after year, until eventually the entire lake was shallow enough to support water plants. At that point the water vegetation shifted into high gear, and it is right now filling in Little Castle Lake faster than ever. Eventually there will be no water here at all—just a rich meadow filled with the kinds of plants that you see growing along the far shore of the lake. With a slow wave of nature's wand, it will one day be as if Little Castle Lake never existed at all.

If you go past the lake a short way and look to your left, you'll be able to see Mount Shasta off to the northeast and behind it Alder Creek Ridge in the Klamath National Forest. A short distance to the southeast (hidden from the lake) lie the Castle Crags, a fantastic collection of massive boulders and soaring granite spires. While such granite intrusions are not rare here, what makes Castle Crags unique is that the blanket of soil that once covered them has washed away. There are undoubtedly countless other such wonders in this area that have yet to be exposed by the relentlessly probing fingers of erosion.

LAKE ELEANORE

Distance: 1.8 miles
Location: Head west up Swift Creek from State Highway 3 near Trinity Center Picnic Area, on the west side of Clair Engle Lake. Signs are located along the roadway to mark turnoffs. A small, aging trail sign points out the pathway, which runs due north. (Note: It is recommended that you drive to this trail head armed with a Shasta-Trinity National Forest map.)

Before going on any walk deep in a national forest, it's a good idea these days to give the local ranger station a call to check on the conditions of the roads leading to the trail head, as well as on the trail itself. (For the Lake Eleanore walk call the Weaverville Ranger Station at 916-623-2121.) Logging operations are creating more and more roads, and a severe lack of Forest Service funding does not allow for producing either updated maps or adequate signs to direct the visitor to the proper place. Disturbing rumors were going around about increased logging in this area, which could create confusion for anyone trying to find the Lake Eleanore trail head.

The walk, although very short, is extremely pleasant. There are corn lilies, willows, and a variety of wild flowers along the lakeshore, and along the trail, ceanothus, currant bushes, and an occasional madrone spreading beneath the high canopies of Jeffrey pine and incense-cedar. The beautiful incense-cedar (which is really not a true cedar at all) never occurs in pure stands but is always mixed with other conifers in an arrangement like the one you see here. This is the tree from which nearly all pencils are manufactured, since it is easy to cut the wood in any direction without its splintering. The heartwood of the tree is used to produce the fine, aromatic boards used in cedar chests and closets.

Many of the Indian tribes for whom acorn meal was a very important dietary staple used incense-cedar in another way. Ground acorns are initially very bitter, primarily due to the quantity of tannin present in the nuts. More than just tasting bad, tannin can also cause serious digestive problems. To rid their acorn meal of tannin-caused bitterness, Indians would typically dig a shallow depression in sand, place the meal in the bottom of the hole, and pour fresh water over it. More water would be added as the tannin-laced liquid percolated through the sand; the entire process would take about two hours. Boughs of incense-cedar laid on top of the ground acorns at the start of this operation primarily dispersed the water across the entire surface of the meal and also imparted a subtle aromatic taste to the final product that was favored by the people.

Up the trail 0.4 mile you can catch views of Clair Engle Lake through the trees off to the right. (Clair Engle was a U.S. senator from California.) The Trinity River was dammed here in 1965 as part of a multimillion-dollar project to transfer its water under a small section of the Klamath Mountains into the Sacramento River, then to be carried via the elaborate Central Valley Project into the southern part of the state. Recreational opportunities aside, Clair Engle Lake is a monument to the long-held Western preference for spending millions of federal dollars to manipulate nature in order to sustain growth and profit, rather than developing a system of sound conservation practices that would help to preserve an irreplaceable wild heritage.

Lake Eleanore itself is small but a true gem—a lake rich with nutrients, supporting so much life that one day the sediments from dying plants will turn it into a marsh, then a meadow, and finally a forest like the one you see around you. For the time being, though, it is truly the water of serenity, leading the quietest of lives in a hidden pocket of the high woodlands. Berry bushes and corn lilies line the trickling outlet stream on the far side of the lake; small fish do cartwheels in the evening air, snapping at a layer of insects that hover above the glassy surface of the water.

To the north and west of Lake Eleanore lies the Salmon-Trinity Alps Primitive Area, parts of it accessible from the same pathway you are on now. More than 200,000 acres of rugged, glaciated mountain country are there, where even the most demanding seeker of solitude can lose himself among a tapestry of alpine lakes, meadows, snowfields, and sheer, snow-capped mountains. You should be aware that the deeply eroded canyon systems of the Salmon-Trinity Alps make hiking a strenuous proposition. But even if you never set foot in this high, lonesome country, it's exciting to think that places like Forbidden and Rattlesnake lakes, Little Grizzly Creek, and the China Gardens are up there, forever wild and waiting.

230

Several kinds of birds can be seen around Lake Eleanore as well as on the pathway to the trail head. Watch carefully for flycatchers, woodpeckers, warblers, and chickadees, and listen for the raucous calling of the Steller's jays.

North Sierras—
South Cascades

LAKE EILER

Distance: 4.4 miles

Location: From State Highway 89 north of Lassen National Park, turn west approximately 3.4 miles north of Bridge Campground. Follow signs for Thousand Lakes Wilderness. (Note: The Lassen National Forest map is highly recommended for the drive to the trail head. The dirt road up is steep in places. The last mile to the trail head, which comes after a right-hand turn off a graded dirt road, is appropriate for cars or pickup trucks only.)

Lake Eiler is located in the northeast section of the Thousand Lakes Wilderness, a small but beautiful slice of high country perched on a soaring crest of mountains that border the east side of the Central Valley.

With the exception of a short climb that begins about 0.1 mile down the trail, the walk to Lake Eiler is nice and flat, a wonderful opportunity for people of virtually any level of physical ability to sample the offerings that beckon on the edge of a high forest wilderness.

If you've done much walking elsewhere in Lassen National Forest, perhaps you'll notice that lodgepole pines, as well as red and white fir trees, are more common here, while the great stands of incense-cedar and ponderosa pine have been all but left behind in the lower elevations. Firs—the only conifers in America that bear their cones upright on the branches—tend to like high, cold, well-drained environments. (Much of the soil here is volcanic, and water percolates through it easily.) While lodgepoles can also thrive

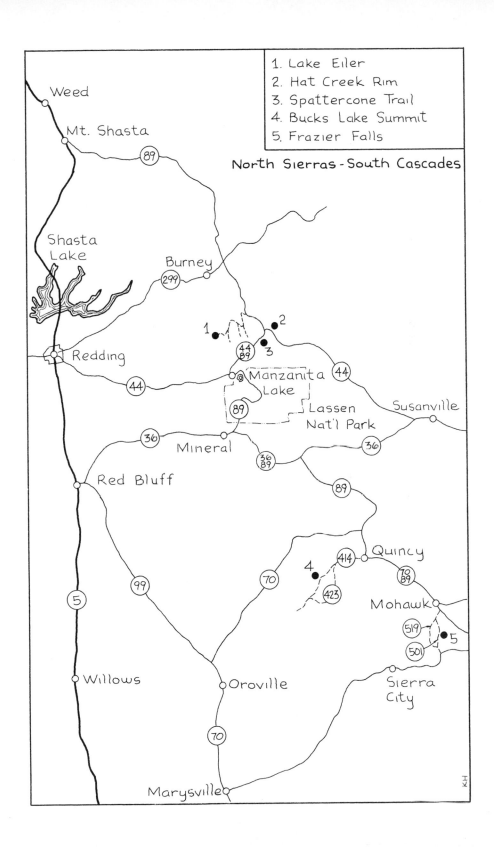

1. Lake Eiler
2. Hat Creek Rim
3. Spattercone Trail
4. Bucks Lake Summit
5. Frazier Falls

North Sierras - South Cascades

Weed

Mt. Shasta

89

Shasta Lake

Burney

299

1

2

44
89

3

Redding

44

Manzanita Lake

44

89

Susanville

Lassen Nat'l Park

36

Mineral

36
89

36

Red Bluff

89

Quincy

4

414

70
89

70

423

Mohawk

99

519

5

5

501

Willows

Oroville

Sierra City

70

Marysville

KH

here, unlike the firs, it is difficult for their seedlings to sprout in a mature forest where there is a shortage of sun. Once the old lodgepoles within these fir forests die, it is unlikely that they will be able to come back until a sunny spot opens up again.

Take a look at the dead trees lying along the trail, many of which have been toppled by the rampages of winter. The increased number of storms at this elevation not only knocks more trees down, but the moisture they release also helps the forces of decomposition turn them back into soil, where the minerals and nutrients they once contained will one day be taken up by still other life forms. If you look closely at one of these trees, you may be able to see signs that one or more of the breakdown processes are already at work. Lodgepoles or Jeffrey pines that have fallen fairly recently may have nothing more than a series of smooth holes drilled in their bark from bees or boring beetles. But if the outer portion of the tree has been eaten away, leaving only the center—what is called the heartwood—then you may see tiny chambers that have been excavated by hundreds of termites and carpenter ants. If the tree has been dead for a very long time, long enough to have wood like sponge or powder, then the tentacles of fungi have been at it, secreting enzymes that break down the tree's last remaining cellular structures.

Life and death here are happening at a particular rate, to a collection of plants and animals that are quite different from the ones you left behind down in Hat Creek Valley. In many ways the out-of-doors is rather like a collection of rooms, each with slightly different climatic and geological conditions. Rather than a tooth-and-nail struggle for survival, plant communities, as well as the birds, mammals, and insects they support, tend to evolve in a way that allows them to take advantage of those rooms that are not already overcrowded with tenants.

About 1.5 miles in on the left side of the trail you will see the first of several ponds, typical of many of the area's "thousand lakes." Each of these small bodies of water has different characteristics, but all are in some stage of going from liquid to solid. There was a time when many of them were deep enough at their centers to prohibit the growth of any bottom-rooted plants. As the willows and corn lilies that grew around the perimeter of the ponds died, they began slowly to fill in the edges of the depression. Before long, even the center of the pond had received enough sediment from dying pond lilies and water weeds to make it possible for rooting plants to take hold there. One day there will be no pond left here at all. Can you see any open meadows along the trail that may once have been filled with water?

Lake Eiler lies just a short way beyond the point where our trail meets another pathway heading off to the left toward Barrett Lakes (keep going straight). Just past here you will see the ever-present colonizer, manzanita, lining the trail in scattered patches. If we return to our analogy about the out-of-doors being a series of rooms with different environmental conditions, the first reaction of anyone who is familiar with the California landscape is that the manzanita isn't at all particular about what room it gets! It may be more accurate to say that after the "rooms" are remodeled—through fire, logging, or disease—the manzanita ends up beating everyone else to the check-in desk. There are about forty different species of this plant, each very good at mastering the conditions of the particular environment in which it is found. The word manzanita, by the way, is Spanish for "little apple," which refers to the apple-shaped fruit produced by the plant during late summer.

Two trails will allow you a close exploration of Lake Eiler. The main pathway that you've been walking follows along the south shore of the lake, eventually joining a trail that runs southwest into the heart of the wilderness. Another path leaves the main trail at the east end of the lake and follows the shore for 0.4 mile. A fine open area is at the end of this path, perfect for picnics or quiet relaxation.

Much of Lake Eiler is framed by fir forest, with the northwest corner dominated by a large talus slope of volcanic rock running all the way down to the water's edge. This rocky slope is slowly being split into smaller and smaller pieces by the freezing and thawing action of water in winter. Someday plants and tree seedlings will begin to grab hold of the hillside, colonizing it until it looks very much like the vegetated slope that you can see just to the south.

HAT CREEK RIM

Distance: 3 miles

Location: Turn east onto State Highway 44 from State Highway 89, approximately 14 miles north of Lassen National Park. About 2.5 miles from this turnoff, watch for a dirt road heading north. (There should be a sign here for Plum Valley Reservoir). After making this left turn, make another left at the second dirt road you come to, just a short way from the highway. Walk north from the camping/picnic ground, following markers for the Pacific Crest Trail.

The Hat Creek area is one of the most beautiful in all of Northern California, and this trail, perched on the edge of an escarpment overlooking the entire drainage area, is a pure pleasure to walk. You will again be on the Pacific Crest Trail, which is a major recreation path that runs 2,600 miles from the Canadian border to Mexico. Be sure to take sunscreen and drinking water with you, since much of this walk crosses areas that are fully exposed to the summer sun.

The very beginning of the Hat Creek Rim walk is through a stately forest of ponderosa and Jeffrey pine. It seems that there are no trees that better invoke fanciful images of the unspoiled West than these two. Jeffrey pine extends into higher mountain zones than ponderosa pine, but there are many places such as here in Lassen National Forest where they occur together. (They are described under the Scott Mountain walk.) Both have thick, reddish bark that is very effective in protecting the trees against fire, and each bears its 7-to-10-inch needles in bundles of three. (The easiest way to distinguish the two is by their cones; the ponderosa has much smaller ones, with spines that stick outward, instead of down.)

During the 1960s it was discovered that there is yet another, rather unfortunate trait shared by the ponderosa and Jeffrey—one first noticed by scientists studying the two species in the San Bernardino Mountains northeast of Los Angeles. Both trees are very sensitive to smog. In fact, when the first surveys were conducted in 1970 to determine the extent of the damage from such pollution, it was found that more than a million of these great trees were already either sick or dying.

About 0.1 mile along the trail you will come to a faint road heading straight north. Stay on the Pacific Crest Trail, which makes a gentle turn to the left. In another 0.2 mile the pathway breaks out onto the edge of the Hat Creek Rim, a fault escarpment that offers stunning panoramic views of the wild country to the west and north. Directly opposite you on the other side of Hat Creek Valley is the Thousand Lakes Wilderness. The two tallest mountains within this wilderness are Magee Peak, at 8,550 feet, and just to the north of that, Crater Peak, at 8,677 feet. Both stand sentinel over a beautiful glaciated valley that offers superb hiking opportunities.

At the bottom of Hat Creek Valley and slightly to your left is the village of Old Station, which in 1856 and 1857 was a way station for the California Stage. But for the occasional reflections of cars along Highway 89, it's not too difficult to stand here and imagine the old rumble-buggies rolling northward along Hat Creek, a cloud of fine volcanic dust licking at their wooden wheels.

As you make your way along the rim, the feature that commands more attention than any other is mighty Mount Shasta, which lies approximately 60 miles north-northwest of where you now stand. A million or so years ago, a great hodgepodge of molten rock began to boil and blow out of cracks and fissures in the earth, no doubt to the complete wonderment of the strange birds and great mammoths that roamed the region. Before it was all over, the valleys and rolling hill country of the Cascade Plateau had been transformed into the magnificent peaks of the Cascade Mountains. Mount Shasta itself had many fits of activity during this period; it had spewed out virtual rivers of lava and rained great clouds of gray volcanic ash over hundreds of square miles of land. The volcano's last eruption is thought to have been about two hundred years ago.

At 14,161 feet above sea level, Shasta is only 332 feet lower than Mount Whitney in the Sierras, which is the highest peak in the continental United States. Even though Shasta is slightly less in elevation, it is thought by many to be much greater in stature. While Whitney is surrounded by other peaks that are 500 to 1,500 feet lower, Shasta stands alone, towering 10,000 feet above the surrounding terrain.

In 0.75 mile you will be walking through open grassy areas that are liberally sprinkled with a beautiful yellow sunflower that

237

sports large, oblong, basal leaves. This is wyethia, or mule ears, of which there are several different species. This particular plant was undoubtedly important to local Indian tribes, although some of the most complete records of the uses for mule ears concern a sister plant found in the mountain ranges of the central coast. The Yuki, Wailaki, and Yokia Indians of that region ate the seeds, stems, and young leaves of the local wyethia. The plant's fibrous roots were especially important. Prepared as either a decoction or a poultice, they were used to treat stomach complaints, rheumatism, and headaches, as well as to help heal cuts and burns. They were also reported to be effective in the treatment of skin rashes caused by poison oak.

In about 1.2 miles you'll cross a fence line, and in another 0.3 mile the trail makes a right turn away from the rim. This is our turnaround point. In this area you can usually find paintbrush dotting the dry ground with splashes of crimson. Notice how many of these flowers are growing beneath stands of rabbit brush, a tidy arrangement that allows the paintbrush to utilize some of the moisture gained by the roots of its shrubby neighbor.

On the way back, Mount Shasta will have been traded for a view of yet another beautiful volcano, 10,457-foot Mount Lassen. The northeast flank of Lassen is where Hat Creek originates, each spring running fast and furious through the valley below, swelled with a fresh, cold cargo of melted snow.

SPATTERCONE TRAIL

Distance: 2.5 miles
Location: On the east side of State Highway 89, approximately 12 miles north of Lassen National Park. The trail begins at a turnout area directly across from Hat Creek Campground.

As you'll note from the interpretive sign at the beginning of Spattercone Trail, you are entering what is believed to be the source of the great lava flows that less than two thousand years ago, wrapped the Hat Creek Valley in a thick blanket of black basalt. Although much of the area north of here has been colonized by

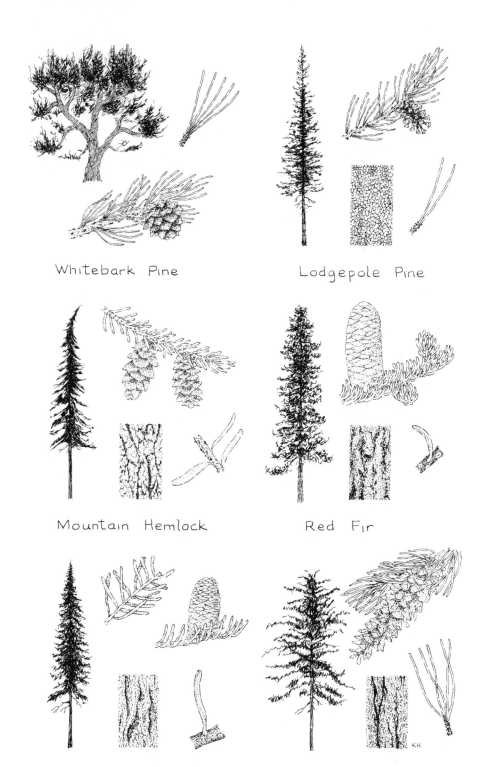

Whitebark Pine

Lodgepole Pine

Mountain Hemlock

Red Fir

White Fir

Sugar Pine

pines, the layers of volcanic rock that underlie these forests still have an influence on their character. Most noticeable, perhaps, is what you *don't* see. Many of the ground plants that would normally grow among the pine trees, called understory vegetation, cannot survive on volcanic ground because the rocks are so porous that moisture seeps quickly through the ground and out of reach of most root systems. This will change as the soil base becomes thick enough to retain water for longer periods of time; unfortunately, soil here is built at a rate of less than 1 inch every two hundred years.

The Forest Service has made this into a fine educational trail, placing signs along the path that identify many of the area's more common plants and geologic features. We'll take this concept a bit further and discuss a few of the traits attached to some of the names. Although this walk is short, it is quite rocky in those places where it crosses old lava flows. People with weak ankles will want to be especially careful.

One of the first residents with a name tag you'll come to is the magnificent ponderosa pine, the common king of the western forests, which takes its name from the Latin *ponderosus*, meaning "heavy" or "massive." This tree is one of the more drought-resistant conifers in America. Consequently it's often the last pine you'll see on your way down out of the mountains and into the desert and the first one to welcome you on your way back up. What makes the ponderosa (also called yellow pine) able to beat the dry conditions of this porous basalt ground is its extensive root system. During the first year of growth, a seedling will typically develop taproots that are seven times as long as the above-ground tree. In a few short years the tiny ponderosa will already have sunk its fingers 4 to 6 feet into the earth. Chipmunks, squirrels, and several types of birds make regular feasts out of ponderosa seeds, though many Indian tribes considered them too small for regular harvesting.

A very similar tree, the Jeffrey pine, is a short way down the path. From a distance it is difficult to tell the two apart, but anyone armed with the senses of smell and touch should be able to make the distinction. The fresh bark of Jeffrey pine has a scent that, depending on your smeller, brings to mind either vanilla or lemon or pineapple, or perhaps some combination of the three. In addition, the cones of the Jeffrey are much bigger than those of the ponderosa, with spines on the scales that point downward instead of outward. Picking up a ponderosa cone and squeezing it in your hand will hurt; doing the same with a Jeffrey cone will not.

A little farther on are currant, which, along with related gooseberry, have formed many a tasty dish for California Indian and pioneer settler alike. The nearby bitterbrush is not so tasty, at least to humans. To deer, pronghorns, elk, and bighorn sheep, however, it is a gourmet delight. If you were to sit next to one of these bushes long enough, you'd almost certainly see a golden-mantled ground squirrel, chipmunk, or deer mouse come calling to carry off the seeds of the bitterbrush for future dining.

The trail continues past the remnants of spattercones, lava domes, and collapsed lava tubes. These domes were formed as thick, pasty lava pushed upward, popping off large slabs of rock from the outer crust of the earth. The lava tubes are the result of the fact that lava tends to cool from the outside in. This means that there may be streams of lava flowing inside of a hardened outer shell. A wonderful example of this phenomenon can be seen at Subway Cave, a very large lava tube located about 3 miles north of here on the east side of the highway. (Bring a good lantern or flashlight.)

Climb up through the rocky basalt dotted with manzanita and mountain mahogany until you reach the South Vista, about 0.6 mile into the walk. Here you will have a superb view of Lassen Peak. Lassen is the southernmost of the large volcanoes making up the California portion of the Cascade Mountains. Known as a plug-dome volcano, it was formed when thick lava pushed its way out of a vent located on the side of another large volcano. This extinct volcano, known as Tehama, sank slowly back into the earth when the molten rock that was inside it withdrew from the interior of the cone.

Plug-dome volcanoes are essentially built from hot magma pushing a skin of earth outward, and they do not have large craters in the top that lava can flow out of to form a mountain. This is not to say that such volcanoes do not have eruptions. Beginning in 1914, Lassen began to blow its top in episodes of varying intensity that lasted for more than seven years. The most violent of these was in 1915, when a giant blast of steam and rock fragments rose

25,000 feet into the sky, forming an ominous dark cloud that was easily seen in Sacramento, 125 miles to the south.

There are several side trails on the upper portion of the walk that will introduce you to a variety of volcanic features. Take a moment to study the rocks; notice how they differ in color, texture, and weight from those that make up other areas of the state. They, along with the steaming vents, and hot springs of the region, remind us that the earth is an ongoing, rather than a finished, work of art.

BUCK'S LAKE SUMMIT

Distance: 4 miles
Location: Approximately 12 miles west of Quincy on Buck's Lake Road. The trail begins on the north side of the highway, just west of the large, paved, summit parking area.

Although the outbound portion of the Buck's Lake Summit walk is an uphill affair, it is nevertheless a fairly easy grade, manageable by just about anyone who is willing to take his time. The route offers shade only in a couple of places, however, so be sure to protect yourself from the effects of the summer sun.

Almost as soon as you leave the highway you'll be entering the Buck's Lake Wilderness, a rather new preserve that gets very little use compared to other wilderness areas. If peace and quiet are what you're after, then this is the place. You'll be climbing up a hillside covered with typical scrub vegetation, much of it having taken firm hold on the land after a fire burned through the area several decades ago. A few young trees can be seen growing in the drainage ravines, but it will obviously be a long time before a true forest will return.

The trail winds back on itself, taking you higher and higher toward the peak that lies just to the northeast of the summit parking area. At 0.25 mile in there is a small spring that runs a short distance along the path. Notice how much larger the same vegetation is here, compared to the size it was farther down the trail. At most locations on this hillside the battle for moisture is made more

242

intense by the fact that the slope has a southern exposure. This means that more sun falls here than on those hills that are oriented toward the north, east, or west. During the winter you'll find less snow on this slope than on the ones across the highway. Likewise, the rain that falls during the summer tends to evaporate much faster.

As you make your way up the path, you can also see the dramatic difference in the size and variety of plant life growing in the small drainage areas and ravines that channel summer rainwater. Even the slightly different exposure of the sides of these drainages can be enough to allow plants to grow there that would not survive on the main flank of the hill.

A mile into the walk some fine views open up to the west. In the distance, beyond Buck's Lake, is a set of pink cliffs. This is part of a massive block of granite that at one time was fiery hot liquid lying beneath a collection of active volcanoes. Volcanic activity subsided and the dark lava cooled. Over thousands of years these fairly soft volcanic rocks eroded away, leaving blocks of granite exposed.

Many of the rocks in this area were shaked and baked in a most unmerciful manner. Two hundred million years ago the dark slates and schists you see in these mountains were part of the ocean floor, a collection of layers made up of sediments that had fallen to the bottom of the sea. Rather than becoming simple sedimentary rocks, however, they ended up being compacted under terrific force as the sliding floor of the ocean collided with the continental shelf. Millions of years later, they were heated to fantastic temperatures. The result of all this heat and pressure is metamorphic rock, which resembles very little the layers that were slowly formed at the bottom of the sea so long ago.

In 1.25 miles you pass a full-fledged stream environment, which on a hot summer day can seem as welcome as an oasis in the desert. Spring-fed streams such as this one are actually kept going by winter snows. Each year much of the snowpack percolates down through the soil into underground reservoirs, where it is released throughout the year in the form of springs.

A crucial factor in this "spring equation" is the presence of plants or trees. Without them rain and snowmelt would simply run over the surface of the land, eroding it severely in the process. Vegetation slows down these cascades, allowing the water to percolate into the soil instead of merely across it. You can best see the severe effect of unchecked runoff in the desert, where sandy soil void of vegetation allows violent flash floods to form, with very little of the water staying where it is needed the most. It was primarily because of this very important effect of trees and plants that the national forest system came into being.

The path continues to wind upward, crossing this same stream again at a higher point. Roughly 0.25 mile from this second crossing the trail emerges on the south side of a broad knoll, offering superb views to the east, south, and west. This is our turn-around point. Just about 7 miles in front of you, toward the southeast, is the Middle Fork of the Feather River, a watercourse that once had miners feverishly crawling over every foot of it looking for the "color" they hoped would make them rich. They were also up in the high peaks that you can see beyond the Feather, chiseling roads into the sides of mountains and running gravel through their wooden rockers along the streams that fell from the shadows of Mount Etna, Pilot Peak, Beartrap Mountain, and Mount Fillmore.

On a very clear day you can look past this distant line of peaks much farther, to a snow-covered slice of the high Sierras not far from Lake Tahoe. The gold seekers were here too. Miners, thousands of them, poured over Carson Pass, planning to stay just long enough to make a few thousand in gold and take it back to the farm in Indiana or New York, to the families who sat up at night in their white wooden houses and waited for some kind of word.

FRAZIER FALLS

Distance: 1 mile

Location: From State Highway 89, 1.5 miles from the town of Graeagle, head south on Forest Road 519 toward Gold Lake. Approximately 2 miles from this turn, take a left on Forest Road 501, and follow it south about 4.5 miles to Frazier Falls, on left side of the road. (Note: This road turns to dirt and continues south for 2 miles, coming back out of Forest Road 519 at the northeast corner of Gold Lake. Large vehicles would do better to approach Frazier Falls from this southern end.)

The path to Frazier Falls, although short, contains a delightful array of mountain spectacles. Massive hummocks of bare rock are softened by rich pockets of red fir and Jeffrey pine, and the streams are flanked by splashes of wild flowers. You will be walking on what is known as the Sierra Nevada granite batholith, an enormous collection of granite fields that actually make up the spine of this mighty mountain range. It is this rock, and the way that it breaks down under the thumb of weather, that is responsible for creating the unique, soaring grandeur that we have come to associate with the high country of the Sierras.

Granite has a tendency to break down in two important ways. Sometimes it forms cracks, called joints, which basically run parallel to one another either vertically or horizontally. Look for this jointing in the large blocks that frame much of the first 0.2 mile of the trail. Small cracks are often pushed farther apart by tenacious tree roots, in this particular area, those of the Jeffrey pine.

Another kind of breakdown caused by weathering, which is much less understood, is exfoliation. Under this type of splitting, the granite actually peels off in layers. Sharp edges are rounded in the process. This action is much the same as peeling away the layers of an onion, and it is responsible for the dramatic loaf-shape domes common in the Yosemite region. Though such weathering is continually at work in these mountains, it's important to remember that these rocks are actually quite young compared to the granite found in, say, the Rocky Mountains, and they are therefore breaking down at a comparatively slow rate.

Take a close look at the small stones lining this path. The

245

main visible components are quartz, which look like pieces of glass, and chalky-looking bits of white, pink, or gray feldspar. Most batches of this rock also contain varying amounts of black or brown mica, horneblend, or pyroxene. Generally speaking, it is the concentration of these latter minerals that determine whether the rock surface appears light or dark. On occasion you will see a thick brown or dark red wavy stripe coursing through the Sierra granite, which is likely the remains of old sedimentary rock that once lay on the floor of the Pacific Ocean.

This area was first thoroughly explored by white men during the gold rush of the middle 1800s. Streams and rivers that carried gold-bearing gravel, along with certain types of opaque quartz veins found in slabs of granite, are the signs that made many a restless miner stop long enough to set up a wooden rocker for sifting gravel or else swing a pickax for a couple of days. The name of the game was to work fast and furiously, to find the "color" before the snow began to fly.

For the thousands of miners who worked rivers and streams at elevations of 3,000 and 4,000 feet, the most frustrating aspect of winter was that it greatly reduced the volume of water available to them for their streamside operations. For those who chose to hang out at the 5,000-to-6,000-foot level, however, winter was much more a force to be reckoned with. To make their way across the snow the miners used what were known as Norwegian snowshoes— thick boards 10 to 14 foot long that could be strapped to the feet in much the way that cross-country skis are used today. Off across the powder-laden slopes they would go, most armed with a long stick that they used as both brake and steering rudder. It is thought to have been the men of nearby La Porte, Onion Valley, and Johnsville that first had the notion to hold races with one another, creating what many historians believe to have been the first competitive skiing events in the world.

In a short 0.5 mile you will reach the overlook point to Frazier Falls, a silvery ribbon of water plunging head over heels toward its rendezvous with the Feather River, 6 miles to the north. Since we've been speaking so much of gold and miners, you might wonder how the Frazier River is for such riches. As the forty-niners found out rather quickly, streams that flowed over smooth, glacier-

246

polished granite, like this particular stretch of stream, were rarely worth wasting their time on. Far better to find water with rough, irregular bottoms, that, just like the old rockers and sluice boxes, tended to act as traps for the heavy particles of gold. A few turns in the watercourse were nice, too, since gold tended to settle on the inside of curves.

Early visitors to this small stretch of the Frazier River would have had to have been satisfied with the sheer beauty of the place, which, even for a crusty old miner, is payment of a very special kind.

South-Central Sierras

SONORA PASS

Distance: 3.6 miles
Location: Take State Highway 108 to Sonora Pass. The parking area is located on the north side of the road. The trail takes off to the west from beside the rest rooms.

Welcome to the High Sierras. The Sonora Pass walk will take you through one of the most stunning pieces of high country on earth. Here is a land with snowfields that never yield to summer, where ice water trickles quietly past fresh gardens of primrose, paintbrush, and heather. The trees here grow thick and gnarled, huddled together like old men telling tales on a cold winter night. Surrounding the scene is a soaring, vertical world of granite and basalt, standing silent as the passing seasons etch line after line in the ancient mountain faces.

Near the beginning of this walk are many black-barked trees with checkerboard patterns on their trunks, standing sharp against the alpine sky like ballerinas frozen in the middle of a dance. These are western white pines, and, along with lodgepole pine, whitebark pine, and mountain hemlock, they form one of the last, successful attempts to stand upright in the face of a mountain winter.

The white pines here are the same as those eagerly sought after by lumbermen of the Northwest; they are cousins to *Pinus strobus* of the East, whose clear, easily worked wood has been prized since the days that the first colonists made their way into the woods of New England. Unfortunately, the white pines are under

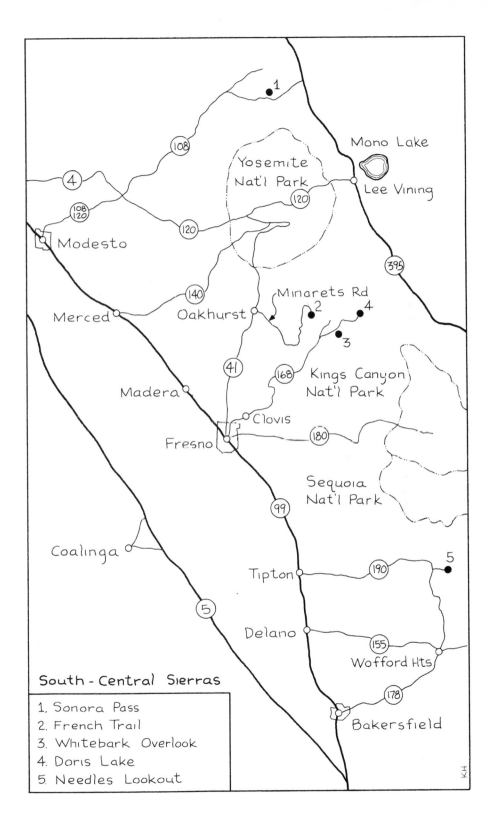

South - Central Sierras

1. Sonora Pass
2. French Trail
3. Whitebark Overlook
4. Doris Lake
5. Needles Lookout

heavy attack by a disease known as blister rust, a European fungus that was accidentally brought to the United States around the turn of the century. Strangely, this fungus needs two hosts in order to survive—the pines themselves and a currant or gooseberry shrub. Reproduction is a two-part affair, with the fungus in the pine producing airborne spores that then infect the leaves of the currant bushes, which produce a second level of spore, which in turn affects more pines. For this reason the Forest Service has launched extensive programs to eradicate currants or gooseberries growing in the same area as any susceptible pine species.

Near the snowfields that usually lie through midsummer along the first 0.5 mile of this walk, look for series of small, twisting ridges of fresh soil running along the ground. These are the signatures of pocket gophers, and they can be found written in alpine meadows throughout the West. When winter makes digging too difficult at the depth at which this tiny bulldozer normally works, he will instead conduct his business in the snowpack. Tunnels are excavated in the snow and then lined with soil from a nearby, workable digging. These soil casts sink to the ground during the spring melt, leaving the crisscross of tiny dirt hummocks that you see lying on the ground.

Pocket gophers spend most of their lives underground and are very sensitive to the vibrations caused by an approaching animal. So efficient are they at moving earth (one animal can dig a hundred feet of tunnel in a single night), that they form a very important link in the vegetative processes of an alpine meadow. Besides aerating the soil, the plants they carry down and the waste products they produce help to enrich the dirt. They also haul into the depths a great number of seeds, some of which end up sprouting as new plants.

Also on the snowfields along the first 0.5 mile of the walk, you may spot another strange phenomenon of the alpine world, pink snow. This is actually a tiny algae living inside a sturdy coat of pink-colored cells. It begins life during late spring, when the melting snowpack can provide enough water for the algae to grow. There are several explanations for the pink casings. A likely one is that the color is very effective in shielding the algal cells from the damaging effects of radiation. (At this elevation, the radiation level from the sun is many times higher than that found at lower altitudes.) Researchers have definitely established that the pink casement cells do concentrate airborne radiation. You may meet backpackers who actually eat pink snow, claiming that it has a pleasantly tart taste. A word of caution, though; for some people, too much pink snow acts as a strong laxative.

The wild flower lover should not expect to make too hasty progress along this trail, since bright palettes of color seem to show up around every bend. Keep an eye out for lupine, larkspur, scarlet gilia, mule ears, creeping penstemon, alpine forget-me-not, saxifrage, monkeyflower, phlox, and shooting stars.

The trail climbs steadily throughout this walk, but the steeper sections are always quickly relieved by a stretch of relatively level ground. Do keep in mind, however, that you're hoofing it at an elevation of more than 9,700 feet. Unless you are quite used to this, you will feel much more out of breath than you would were you at a lower altitude. Take your time; heaven knows you could never find a more perfect place just to sit and gawk.

At about 1 mile the trail begins to wind up in earnest toward a saddle that lies just north of where you parked. Here streams plunge down the faces of sheer cliffs. The rocks have been fractured into stunning collections of spires, looking like fortifications for some mythical mountain kingdom. Notice how plants and trees become shorter the higher you climb, until you reach a point where the sheering effects of winter winds have reduced plant life, even trees, to a world not more than a foot or two in height.

The view from the saddle, our turnaround point, is magnificent. To the east are Wolf Creek and Leavitt Meadow, where in 1853 a survey party struggled through the mountains looking for a railway route to connect San Francisco with the lands east of the great Sierra Divide. Beyond the meadows is range after range after range, some sporting scattered white coats of snow even in July, all looking bold and impenetrable. As I viewed this scene, my awe at the incredible beauty of the landscape was mixed with the slightest feeling of unease—perhaps an echo from a time not so long ago when such sights brought settlers to their knees, asking God for deliverance from nature's stern hand.

251

FRENCH TRAIL

Distance: 2.5 miles

Location: North of Oakhurst 3 miles on State Highway 41, head east toward Bass Lake. Follow this road approximately 5 miles past the lake and turn left toward South Fork. From here follow the winding Minarets Road north into the Sierra National Forest. Turn right at the sign for Mammoth Pool, taking a left in several miles at a fork in the road beside a small store to the east. You will soon come to a sign on the right side of the road that says French Trail. Turn left exactly opposite this sign, drive for 40 or 50 yards on a small dirt road and park. Join the trail by walking up around the switchback instead of climbing up the steeply eroded section that lies immediately in front of the parking area.

The French Trail begins with a short but steep climb through manzanita and incense-cedar, but in less than 0.2 mile it turns into a relatively flat walk framed on the left by beautiful park land that is ideal for watching deer feeding during late evening. A short distance past the meadow you will catch glimpses of the sheer, forbidding scarp of Chiquito Ridge to the west and further north a bold rise of granite peaks, which flank the southern end of Yosemite National Park. "The scenery is magnificently wild," reads one of the first-known diary entries describing the country before you. It was written by a soldier, Robert Eccleston, who in 1851 was one of the first Americans to lay eyes on this soaring landscape. Unfortunately, at the time, the scenery was one of the few pleasant aspects of Eccleston's assignments. He was here as a member of a battalion assigned the duty of rounding up the Yosemite Indians, who were more than a little unreceptive to the idea of being moved to a reservation in a place they didn't belong (along the Fresno River), led by chiefs that they didn't even know.

As you make your way along the French Trail, you'll be traversing a veritable garden of granitic rock. In fact, if you look beneath your feet, you'll see that you are helping to turn tiny pieces of it back into soil as you walk along this path. Granitic rock is composed of colored grains of quartz and feldspar that 150 million years ago turned to crystal as they cooled inside the earth in a fiery hot stew of magma. The rock of the Sierra is quite young compared to that of other mountain ranges, and as a result, much of it is still relatively impervious to weathering. The smooth, granite fields (called plutons) found here on the west side of the Sierras were once important as a source for construction material; a fair amount of it ended up as exterior surfaces on buildings in cities throughout the state.

It's important to remember that beside being affected by the composition of the granite, a great deal of the scene before you was sculpted by glaciers, a concept that John Muir was largely responsible for establishing during his incredibly thorough explorations of the Yosemite country during the 1870s. Remnants of glaciers still remain high in the mountains east of here, where they began forming more than a million years ago; some reach depths of several thousand feet. Gravity moved these massive blocks of ice and boulders down from the high country, scouring the landscape like a giant ice cream scoop.

Here along the lower part of the French Trail you can sometimes spot evidence of glaciers in another form, called erratics. These are large boulders composed of material completely different from anything surrounding them, and they arrived here from the high country by riding on the backs of glaciers. Particularly fine examples of erratics can be seen near Balloon Dome, about 10 miles from where you now stand, on the east side of the San Joaquin River.

Speaking of the San Joaquin, it is roughly parallel to your route of travel, hidden from sight by a narrow, 400-foot ridge that runs to the northeast. Hudson's Bay Company trappers made their way along this watercourse during the late 1820s and early 1830s, as well as the famous trapper Kit Carson. The area did not prove to be particularly rich in beaver and had a brief rest from any type of harvesting until about twenty years later, when the cry of "gold!" rang down the valley walls. Miners new to the area were often told that the San Joaquin contained so many riches that during the spring runoff, gold dust washed in sheets onto the Central Valley. Like most such rumors, this one was about as far off the mark as you could get. As one French fortune seeker commented in a letter to a Paris newspaper, "as with almost everything that is said about California: one can find out the truth only in the place itself."

At 0.5 mile into the walk you will gain a slight divide, with a flat spot on the left that affords striking views of the magnificent granite spires and abrupt escarpments of the country to the west and northwest. Just past this view area, about 30 yards after crossing between the cut trunk of a fallen pine, the trail becomes faint. The path dips down to the left here and then continues on in the original direction. This is a relatively short section in which you may become confused, but those who do not feel comfortable navigating it can turn around here for a fine round-trip walk of 1 mile. Those who continue on will come upon a pleasant, wooded drainage area at 0.7 mile, and 0.2 mile after that, a T junction located in a fine oak forest. This is the recommended turnaround point.

This walk is quite exposed to the sun, so be sure to carry water with you if you are making the trek during the heat of the day. Photographers should plan to hit the trail in the early morning; the distant peaks off to the left will light up with a flush of apricot, turning a rich gold as the sun tops the high ridge lying immediately to the east.

WHITEBARK OVERLOOK

Distance: 2 miles
Location: Take State Highway 168 east to the top of Kaiser Pass. Park on the west side of the highway and follow the signed road east toward the overlook.

The old road to the Whitebark Overlook winds its way through an open pine forest, coming out in 1 mile at a vista point that provides extraordinary views of the striking high country to the northwest. Because you are on a four-wheel-drive road you may see an occasional jeep or truck rumble by, but the traffic is rarely heavy enough to distract you from the grandeur of the surroundings.

The overlook at our turnaround point derives its name from the five-needled whitebark pine, a hardy conifer that surely must be among the two or three most indomitable trees in America. Whitebarks are masters at growing in the scantest amounts of gla-

Yellow - bellied Marmot

Mule Deer

Pocket Gopher

Meadow Mouse

Pika

Golden-mantled Ground Squirrel

cial soil and under the most severe climatical conditions to be found anywhere in the state. At this rather protected location the whitebark grows into a full-bodied tree from 20 to 40 feet tall. On the tops of high, exposed mountains, however, a whitebark several centuries old will appear as a 2- or 3-foot-high creeping shrub, pinned to a prone position by the bitter hand of winter.

Such small, shrubby alpine versions of normally erect trees are known as *krummholz,* a German word that means "elfin timber." Conditions high in the mountains are usually too severe for krummholz to produce its own seed; nearly all of the trees that you see hugging the earth at such elevations have sprouted from seeds carried up from lower elevations by the wind. Such propagation is a chancy affair at best, since the seed must first land in a place that offers complete protection from the searing winter winds, usually on the lee side of a large boulder. Once the tree reaches the height of the rock that has sheltered it, it will begin to grow laterally, new growth sprouting only from the most sheltered side of the plant. In this way the whitebark will literally "travel" across the tundra in the same direction as the prevailing winter winds.

For some mountain Indian tribes the seeds of the whitebark pine were a source of food, and you may see a Clark's nutcracker flitting through the branches of this forest looking for just such a meal. Whether man or beast, though, eating these seeds requires real effort, since the cones of the tree never really open but release their bounty only through the slow process of decay.

Look closely at the lower branches of the young pine trees growing along this roadway. On some you will see accumulations of mottled black or brown branch tips, which look as though they've been dipped in molasses. During the spring these limbs were pinned against the moist ground by heavy snow packs, enabling a dark fungus to attack the needles.

The lodgepole pine, also lining this roadway, is the only pine in this region whose needles grow in bundles of two, and its cones, at $\frac{3}{4}$ to 2 inches, are smaller than those of any other western pine. Many of the standing dead snags you see along this walk are lodgepoles, killed either by pine beetles or needle-miner moths, the first destroying the tree by larvae eating through the needles, and the second by larvae boring tunnels beneath the bark. (This latter insect leaves distinct grooves, which you can still see etched in the snags' weathered trunks.) These dead trees provide homes for birds such as the Williamson's sapsucker and three-toed woodpecker, and hawks can often be seen perched quietly in their upper branches.

By the way, you will run across many lakes, campgrounds, streams, and other features that bear the name Tamarack. In fact, there are no tamaracks (also known as western larch) even close to the Sierra Nevada; the name actually refers to lodgepole pine. It is not known precisely how the lodgepole came to be called tamarack, although John Muir often referred to them by this name.

Into the walk 0.8 mile there is a fairly steep climb, but your efforts up this 0.2-mile stretch will be rewarded by stunning views from Whitebark Overlook, perched 9,400 feet high on Kaiser Ridge. Standing at the vista point, line yourself up with Lake Thomas A. Edison, the long body of water lying about 9 miles to the northwest. The large tongue of land to the right of the lake is Bear Ridge, which climbs gently to the northwest until it reaches the sheer southern flank of the Mono Divide. This grand, 12,000-to-13,000-foot ridge forms a gently curving crescent running through the middle of the John Muir Wilderness. The Pacific Crest Trail winds among the dozens of icy streams and dazzling blue glacial lakes of this wild high country, and is located just about 1 mile past the far end of Lake Edison.

Lake Edison lies in a lush area known as Vermillion Valley, which was a layover place for the men of the famous Whitney Survey of 1864. This small group of stalwart geologists were the first to make detailed maps of much of this country, and in the process they gave names to many of the mountains before you.

There is truly an abundance of water running off this high line of the Sierra Nevada, a fact that did not go unnoticed by Southern California Edison power company. Besides what you can see from here, another large body of water, Florence Lake, lies just behind the high ridges to the east of where you now stand. All of these lakes have been tied together through a system that carries water *under* Kaiser Ridge and into Huntington Lake, which you passed on the drive up. From there it is used to feed power generators that deliver electricity to the cities of Southern California.

257

DORIS LAKE

Distance: 2 miles
Location: Take State Highway 168 northeast past Huntington Lake, across Kaiser Pass and down to Mono Hot Springs. A small dirt road takes off north just west of Mono Hot Springs Cabins and Lodge. The road is quite rough, so park just outside of the Forest Service campground and walk the 0.25 mile along this road to the trail head. Be careful not to block traffic in any way. (Note: The Road over Kaiser Pass is very narrow and not recommended for vehicles pulling trailers.)

Though there's a lot of competition in California for the title of "most intriguing mountain road," the one over Kaiser Pass is certainly a serious contender. It is hardly a route for anyone in a hurry. Better to stop often and savor this wild maze of high country cradling the South Fork of the San Joaquin River. This magnificent region is every bit as astonishing to today's viewer as it was more than a century ago, when, in 1864, the rough and ready California Geological survey party mapped their way from east to west across this yawning landscape.

A couple of weeks before he had reached this particular area, while standing on a peak 25 miles southeast of here that now bears his name, the geologist William Brewer made a diary entry that rings true for this entire region. (Brewer was the survey field supervisor under the state geologist Josiah Whitney, for whom he had just christened the highest peak in California.) He writes: "The view was wilder than we have ever seen before. Such a landscape! a hundred peaks in sight over thirteen thousand feet—many very sharp—deep canyons, cliffs in every direction, sharp ridges almost inaccessible to man on which human foot has never trod—all combine to produce a view the sublimity of which is rarely equalled, one which few are privileged to behold."

The short section of road you will be walking along on your way to the trail head is flanked on the right by a beautiful grassy meadow, with wild roses lending splashes of soft pink to the green and gray of meadow grasses and jointed blocks of granite. Rose hips, the "fruit" of the rose, were a fairly common food source for some Indians, as well as for early settlers throughout the West. Teas made from the hips were frequently given to people as a cure

258

for a variety of ailments. (Rose hips contain vitamin C in concentrations many times greater than oranges.) Some Indian tribes also made medicines from the blossoms. Wildlife of the area, such as black bear and blue grouse, can be seen dining on the hips in late autumn.

On a small hill to your left, just past the parking area at the end of this dirt road, is a sign that marks the beginning of the trail to Doris and Tule lakes. The first part of the path rises steadily through giant, rounded columns of granitic rock. This granite has weathered both by jointing or (cracking) and exfoliation, a process of breaking away in layers, which tends to turn sharp edges into rounded ones. You can see this phenomenon here and in more dramatic proportions in the domes of Yosemite. Notice how the Jeffrey pines of the area aid vertical jointing by establishing root systems in the cracks of the rocks. No tree in the Sierra is more effective at this type of anchoring system. Other large plants growing along the path here are the extraordinarily sturdy canyon live oak and the ever-present manzanita.

Just before reaching the lake, on the right side of the trail, you will come to a marsh that is covered with thick stands of rush. Young rush plants are consumed eagerly by grazing animals, and Sierra Indians used the tough, leafy stems to weave such items as baskets and mats. Notice how the rushes around the lake have colonized every available pocket of the rocky shoreline.

Another plant you'll see here, though not nearly in such quantities, is the cattail. Cattails have been used extensively for centuries by European settlers and Indians alike. In the spring, before the stalks begin to grow, the white inner core of the plant is very tasty either eaten raw or cooked in soups or stews, as are the young tips of the root system. (The roots and lower stems of the cattail are almost pure carbohydrate.) The yellow pollen from the tip of the male plants is still used by some people as a flour substitute, usually as an additive to other types of flour. The brown, downlike material of the tubular female heads is extremely soft and absorbent, and settlers and Indians alike frequently made beds from it. Indians also favored it for lining the cradles of their infants. If all that is not enough, these same heads are quite effective when used as tinder to start campfires.

259

Many bodies of water in this region, such as Doris Lake, lie in the hollowed-out basins of granitic-basalt rock, neither fed nor drained by inlet or outlet stream. The summer sun beating down on these basins day after day warms the water, until by August, it reaches a very pleasant swimming temperature despite the rather high elevation.

As you stand on the northwest corner of the lake, you can see a fine ridge of high mountains off to the east. This is the wildly beautiful country of the John Muir Wilderness—stately peaks, glacier-carved valleys, and dizzying cliffs bound together in an alpine tapestry that is among the most magnificent on earth. Up among these high palisades—the Mono Divide, Turret Peak, the Seven Gables—winds the John Muir Portion of the Pacific Crest Trail. It seems likely that anyone up there rubbing elbows with such unleashed beauty would at some point stop in his tracks, look around him, and break into a beaming smile at having at last come to the western version of what John Bunyon, writing in the seventeenth century, called the "Delectable Mountains."

NEEDLES LOOKOUT

Distance: 4 miles
Location: From Tipton or Porterville take State Highway 190 east into the Sequoia National Forest. Where 190 ends, take a right and proceed south for about 1 mile to a signed road heading east toward the Needles Lookout. The trail head is at the end of this road.

If ever there was a threshold over which you could pass easily into the magic of a mountain wilderness, this is it. The beginning of the Needles Lookout walk starts out through a typical, but by no means mundane, array of southern Sierra high country life. Jeffrey pines stand at attention in the cool mountain air, patches of manzanita huddled at their sturdy feet. Purple lupine gardens line the open trail, while an occasional outcropping of weathered brown granite can be seen protruding from the southern hillside, looking like soft, suntanned shoulders in the early morning sun.

Then, at 0.4 mile, the world falls away. Off the left side of the trail is a deep, southward-tilting valley drained by the Kern River, the far side of which is skirted by three sets of high ridges that crest like waves slapping against an invisible shore. The first ridge lies near the southern border of the Golden Trout Wilderness, and the peaks behind that, which include the Toqwa Range, cut a line through the heart of this same wild preserve. The most distant chain forms a snow-capped ridgeline that rises higher and higher as it moves north, culminating in 14,495-foot Mount Whitney, which rises along the border dividing the John Muir Wilderness from Sequoia National Park.

If you have walked in the more northern area of the Sierras, you may be used to seeing gray granitic rock interspersed with dark brown or black volcanic basalt. There are certainly some remnants of volcanic activity in this area; a large flow can be found along Golden Trout Creek 25 miles to the northwest, and fairly recent cones and small flows are fairly common along various stretches of the Kern River watershed. As a rule, however, the most abundant evidence of volcanic activity is found from the Stanislaus River northward.

At 0.75 mile the trail makes a short climb across an outcropping of jointed granite. Here the forest begins to thin out, the rocks offering only a few pockets of soil or large cracks for a scattering of firs and Jeffrey pines to gain a foothold. Keep your eye out through here for the uniquely beautiful red snow plant. This entirely red member of the heath family is among a group of plants known as saprophytes, which take their nourishment from decaying organic material. In another 1.1 miles is the first, somewhat shocking view of the Needles Lookout. The tiny station is perched on a large, bare granite knuckle that soars alone over the valley to the east. You will first descend into a small ravine and then make a switchback up to the lookout itself.

You'll be in for an unforgettable experience when you reach the first in a series of platforms that are strung together by a long chain of metal steps leading up to the lookout itself. The feeling when climbing here is like that of being an acrobat en route to the ultimate trapeze, the land falling away with each step in a dizzying rush of sky and mountains. The panorama from this lofty perch is

261

nothing short of glorious. To the northeast lie clear views of Mount Whitney, Mount Muir, the Kaweahs, and the wind-scoured portal of Farewell Gap. To the south lies the long green reach of the Kern River Valley, a fast passageway to the Central Valley for snowmelt and high-country spring water, some of which comes from as far away as northwest of Mount Whitney.

This fire tower is manned during the summer, so try to be as considerate as possible to the lookout working there. If the station is already busy with visitors, you can give the person a break and still have exquisite views of the surrounding landscape by stopping at one of the various platforms on the way up. It isn't necessary to go all the way to the final deck—the lookout's "front porch"—which surrounds the building.

For decades fire lookouts have been the "eyes" of the U.S. Forest Service. With the advent of high-tech fire-detection equipment, it was beginning to look as if the days of the people who man these towers were numbered. Then, as a result of the severe budget cuts of the last ten years, new life was breathed into this relatively inexpensive means of detection. For the time being, at least, a fairly extensive network of women and men still perch each summer high above the vast conifer forests of the West.

San Bernardino National Forest

MOJAVE RIVER FORKS

Distance: 4 miles
Location: From State Highway 138 on the northwest corner of Silverwood Lake, head east on State Highway 173 to the end of the pavement. Follow Pacific Crest Trail markers north.

The Mojave River Forks walk is for the adventurous among you who are willing to negotiate a few strange twists of the trail in exchange for some fine desert mountain scenery, liberally seasoned with history. Because of the low elevation, this walk is best done in late fall, but hikers who can go in and out early on a summer morning will not suffer if they carry adequate water with them. The walk heads north from the end of the paved portion of Highway 173, traversing a wide, yawning expanse of the Mojave Desert. A trail branches off to the left about 40 yards in, but you continue right, along a ridge overlooking a grassy parkland studded with gnarled cottonwoods, their leaves shimmering in the slightest breeze. The water channel below, which in summer will be nothing more than a dry bed of sand, belongs to the Mojave River.

Toward the setting sun lies the high, northwest-tilting ridge of the San Gabriel Mountains, a grand uplift of extremely old rocks framed by valleys of gravelly sediment that were first laid down in the dark waters of ancient oceans. At the eastern edge of these mountains is a low saddle, which separates them from the peaks of the San Bernardino. This saddle, heavily eroded by the San Gabriel River, lies along the infamous San Andreas Fault. It is the path that the Old Spanish Trail followed on its way into the Los Angeles Basin, and it is the route (Interstate 15) still used for the vast

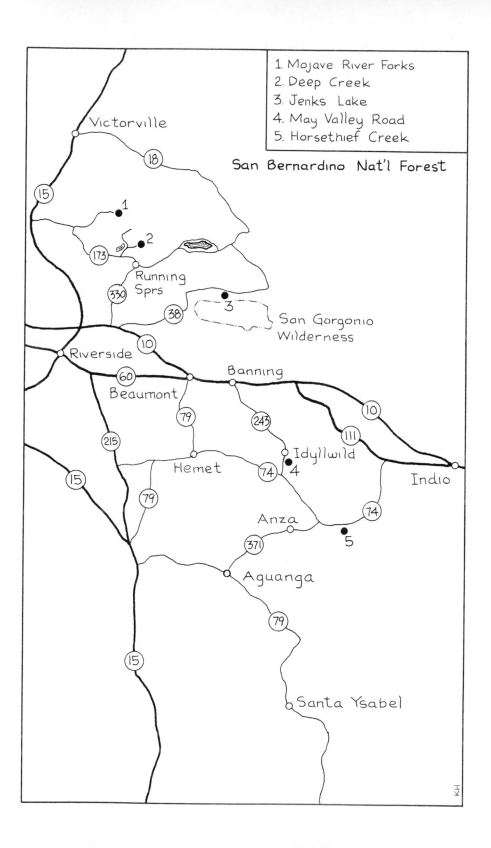

majority of vehicular traffic, as well as for all major rail lines coming in from the northeast.

In about 0.7 mile you'll leave the more exposed desert behind and enter a soft, stream-side corridor of willows and Frémont cottonwoods. This type of cottonwood was named, as you might have guessed, for that intrepid explorer Captain John C. Frémont, who discovered the species during a trek to California in 1844. (Frémont actually called the tree sweet cottonwood because the inner bark lacked the bitter taste that marks most other species of this tree.) It is a very common resident of watercourses throughout the southwest lowlands; its relative, the black cottonwood, takes over along the rivers and streams of the higher mountains.

Indian tribes along the coast soaked the bark of the cottonwood tree in water to make a solution that was reportedly quite effective in healing skin cuts and lacerations. European settlers later borrowed this bit of knowledge, finding the decoction to be useful for treating saddle sores on their horses. The Cahuilla Indians to the south made food-grinding mortars out of the heart of Frémont cottonwood, and the wood was a major source of fuel. These people also discovered an indirect use for the cottonwood by way of the fungus that often grows on dead limbs. These "tree mushrooms," as they have been called, were highly valued as food, most commonly in the spring when they are a fresh, ivory color.

The trail crosses the Mojave River bed, at which point you will wind your way up to the top of a large rock spillway located on the other side. Crossing westward over the top of this spillway, you'll reach a small parking area, with Pacific Crest Trail markers on the other side. A short climb from here leads to a point where the trail joins, of all things, a water flume that has been carved out of the bare mountain.

This flume was built by Chinese laborers during the Depression years to bring irrigation water to the dry lands to the west. It takes very little imagination to appreciate the incredible amount of work that went into blasting and chipping this channel out of solid rock. As you can see, it sports more than a few patches, some of which still bear the date of the repair. It has not been used to carry water for many years, reaching perhaps its ultimate function by forming this strange, stony section of the Pacific Crest Trail.

You can turn around anywhere near the mouth of the stream canyon. This rugged, boulder-strewn channel, which was carved out by the patient hand of Deep Creek, delivers water to this point all the way from a cool patch of high pine forest located southeast of Lake Arrowhead.

On your way back along the streambed of the Mojave River, it's interesting to consider that you are retracing one of the most heavily used Indian trading paths in all of Southern California. Indians would follow the Mojave River up into the San Bernardinos, cross the high ridge on the east side of Monument Peak, and then make their way down into the San Bernardino Valley and onto the coast. Considering the windswept tableland that reaches westward to the San Gabriel Mountains, or the high line of the San Bernardinos, laced with quiet pools of clear water and hidden pockets of game-filled pine forests, a run along the ancient trade routes must have been far more inspiring than the fast lane to Los Angeles on Interstate 15. Could there then have been even one ordinary, uneventful trip, when men who were attuned to the slightest changes traveled through a land so thick with mystery?

DEEP CREEK

Distance: 3 miles
Location: From State Highway 173 on the east side of Lake Arrowhead take Hook Creek Road, which is located just about 1.75 miles from the downtown "traffic light" district. Keep following this road, which becomes Forest Road 2N26Y. Just past a small Forest Service cabin is a fork; stay left. At the next small fork take a right. About 0.4 mile past the Forest Service cabin you will come to the top of a steep hill. This is 0.2 mile from the parking area for the walk, and people in small, low-clearance cars may want to park here and walk down to the creek. An old cabin is adjacent to the trail head.

Deep Creek is easily one of the most beautiful watercourses in the San Bernardino Mountains, draining a vast, rugged region of forest and high desert running east and north of Lake Arrowhead. This stretch of the Deep Creek Trail is particularly varied, beginning in the cool pine forests that frame the creek for the first part of its northward run and ending at the edge of the boulder-strewn, high desert canyons that accompany the watercourse until its eventual rendezvous with the Mojave River. Incidentally, fifteen or twenty thousand years ago—very recently geologically speaking—the water from Deep Creek entered the Mojave River and then, through a series of lakes, flowed all the way to Death Valley.

Just a few yards from the beginning of the walk at Splinters Cabin, the trail splits into several different paths, most of which head off to the right along the east side of Deep Creek. You will want to take the left path, which crosses the creek almost immediately and then winds downstream along its western edge. Here is a beautiful collection of moisture-loving grasses and wild flowers, as well as scattered willows and oaks. About 50 or 60 yards into the walk you'll be able to see a large metal expansion bridge a short distance ahead. You will want to follow any of several small paths that lead up to the point where the horizontal bridge planks join the left side of the canyon. It is here we will pick up the Pacific Crest Trail, which continues north along the west side of Deep Creek.

The San Bernardino Mountains are a hodgepodge of metamorphic (changed by heat or pressure) and igneous (cooled from a hot liquid state) rock collections, many of which are among the oldest to be found in this part of the state. About 0.2 mile into the walk on the far side of the canyon you can see slabs of igneous rock breaking away from the sheer cliffs that make up the parent rock. This process is aided to a great extent by the strong fingers of tree and shrub roots, which find their way into tiny cracks in the rock faces, splitting them open as they grow. Once the slabs break away from the parent rock, they will continue to weather slowly into smaller and smaller pieces, many of which will fall to the bottom of the canyon and be carried away by the waters of Deep Creek.

Just past this weathered canyon wall you will begin to catch glimpses of the parched, rugged mountain country that lies to the north. Even the names of the features in this distant landscape—Rattlesnake Mountain, Juniper Flats, Devil's Hole—hint at a rather severe change of character when compared to the cool tapestries of oak and pine you are leaving behind to the south.

267

At 0.7 mile in look to your right across the canyon and you'll see a deep, east-west ravine. Notice how the north-facing slope is covered with pines and large shrubs, while the one that faces south is much drier and rockier looking. The sun traces a path through the summer sky in such a way that it does not shine directly on north-facing slopes. The moisture that falls here won't evaporate as quickly as it does on south-facing slopes—a condition that allows a much greater variety of plant life to survive here. This rather simple concept of orientation explains the extraordinarily diverse collage of mountain plant cover. Through the ages it has also been an important consideration in man's selection of caves to live in and later in choosing sites for his erected structures.

Earlier we spoke of how large slabs of rock tend to become smaller when exposed to the breaking action of tree roots and weather. Obvious effects of one aspect of the weather equation, rain, can easily be seen 1.2 miles into the walk on a hillside across the canyon marked by eroded shallow ravines. Each rainstorm takes more and more of this hill into the creek below. Realize that not only hills and mountains are eroded in this way, but water also cuts downward to form the stream channels that you see—from the mighty Grand Canyon to this more modest one carved out by Deep Creek. Rain and rivers are slowly washing away all this vertical land, which, if not stopped by dams, eventually finds its way back to the ocean from where it originally came. If mountain uplift does not proceed at a rate similar to that of erosion, the earth will eventually turn into a flat landscape.

At 1.3 miles the trail makes a sudden turn to the west, passing a small stream drainage area before coming out on the edge of the canyon, heading north once again. Less than 0.2 mile from here you'll come to a point where the path passes between a large rocky slope on the left and a small, pillar-shaped outcropping on the right. This is our turnaround point, and it serves as the best example of all for illustrating to what a great extent these mountains are being broken apart by erosion. Several large pieces from the hillside above you can be seen laying in or near the creek below.

Before turning around for the walk back, take some time to ponder the wild, untrammeled vista spread out before you. Not many miles to the north lie the faded ruts of the Old Spanish Trail, the Colorado and Utah sections of which were first established by Father Silvestre Vélez de Escalante in the same year that the Thirteen Colonies signed the Declaration of Independence. Along this parched path thousands of immigrants made their way into California, some turning north toward the gold fields, others continuing on into the rich agricultural lands to the west. How good the San Bernardino peaks must have looked from the Mojave Desert, appearing as a long, magnificent ridge of high country, marking the end of a long, hard journey and the beginning of a new life to come.

JENKS LAKE

Distance: 2.4 miles

Location: On the south side of State Highway 38, 0.25 mile east of the Barton Flats Visitors' Information Station (north of the San Gorgonio Wilderness). Begin the walk across the highway from Camp Arbolado, which lies just west of the Barton Flats Campground. There is a small hiking trail sign on the south side of the road marking the trail head. On the other side of Highway 38 from here (facing west) is a sign reading "Telephone: $\frac{1}{4}$ mile." There are small pullout areas on both the north and south sides of the road.

Though the Jenks Lake walk involves some climbing, it offers an exquisite sample of the San Bernardino high country. Since our turnaround point at the Jenks Lake Picnic Area can also be reached by a good road from the west, this is a perfect trip for walkers who wish to rendezvous with nonwalking members of their party.

Begin this trek at a small trail marker on the south side of Highway 38, at 0.25 mile east of the Barton Flats Visitors' Information Station. There are a couple of small turnouts here that can be used as parking places, though you should be careful that you don't block the entrance to Camp Arbolado on the north side of the highway. You are actually beginning this walk along the western section of a nature trail that crosses the highway at this point. There are a few interpretive signs here, which will give you a bit of nature and historical information before you start your ascent into the mountains.

There are some fine open parklands along this first stretch of trail, liberally sprinkled with pines, manzanita, white fir, and black oak. Black oak was once an extremely important food source to the Serrano Indians (*Serrano* is Spanish for "mountaineer"). As you'll note from one of the nature signs along the path, this forest is of the type known as mixed conifer. The mixed-conifer belt that you see here has a different blend than you would find in the Sierra Nevada or Klamath Mountains, although there is some overlapping of individual species. The particular section that we'll be walking through is composed primarily of ponderosa pine, incense-cedar, and white fir, along with Coulter, Jeffrey, knobcone, and sugar pine.

In 0.2 mile is the east entrance to the Barton Flats Visitors' Information Center. When I was here this fine facility, which was ideally situated for answering the plethora of questions that people have about trees, campgrounds, fires, fish, flies, birds, bees, berries, brambles, and bears, was closed owing to lack of funding. It is a grave injustice that this forest—among the busiest in the country with more than 6 million visitor days per year—is not given money for even the most basic information centers like this one, when the integrity of the resource and the assistance and education of the public who own the property so desperately depend on it.

The trail for Jenks Lake takes off from the back of the information center on the east side of the main buildings. In no way should you disturb anything in this complex, especially since what is here is not likely to be repaired or replaced if damaged. The first part of the lake trail is quite steep, though this portion lasts for less than 100 yards. After it you will climb more gently, coming out 0.2 mile from the visitors' center in front of a Y junction on a dirt forest road. Take the right fork here—yes, the one that climbs.

From this point the walk, although still uphill, is an extremely pleasant one, wrapped in the typical, shimmering green coat and thick shadows of a north-slope, high-country forest. There is no shortage of surprises along this road, from grand willows huddled along tiny roadside seeps to the soft purple heads of iris and blue-eyed grass swaying their soft purple heads in the after-

Gray-crowned
Rosy Finch

Clark's Nutcracker

Golden-crowned Kinglet

Cassin's Finch

Mountain Bluebird

Pine Grosbeak

KH

noon breeze. The plant life of this island of mountains called the San Bernardinos is quite extraordinary. There are more rare plants here than in any other national forest in the United States, as well as some of the oldest (more than two thousand years) limber pines to be found anywhere in the world.

It is hard to believe that this tapestry is woven so thick with life when a short way to the west in the Los Angeles Basin, there is not a quarter of the moisture needed to grow this kind of garden. You are seeing one of the simplest but greatest miracles of mountain ranges, their ability to force air masses up to higher, cooler levels where they can no longer hold the moisture they are carrying and so proceed to drop it in the form of rain or snow, bringing forth a riot of life.

A short distance from where you joined this roadway is a path going straight up an eroded hill. Our route takes a sharp right, narrowing for a short distance into a footpath. Yes, the straight path is a shortcut, but you'll miss the best scenery of the entire walk by taking it, and you will also be contributing to a bad soil erosion problem.

As you make your way to the west along this peaceful stretch of trail, views will begin to open up to the north. Here Grand View Point, Clark's Summit, and Lookout Point form a bold east-west ridge that frames the soothing green and gold valley bottom of Barton Flats and Jenks Meadow. Just 7 miles northeast as the Cooper's hawk flies is the bustling resort of Big Bear Lake, which, from this quiet lookout, may as well be 700 miles away.

Continuing this gentle climb, you'll reach a hairpin left turn about 0.8 mile from the parking area. From this turn you will be afforded spectacular views of the high peaks that form the western spine of the San Gorgonio Wilderness. This line of peaks, capped farther to the east by 11,502-foot-high San Gorgonio Mountain, forms the highest group of mountain summits in Southern California. Fifteen thousand years ago, the highest portion of this ridge supported seven small glaciers.

After drinking your fill of this fine, wild view, continue uphill for 0.3 mile more to Jenks Lake. This is a lovely picnic spot, though after a nice, quiet walk up, it can tend to seem a bit harried and hurried by the numbers of people who drive up here on summer days for a bit of fishing and picnicking. As one of the signs along the beginning of the walk related, an attempt was made by Lester Jenks in 1878 to turn this into a getaway place for the people of the Los Angeles Basin. Alas, it failed because the three-day burro ride was too much of an ordeal for the vast majority of his prospective clients. Something tells me that were this today the same grand slice of undeveloped backwoods that it was then, Jenks would run out of burros long before he ran out of customers.

MAY VALLEY ROAD

Distance: 3 miles

Location: A little over 1 mile south of Idyllwild, turn east off the Idyllwild-Hemet Highway onto Saunders Meadow Road. (There is a sign here that says "May Valley.") It is 1 mile from this point to May Valley Road, which is also known as Forest Road 5S21. Go southeast on May Valley Road and stop at the first available parking area, 50 yards or so from the highway.

This trek on the May Valley Road begins in a very attractive open forest of black oak and ponderosa, Jeffrey, and Coulter pines, with a scattered understory of manzanita and deer brush. To the right you can gain glimpses southward through the trees into the dryer valleys below covered with greasewood, manzanita, and ribbonwood. Such vistas are very effective in driving home the point that in mountainous terrain vegetation does not grow haphazardly but exists in general belts of reference called life zones.

Life zones are based on climatical changes that occur with increases in altitude, specifically a decline in temperature (about 3 degrees per thousand feet gained), with a resulting increase in annual precipitation. Traveling up the side of a mountain is, as far as plant life is concerned, very similar to traveling north in latitude. A couple of the names given to the five most common life zones suggest just this tendency. We begin in what are called the Lower and Upper Sonoran Zones (as in the Sonoran Desert of the southwest), move up through the Transitional Zone and into the Canadian Zone, finally topping off at the Alpine, or Arctic Zone. It's astounding to think that in the San Jacintos you would not have to go farther than 30 miles from where you now stand to make a trip that would be the ecological equivalent of traveling from the Mexican border to the Arctic Circle.

The principles of such transitions were understood for countless centuries by Indian peoples such as the Cahuilla. In the summer they could stay in the cool Transitional Zone, where they would find elderberries and manzanita, along with an abundance of game animals. In the fall they would move down into the Upper Sonoran Zone to collect acorns, and in the winter in the Lower Sonoran Zone they could harvest desert plants like the mesquite, agave, and jojoba. The richest life zone for the Cahuilla, where they collected more than half of their food plants, was the Upper Sonoran Zone, which in this area extends roughly from 3,000 to 5,000 feet. Technically you are now a little above the limits of the Upper Sonoran Zone, but it would be unwise to think of life belts as being that precise. The hillsides on your right that have dryer southern exposures, for example, will tend to contain more Sonoran Zone plants than the more protected, north-facing hills that lie at the same elevation.

About 0.6 mile into the walk you can study such life zones even more clearly, as the forest peels away from the right side of the road and spectacular views of Garner Valley open up slightly to the southeast. This pine-studded valley is framed on the far side by the lovely Santa Rosa Mountains, which, like the San Jacintos, form some of the northernmost uplifts of the Peninsular Ranges, stretching more than 800 miles to the south along the peninsula of Baja California.

It is thought that the mountain ranges immediately surrounding you began uplifting approximately 95 million years ago, a process that was not continual but was broken by 10- to-20-million-year periods where there was little or no activity. Some scientists believe that these Southern California ranges are in the process of coming out of one such resting period. Over a fairly recent 150-year block of time, activity along the San Jacinto Fault zone averaged six times the activity found on any other fault zone in the state. (The San Jacinto Mountains, by the way, lie between the San Jacinto Fault line on the west and the San Andreas Fault line on the east.

There have already been two major earthquakes along the San Jacinto Fault in the last hundred years, each causing a great deal of damage to the nearby town of Hemet.)

Off in the distance to the west lie the Santa Ana Mountains and to the north of those, the San Gabriel Mountains. The city of Los Angeles is sandwiched right between the two. Interestingly, fairly young batholith and sedimentary rocks 80 to 100 million years old dominate much of the Santa Ana Mountains, while the San Gabriels include combinations of rocks that, at 1.7 billion years, are among the oldest to be found anywhere in Southern California. One other feature worth noting from this high point is the Agua Tibia Mountains, which are located about 25 miles due southeast. This is where the Palomar Observatory is located, which contains one of the largest reflecting telescopes in the world.

At 1.3 miles into the walk you will see your first views of the rugged pinnacles to the northeast that make up the southern spine of the San Jacinto Wilderness. In just another 0.2 mile you'll reach our turnaround point at the intersection with the South Ridge Trail, set in a beautiful, grassy saddle dotted with oaks. Here again are fine views of the soaring high country to the northeast, a rough ridge with Tahquitz, South, and Apache peaks ripping through the pine and chaparral canopy like stalagmites through tattered fabric. The South Ridge Trail goes from here up to Tahquitz Peak Lookout. Tahquitz, incidentally, is the name of a powerful evil spirit of the Cahuilla Indians. This peak is said to be one of several resting places where Tahquitz would recuperate from his savage hunting forays, during which he sought out unwary human beings and drifting lost souls.

HORSETHIEF CREEK

Distance: 5 miles

Location: Take State Highway 74 south from Palm Desert 16 miles to a paved road on the south side of the highway, directly across from Pinyon Flat Campground. (Coming from the west on Highway 74, the turnoff is about 9 miles past the State Highway 371 junction.) Head south on this paved road 0.3 mile; then turn left onto a dirt road, following signs for Elks Mountain Retreat. The road to Elks Retreat turns left; you keep going straight (east) 0.15 mile and park just this side of a large bulldozed hill blocking road. (Note: People with low-clearance cars should not proceed this final 0.15 mile but instead park up near the Elks turnoff and walk the additional 0.15 mile.) On the other side of the bulldozed hill is a road running north-south. Follow it south (right turn) on foot for 125 yards to a sign on the left indicating the trail head for Horsethief Creek.

The extreme southern portion of the San Bernardino National Forest is a handsome medley of desert mountains and swales, carved by wind and water into polished canyons concealing woodlands, cool springs, and fine, green gardens of plants of the dry Southwest. The Horsethief Creek walk is ideally done from autumn through late spring, but on occasion summer temperatures will be moderate enough to make an early morning or late evening trek quite enjoyable. At any time of year, however, you are advised to carry water with you.

Directly before you as you walk south on the first stretch of roadway is a fine view of Santa Rosa Mountain and, just to the east, Toro Peak. These mountains, like all those in this area, are members of what are commonly referred to as the Peninsular Range. This name hints at the fact that the majority of this 800-mile-long uplift is located south of here, forming the spine of the Baja California peninsula. The rocks that make up these peaks are part of a giant batholith, which is hot liquid magma that has cooled slowly inside the earth into a crystalline state, later uplifting to form mountains. The large grains that you see in this rock, as well as much of the rock in the Sierras, are the result of this crystallization process. This type of formation is of more than casual interest to many people, since it is what gives birth to a myriad of precious gems. In fact, a small mountain region to the west of here was once one of the most popular gem-collecting areas in the country.

There is something else worth noting about this mountain vista. Look at the way the top of the high ridge in front of you is capped by a thick stand of trees, compared to the more typical desert collection of yucca, agave, and prickly pear that covers the land below. This is the result of two important principles that go a long way in determining what plants (and therefore what animals) you'll see in any natural area in the world. The first is elevation. As you have probably noticed, air temperature tends to become cooler the higher the elevation. Cold air is not able to hold as much moisture as warm air, so the water inside of a cloud tends to condense as the cloud rises over the higher, cooler terrain. Sometimes these condensed droplets fall to the ground as rain, which is the single magic ingredient that gives these two landscapes such different looks.

Also in favor of the trees above you is that they are growing on terrain that slopes gently toward the north. North slopes are protected from the full impact of the summer sun, so whatever moisture falls there tends not to evaporate as quickly. Were you to cross over this mountain ridge and look at the south side, you'd find that the trees there grow in much more scattered groves, simply because there isn't as much ground moisture to go around.

Up this dirt road 125 yards you'll come to a trail sign on the left marking the route to Horsethief Creek. Then this road gently descends and about 0.25 mile down are fine stands of the red, papery-barked ribbonwood, or red shank. The wood of this fairly common plant is extremely hard and gives off a very intense heat when burned. Cahuilla Indians roasted meat over ribbonwood and used it for caps on reed arrow shafts to which stone arrowheads were then fastened. The plant was also used a great deal for medicinal purposes. Leaves were made into a tea, which reportedly was effective in the treatment of ulcers, and some medicine men also used ribbonwood to treat arthritis.

A bit under 0.5 mile away from the trail sign you will come to the rusty remains of the Dolomite Mine. Dolomite is a carbonate found in certain sedimentary rocks, which contains high levels of calcium and magnesium. There is a fork at the west end of the mine itself; take the right branch. About 0.1 mile past this fork you'll see a sign-in box on the right for the Santa Rosa Wilderness. This marks the beginning of the trail portion of the walk.

The walk from here goes through some surprisingly thick stands of nolina, yucca, agave, manzanita, prickly pear, and chamise. Considering the many kinds of foods that the Cahuilla Indians were able to harvest from desert plants, it's easy to see how this rather lush high desert, commonly referred to as the Upper Sonoran Zone, was among the most frequently utilized parts of the desert. It has been estimated that well over half of all the plants that the Cahuilla used for food were taken from the vegetation communities like this one.

The mountains ahead of you form the territory of the largest herd of desert bighorn sheep in the state of California. The first recorded sightings of these magnificent animals were made by the famous Spanish explorer Francisco Vásquez de Coronado in 1540. The numbers of bighorn have declined dramatically during the past century, and since their nimble rock dances make them all but free from natural predators, it seems obvious who's to blame for their demise. The Santa Rosa herd, currently numbering more than five hundred, is extremely secretive, making bedding areas in the most remote, inaccessible rock fortresses imaginable. About the only chance you'll have to see a bighorn is at one of several springs in the area, where the sheep come regularly to drink.

The trail has a slight downward tilt to it for much of the outbound walk, cutting against the natural lay of the land. In 2.5 miles it drops down into Horsethief Creek.

This creek comes by its dishonest name very honestly. Horse thieves during the late nineteenth century drove stolen stock here from the coast, changed their brands, and then drove them north to San Bernardino to sell to unsuspecting customers.

Though there are small pools scattered in this wash even in summer, the watercourse is at its best in the early spring, when snowmelt and spring water from the eastern flank of Toro Peak cascade through these rugged canyon walls with true abandon. The cottonwoods lining the creek are especially beautiful spring through fall, and the wind can nearly always be heard whispering music through their sunlit canopies.